The Chicago School

Theoretical Traditions in the Social Sciences

This series introduces the work of major figures in social science to students beyond their immediate specialisms.

The Chicago School

A Liberal Critique of Capitalism

Dennis Smith

St. Martin's Press   New York

First published in the United States of America in 1988

Printed in Hong Kong

ISBN 0-312-00384-6
ISBN 0-312-00386-2 (pbk)

Library of Congress Cataloging-in-Publication Data
Smith, Dennis, 1945–
The Chicago school.
(Theoretical traditions in the social sciences)
Bibliography: p.
Includes index.
1. Sociology—United States—History.
2. Chicago school of sociology. 3. Liberalism—
United States—History. 4. Capitalism—United States
—History. I. Title. II. Series.
HM22.U5S57 1988   301'.0973   87–16680
ISBN 0-312-00384-6
ISBN 0-312-00386-2 (pbk)

Contents

v

For my father

Preface

The front cover of this book depicts Liberty with her torch. In the mid-1880s she was delivered by her European creators to the American Ambassador in Paris. While this book was under way, the rusting statue was given a clean-up and general refurbishment followed by a magnificent firework display. These events celebrated the centenary of the original arrival in New York of Liberty in 1886. Apparently, it was a good deal easier to raise the cash for the fireworks than for the clean-up and refurbishment. Albion Small, the founding professor of Chicago University's sociology department, might well have found that rather symbolic. In fact, cleaning-up and refurbishng American liberty in its various expressions was a central objective of his life's work. He became very disillusioned.

This book discusses the dilemmas and pitfalls confronting Small and a number of other Chicago sociologists who tried to construct a morally-relevant and socially-useful academic discipline. They took very seriously the goals and values lauded as 'the American Way' and wrestled with their ambiguities. In doing so they often came up with conclusions which were unsympathetic to 'vested interests' and dedicated individualists. In other words, being a good American did not mean that you necessarily agreed with the person on the streetcar reading *The Chicago Tribune* – still less with those who owned the streetcar company and the newspaper house.

Jack P. Diggins has recently speculated on the form that the American declaration of Independence might take if it were rewritten by the sociologists: 'We hold these truths to be socially conditioned: that all men are created equal and mutually dependent . . .' and so on (Diggins, 1979, p. 482). The point is that their intellectual and moral location within the tradition of American liberalism provided the Chicago sociologists to be studied here with a critical perspective upon modern American society. However, it also imposed limits upon that critique. Some of these limits become more clearly visible when a comparative perspective is adopted. Like the statue, the rhetoric of 'liberty' was originally European. The fate of liberalism in Europe has been different. The European comparison, especially with Germany, has been stressed here in order to emphasise the extent to which the perceptions of men like Albion Small, W. I. Thomas, Robert Park, Louis Wirth, William Ogburn and Morris Janowitz have been shaped by the fact that they are Americans as well as the fact that they are sociologists.

During a visit to Chicago in 1983, I met Morris Janowitz, Gerald Suttles and Albert Hunter. My conversations with them provided valuable background and insights. Needless to say, they are absolved from any responsibility for the argument of this book. At Chicago I enjoyed the warm hospitality of Bert Hoselitz, his wife Gunhild and their daughter Ann. Their unstinting kindness was greatly appreciated.

Once again, many thanks to Tanya, Penny, Sue, Ed, Freda and Cleo for their benevolent interest. Ian and Butch Riddell were also tolerant and supportive. In particular, I am grateful for the many expert and insightful comments of Val Riddell, head of American Studies at Nene College, Northampton.

D. S.

1

The Chicago Tradition and its Critics

In this book I explore some aspects of the interplay between American sociology, American liberalism and American capitalism. The writings of members of the Chicago school provide a rich source of evidence upon which I draw selectively. Before outlining the argument and justifying the basis of my selection it will be useful to provide a potted history of Chicago sociology.

A beginner's guide

The new University of Chicago was founded in 1892. The enterprise was favoured by a strong tide of Baptist fervour and capitalist philanthropy. Albion Small, the first head of the sociology department, had trained as a Baptist minister. The research carried out by his colleagues and successors was to a considerable degree made possible by funds ultimately controlled by the Rockefeller family. Chicago sociologists were always aware of two potent influences. One consisted of the moral imperatives associated with being 'good Americans', a phrase that could be uttered without irony. The other was the power of private capital. However, that is to anticipate the argument.

Two publications signalled the establishment of a distinctive style and content for Chicago sociology. One was Robert Park's paper entitled 'The City: Suggestions for the Investigation of Human Behavior in the City Environment' (1915). This paper set aside the prevailing tradition of abstract philosophising and sweeping generalisation in favour of sharp, researchable questions about institutions and processes that could be immediately observed and

1

investigated. Park did not pontificate. Instead, he puzzled out loud. The other breakthrough was *The Polish Peasant in Europe and America* by W. I. Thomas and Florian Znaniecki. This was a potent mixture of analytical description, theoretical speculation and – most startling of all – empirical evidence consisting of hundreds of pages of direct quotations from newspapers, social-work agencies, immigrant societies and private letters.

Taken together, the two works just described make up a kind of 'declaration of independence'. Social scientists were shown how to work in a new way, one which allowed them to use their intelligence and senses systematically and with self-confidence in a process of discovery. In more optimistic moments, it must have seemed as if a new urban frontier was being opened up by academic pioneers. Although it was new to the social sciences, this approach drew upon a powerful American myth, partly grounded in historical experience.

For well over a decade after the end of the First World War Chicago sociology *was*, in effect, American sociology. Under the astute administrative guidance of Ernest Burgess and with funds drawn from the Laura Spelman Rockefeller Memorial and similar bodies American social life in Chicago and beyond was mapped, measured, examined and experienced. The energies of scores of graduate researchers were available. Some idea of the range of topics covered is conveyed by the list of doctoral and master's dissertations in the period (given in Faris, 1967, pp. 135–50). They include investigations of: immigrant groups in America such as the Japanese, Czechs, Italians, Swedes, Germans, Jews, Chinese and Estonians; the dimensions of black life including slavery, the press, the family, theological seminaries, prejudice, race consciousness and bi-racial organisation; and aspects of the family, youth and gender such as desertion, personality formation, the play movement, family disorganisation, female mobility, birth control, intermarriage, divorce, demographic patterns.

There are also investigations of: topics relating to deviance and marginality such as the county gaol, the juvenile court, pauper law, systems of punishment, hotel life, hobos, vice areas, gangs, suicide, insanity, prohibition and religious sects; media of communication, collective expression and culture change such as newspapers, religious missions, motion pictures and the radio; economic factors and institutions such as chain stores, the Chicago Real Estate

Board, the money market, strikes and land values; and, not least, studies of specific communities such as the Jewish ghetto in Chicago, the Finns in Michigan, Mennonite settlements in Kansas, Tepoztlan in Mexico, and Jackson in Tennessee.

Lester. R. Kurtz (1984, p. 2) argues that in the period up to 1950 there were three generations of Chicago sociology. Slightly revised, this framework can be extended to apply to the period from the 1890s to the present. During the first generation, which lasted from the 1890s until the end of the First World War, Albion Small maintained an episcopal presence, presiding over both the department and the *American Journal of Sociology*. This generation rubbed shoulders with John Dewey, George Herbert Mead and Thorstein Veblen, none of whom were sociologists but all of whom were powerful intellectual influences upon their academic contemporaries. During this period a strong relationship was established with civic reformers, especially the social workers based at Hull House. This is the Chicago school of Albion Small and W. I. Thomas. Its demise was marked by the dismissal of the latter.

The second generation belonged to the Chicago school of Robert Park and Ernest Burgess which endured through the 1920s and into the 1930s. The graduate researchers whose work has just been illustrated shared the experience of finding their way through the 'green bible', the *Introduction to the Science of Sociology* (1921) put together by Robert Park and Ernest Burgess. The latter had joined the faculty in 1919 and was responsible for considerable empirical research in the spheres of urban social processes, the family and social disorganisation. Burgess did not retire until 1957. However, the great dependence of the department upon the energising intellect of his colleague is shown, in part, by the relative decline in the prominence of Chicago sociology following Park's departure in 1933. By the time this second generation was coming to an end other powerful centres of academic sociology were making themselves felt. From the perspectives of sociologists at Harvard, Columbia and elsewhere, the Chicago school of Park and Burgess began to appear rather old-fashioned: theoretically unsophisticated, politically naive, little acquainted with advanced statistical methods.

During the third generation some of those criticisms were effectively met by the arrival of William Ogburn who served as departmental chairman from 1936 until 1951. Ogburn brought statistical expertise and strong connections with federal government. His colleagues included graduates from 'second-generation' Chicago, for example, Everett Hughes, Samuel Stouffer and Louis Wirth. Students in this third generation included Franklin Frazier, Paul Cressey, Edward Shils, Howard Becker and many other well-known figures in post-war American sociology.

It is tempting to speak of a fourth-generation Chicago school. In fact, there are two. One of them is the Chicago school of Herbert Blumer, a graduate of the department during the 1920s. This school of symbolic interactionism traces its origins to the work of Mead and claims Thomas, Park and Hughes among its list of early contributors. Unlike the second-generation school which directed its attention towards the city, this fourth-generation school concentrates upon the exploration of the self. However, there is another fourth-generation Chicago school associated with Morris Janowitz. He chaired the Chicago sociology department between 1967 and 1972, a period which witnessed a strong revival of a vigorous theoretical and empirical research tradition in the sphere of urban sociology. Apart from Janowitz, its adherents include (for example) Gerald Suttles, William Kornblum and Albert Hunter.

Chicago sociology in these various phases has included several overlapping foci of concern: ecological processes in urban society, social organisation and disorganisation, dimensions of social and personal control, symbolic interaction and the management of the self. Specifically, these themes have been explored with reference to spheres such as race and ethnic relations, public opinion and mass communications, deviance and criminality, and demographic change. Considerable use has been made of research techniques such as the exploitation of public and private documentary sources, participant observation and interviews.

The men and the themes

The Chicago school, as I describe it for the purposes of this present book, contains members of each of the four generations. The argument takes relatively little account of the particular influence of Mead and the special contributions of Blumer and the symbolic interactionists. These themes have recently been well treated (for example, in Rock, 1979; Lewis and Smith, 1980; Joas, 1985;

Denzin, 1984; Kuklick, 1984) and I can make my case without having to enter the recent debate about the timing and degree of influence of Mead's ideas upon the early symbolic interactionists. My Chicago school includes Small and Thomas from the first generation, Park from the second, Wirth and Ogburn from the third, and Janowitz from the fourth. Instead of Mead, I focus attention upon John Dewey and Thorstein Veblen. These men, respectively a philosopher and an economist, offered alternative prescriptions for coping with a problem – central to this book – which faced all the sociologists just mentioned.

In its broadest terms, this problem was, how could social science be used in order to realise liberal values and goals in modern American society? The centrality of this problem to my argument accounts for a major omission from this book. Ernest Burgess, one of the two key sociologists of the 'classic' second-generation school, does not receive special attention despite his massive contribution to the development of empirical research programmes. In his writing, Burgess does not treat the interplay between sociology, liberalism and capitalism as intellectually problematic. Arguably, he was too busy wrestling with this issue in the practical world to spend much time writing about it. In any case, he does not provide much enlightenment on this matter, as will shortly be seen.

The intellectual tradition I am going to explore through the writings of Small, Thomas, Park, Wirth, Ogburn and Janowitz is fundamental to understanding their work. However, it is not a regional or parochial tradition restricted to Chicago. Behind these scholars' practical interest in social disorganisation in Chicago and theoretical preoccupation with the nature of the 'city' or the 'self' there lies an encompassing and still more basic concern which predates the establishment of Chicago University by decades, even centuries. The object of this concern is the nature of America and Americans: what they ought to be, why they are not as they ought, and how they may become more like they ought to be.

I describe the Chicago sociologists being discussed as 'liberals'. By this term I mean no more or less than that they believed American democracy, properly functioning, should enable men and women to achieve the satisfactions embodied in what has become known as the American Dream. They took seriously the obligation to work for the enactment of goals such as social justice and individual happiness as embodied in contemporary interpretations of the American Declaration of Independence and the American Constitution. The above statements are full of ambiguities, some of which will be discussed later.

There is a well-rehearsed argument, set out by (for example) Thorstein Veblen (1965a), C. W. Mills (1943), Alvin Gouldner (1970) and the Schwendingers (1974), which asserts that the concepts and theories developed by sociologists in Chicago, as elsewhere in America, were structured in ways which served the interests of modern corporate capitalism. Furthermore, it is asserted, the ideological glasses through which these sociologists saw the world prevented them from recognising how they were being used. In other words, the liberalism of sociologists smoothed away potential points of moral irritation.

No doubt it would be possible to write a book about social scientists or, indeed, people in many other academic disciplines, past or present, who have readily responded to the wishes of private business interests and found no difficulty in reconciling this with their liberal views. However, I do not think this applies to the men I discuss in this book, all of whom held leading positions in their discipline. This is not to claim that they were especially heroic. Nor have they significantly altered the direction of social change in the United States of America. However, in my view, the liberalism of the Chicago sociologists discussed here caused them considerable moral discomfort when confronting the misery, oppression and frustration imposed by modern America.

Moral discomfort is only interesting in this context because it posed intellectual challenges which were faced in a variety of fascinating ways. It is, in fact, possible that the intellectual contributions made by each would have been much less if he had not come up against these moral issues. Each had a particular reason to be sensitive to the 'promise of America'. Two of them (Small and Thomas) came from deeply religious New England families. Two (Wirth and Janowitz) belonged to recent Jewish immigrant stock. Two (Park and Ogburn) were intensely familiar with the deeply contrasting social orders of the northern and southern regions of the USA.

The argument

As has just been implied, in this book I argue that Chicago sociology illustrates a variety of responses from within American liberalism to the practical and moral challenges of contemporary American capitalism. I begin by noting the long shadow cast forward to the present by the inter-war Chicago school. On the one hand, there is the long-running Veblen–Mills–Gouldner–Schwendinger critique, already mentioned. On the other hand, warm nostalgic feelings for the 'good old days in Chicago' have recently been supplemented by a revival of intellectual curiosity about the work that was done in that era.

Second, I note that the situation of early American sociologists in relation to the dominant political ideology and ruling-class interests of their society was very different from that of their counterparts in European societies, especially Germany. The implications of these differences, especially in the late nineteenth and early twentieth centuries, are illustrated and explored through two related comparisons: between intellectual life in Berlin and Chicago and between the key ideas of Georg Simmel and Thorstein Veblen.

During the 1880s and 1890s, American scholars travelled to Germany in droves in order to savour the products of the most advanced university system in the world. However, by those decades the social and moral order underpinning the work of bourgeois liberal politicians and academics in Germany, as elsewhere in Europe, was rapidly disintegrating. The westward migration of European intellectuals across the Atlantic became a powerful tide after the First World War, bringing to America the challenges of contemporary Marxist and Freudian thought. However, this tide was answered by a strong reverse movement in the late 1940s as American military, ideological and economic domination was imposed over a defeated German nation. These ebbs and flows are noticed throughout the argument since they provided new materials and situations which were selectively incorporated and interpreted by the Chicago sociologists.

The American intellectuals studied in this book had to cope, on the one hand, with the sanctions available to business interests controlling the university's purse strings and, on the other hand, with three dilemmas intrinsic to the inherited liberal tradition. Expressed very simply these dilemmas were: how to criticise a social order in terms of the very liberal ideology with which it was officially justified; how to reconcile the pursuit of harmony within the just community with the defence of individual liberty; and how to combine happiness with efficiency or rationality. In seeking ways to confront the power of vested interests, a common strategy of Chicago sociology has been to emphasise the potential influence and educability of American public opinion (or 'the people'). Public opinion is a major buttress or component of an enlightened civic culture. Enlightenment may, in practice, be produced through a combination of good science and right-thinking professionals. These views were not peculiar to Chicago sociology. Indeed, as I argue, Talcott Parsons built his own approach upon similar assumptions.

The Chicago sociologists responded in a variety of ways to the alternatives imposed by the dilemmas of American liberalism. In part they chose among pathways marked out on native soil by Thorstein Veblen and John Dewey and, abroad, by Marx and Freud. Veblen distrusted the vested interests of professionals and put his faith in the democratising and humanising power of pure science. Dewey placed his faith in the devoted practice of American professionals who would apply the pragmatic test of truth to the outcome of practical experience in the course of problem-solving. Marxian theory demonstrated that the conditions of social justice were inimical to bourgeois individualism. By contrast, Freudian practice offered a means (through therapy) to apply rationality to the pursuit of individual happiness.

Albion Small's pursuit of social justice in the context of a high-minded national consensus led him to disillusionment and Veblenesque irony. By contrast, W. I. Thomas's investigation of the conditions of individual happiness followed a pragmatist route close to Dewey's own. Sharing this Deweyan perspective, Robert Park struggled to reconcile his belief in the power of an educated public opinion with his pessimistic diagnosis of the damage done by the erosion of established folkways in the name of 'progress'. Louis Wirth adopted Small's objective of promoting social harmony through an enlightened civic culture, a goal he sought to obtain through the influence of Deweyan intellectuals over the media. With his 'European' sensitivity to capitalist control over the media, Wirth might be very crudely parodied as 'Dewey modified by Marx'. With similar oversimplification, William Ogburn could be described as 'Veblen modified by Freud'. Ogburn shared Thomas's concern for the conditions under which individual happiness might be promoted but he favoured a strategy of 'setting science free' to do its benevolent work for ordinary Americans rather than following the former's programme of training 'social technicians' to foster more adequate 'personal organisation'.

Morris Janowitz has combined a Parkian belief in the value of the local community with an insistence, reminiscent of Small, that sociologists should inject objective analysis into the political process in order to help to achieve the social control which makes harmony and justice possible. This focus upon social control is complemented by Janowitz's concern, reminiscent of Thomas, for improved controls at the personal level. Dewey and Freud come together, so to speak, in the fourth-generation Chicago school. The absent combination in the above summary is 'Freud plus Marx', a fusion characteristic of the Frankfurt school and its heirs. In the final part of the book I contrast the approaches of Janowitz and Jürgen Habermas to the post-war 'legitimation' crisis within the modern capitalist state and argue that the heirs of two schools, those of Chicago and Frankfurt, may still have much to learn from each other.

A vigorous tradition

Before embarking on the more detailed argument, it is gratefully acknowledged that scholarly and detailed work has been published on many aspects of the civic connections, social background, interpersonal relations and institutional framework within which the Chicago sociologists carried out their research, teaching and administration. All scholars in this area are grateful for the contributions made by Robert Faris (Faris, 1967), James Carey, (Carey, 1975), Steven Diner (Diner, 1975; Diner, 1980) and Martin Bulmer (Bulmer, 1984a), to name but a few. We also owe much to the several volumes in *The Heritage of Sociology*, the series edited by Morris Janowitz, not least the bibliographical guide prepared by Lester Kurtz entitled *Evaluating Chicago Sociology* (1984).[1]

In fact, even the lightest skimming of the literature dealing with urban sociology or sociological theory in the USA uncovers several academic trails leading back to Chicago. The newcomer will find the trails well-trodden and may, if exploring them in the 1980s, catch a faint whiff of nostalgia. For example, in 'a sentimental review' (Guest, 1984, p. 2), Avery M. Guest recently suggested ways in which Robert Park's theory of the natural area might be revived and exploited in the analysis of local culture. Examination of Guest's bibliography leads not only to names from the inter-war Chicago school such as Ernest Burgess, Robert Faris, Louis Wirth, Clifford Shaw and Harvey Zorbaugh but also its well-known critics such as Milla Alihan and Walter Firey (Alihan, 1938; Firey, 1947). Alongside Amos Hawley, specialist in human ecology (Hawley, 1950) is Claude Fischer, who has develped his own approach to urban analysis in part through a sympathetic critique of Louis Wirth (Fischer, 1972; Fischer, 1981). Also to be found are 'neo-Chicagoans' (Matza, 1969, p. 37) such as Albert Hunter (Hunter, 1974), Harvey Molotch (Molotch, 1972) and, of course, Morris Janowitz and Gerald Suttles (Suttles, 1972; Suttles, 1968).

A number of 'Chicago Irregulars' (Thomas, J., 1983a, p. 391) founded the journal *Urban Life* in 1969. In January 1983 a special issue on 'The Chicago School: The Tradition and the Legacy' appeared. It included an analysis of some research replicating Zorbaugh's classic work on 'the gold coast and the slum' (Hunter, 1983; Zorbaugh, 1929) as well as a report by Jon Snodgrass on a fifty-year follow-up on the case of the delinquent child studied by Clifford Shaw in *The Jack-Roller* (Snodgrass, 1983; Shaw, 1966). Some contributors suggested ways of integrating 'the Chicago legacy' (Lofland, 1983, p. 491) with other approaches. For example, Lyn Lofland argued that the members of the inter-war Chicago school focused on primary relationships and the private realm but neglected the sphere of public culture as subsequently explored in different ways by (for example) Richard Sennett (Sennett, 1977), Jane Jacobs (Jacobs, 1963) and Erving Goffman (Goffman, 1963). Jim Thomas suggested that ethnographic sociology in the Chicago tradition was more than a 'romantic curiosity' (Thomas, J., 1983b, p. 477). The 'emancipatory potential of the original Chicago tradition' could be revitalised by the injection of insights from 'Critical theory, especially as shaped by the Frankfurt school' (Thomas, J., 1983b, p. 488).

Other researchers, such as Lawton R. Burns, have discovered affinities between the work of pre-war Chicago students such as Ernest Shideler (Shideler, 1927) and Everett Hughes (Hughes,

1928) and the questions underlying the ecological perspective in current work on 'organisation–environment relations' (Burns, 1980, p. 342). The general point is that Chicago sociology, widely regarded as 'played out' by the 1950s, had acquired new life by the 1970s and 1980s. It had once more become a useful intellectual resource. It was worth analysing and plundering for ideas. Its sympathisers were capable of standing up to a good fight.

David Ward has applied a 'structuralist' interpretation of the Chicago school's approach to urban questions, arguing that its members failed to stress 'the primary causes of poverty' (Ward, 1983, p. 299). In the same year, Peter Jackson directed attention elsewhere, pointing out that W. I. Thomas and Robert Park were particularly interested in the existence of moral order, even in urban areas which were apparently highly 'disorganised' (Jackson, 1983, p. 179). Jackson emphasised the recurrence of a similar concern for order in work by, for example, Gerald Suttles (Suttles, 1968; Suttles, 1972), Elijah Anderson (Anderson, 1976) and William Kornblum (Kornblum, 1974).

Manuel Castells squared up to Louis Wirth's 'myth' of 'urbanism' (Castells, 1976, p. 70) in the late 1960s. He dismissed it on the grounds that it was 'an ideology of modernism ethnocentrically identified with the crystallisation of the social forms of liberal capitalism'. He argued that the urban sociology of Wirth, Burgess and their colleagues had 'no specific real object' (ibid, p. 73). In fact, he missed the point. The principal object of the Chicago sociologists was not 'the city' but human nature and the social order as it was and might be. However, that is to anticipate the argument.

In any event, the 'neo-Chicagoans' were capable of returning blows. Reviewing Castells' *The City and the Grassroots* (1983), Harvey Molotch turned the tables beautifully. His criticisms of Castells' studies of social movements recalled comments that the ethnographers of Chicago were used to hearing about their own work. Castells, in Molotch's view, was:

impressively humane; prone, however, to a romanticism that always seems to deflect his analysis. Paying attention to ordinary people as makers of history can reveal [he continued] just how the material, familial, and ideological variety of their efforts come to count differently under diverse historical circumstances. But Castells ignores the equally creative efforts of those whose duties and institutions create the challenges with which movements must contend (Molotch, 1984, p. 141).

The exploratory ventures and intellectual skirmishes just mentioned are, in part, a response to what Norman Wiley has called 'The current interregnum in American sociology' (Wiley, 1985). In 1985, Wiley noted that the discipline had been 'without a dominant or hegemonic theory for about fifteen years' (ibid, p. 179), in fact, ever since the functionalism of Talcott Parsons and Robert Merton had ceased to hold sway. The last such interregnum had been very brief. The overwhelming influence exercised by Chicago sociology in the years after the First World War was radically reduced during the early 1930s. However, by 1937 Talcott Parsons had published *The Structure of Social Action*, inaugurating the successor regime. During the decade and a half following the decline of functionalism, sociology had arrived at 'a crisis or turning-point'. How was the discipline going to respond to the 'strong and inviting challenge' of 'being asked to explain how the world is changing' (Wiley, 1985, p. 204)? In another article on a related theme, Herman R. Lantz commented: 'We may be at a point of maximum openness in terms of sociological work' (Lantz, 1984, p. 593). As will be seen, during these years of 'openness' Morris Janowitz had been forging his own detailed response to the 'challenge' identified by Wiley, elaborating his own modified version of the Chicago tradition.

Meanwhile, other sociologists have turned towards the task of 'Restructuring the past' (Kuklick, 1980a), examining the social and cultural context in which the discipline took shape in the late nineteenth and early twentieth centuries. In the course of doing this they sought not to destroy but to 'de-sanctify our patron saints'. This has been done by learning to 'recognise these thinkers not as holy seers of prophetic visions, but as creatures of their eras' (ibid, p. 18). Among those engaged in this process of reconstruction, Henrika Kuklick has paid attention to the Chicago school (Kuklick, 1973; Kuklick, 1980a; Kuklick, 1980b; Kuklick, 1980c). As part of the same broad intellectual effort, Fred Matthews has provided a valuable intellectual portrait of Robert Park (Matthews, 1977).

This present study seeks to contribute to this general line of enquiry by, so to speak, taking bearings from a number of strategically-located triangulation points. This project encompasses at one chronological extreme the work of Albion Small, founder of the Chicago sociology department in 1892, and, at the other, Morris Janowitz, whose book *The Reconstruction of Patriotism* was published in 1983. Between the two triangulation points represented by Small and Janowitz there is a clear line of vision. This can be seen by comparing a few passages from two monumental personal testaments: Small's *General Sociology* (1905) and Janowitz's *The Last Half-Century* (1978).

In his book Small asked, on behalf of his fellow citizens, *'At what have we arrived, and in what direction progress?'* (Small, 1905, p. 717; italics in original). He found that confronting this issue was made very difficult for Americans because of their practical and moral disagreements: 'The absence of a central tribunal of moral judgement [he wrote] is the most radical fact in our present social situation' (ibid, p. 660).

In Small's view:

> The distinctive feature about our present situation is its exposure of the poverty of our concept *democracy*. The problems of today are not, in the strictest sense, economic. The economic problems proper are in principle solved . . . The sciences by application of which the resources of the earth are to be appropriated are in our possession . . . But the unsolved question is: How shall these resources be shared? Who shall have them and on what terms? What part shall these material goods play in determining individual men's relative opportunity to get on in gaining health, wealth, sociability, knowledge, beauty and rightness satisfaction (Small, 1905, p. 716; italics in original).

Small looked forward to intellectual and ethical advances which would be implemented through appropriate 'technical social devices' (ibid, p. 716). Above all, 'There must be credible sociologists in order that there may be far-seeing scientists and statesmen and moralists, and that each of us may be an intelligent specialist at his post' (ibid, p. 729).

Compare Janowitz's words over seventy years later. He found that the American political system was undergoing 'marked strain'. One major symptom was 'an increased inability to govern effectively, that is, to balance competing interest-group demands and resolve political conflicts'. Janowitz emphasised the need for more adequate social control by which term he meant 'the capacity of a whole group, including a whole society, to regulate itself. Self-regulation [he continued] must imply a set of "higher moral principles" beyond those of self-interest' (Janowitz, 1978, p. 3).

Janowitz stressed the inadequacy of 'economic' models of politics and the importance of improved 'citizen participation outside the electoral system' (ibid, p. 543). He deplored the fact that many political scientists had become partisan, attaching themselves in many cases to specific candidates. This occurred at the expense of 'the opportunity to serve the citizenry as commentators of the strength and weakness of the political system'. It was desirable, he suggested, that social scientists should take on 'a more explicit concern with broad systemic responsibilities' (ibid, pp. 544–5). Social scientists and political leaders should interact as 'distinct professional groups' (ibid, p. 557).

Small and Janowitz both regretted that higher moral principles were being neglected in the political sphere. Neither thought that existing institutional arrangements were capable of remedying this without substantial reform. Both thought that sociologists could help to remedy this as part of their professional duties. Both men – Small in 1905, Janowitz in 1978 – took very seriously the responsibility of sociology to offer guidance to political leaders and others from a standpoint which considered the best interest of the whole society, not the self-interest of specific groups.

The radical critique

The tradition stretching from Small to Janowitz is complemented by a long-running critique of the Chicago school. Recently, for example, Herman and Julia Schwendinger have argued that its adherents presented a wholehearted apologia for the interests of corporate capital. In *The Sociologists of the Chair* (1974), subtitled a 'radical analysis of the formative years of North American Sociology', the authors argue that between the 1880s and the early 1920s academic sociologists made a major contribution to forging an ideology of corporate liberalism. In contrast to *laissez-faire* liberalism, corporate liberalism accepted that intervention by the capitalist state was needed as one means of managing the relations of large-scale organised labour and gigantic business monopolies. They argued that sociological theories in this period had a strong tendency towards psychological reductionism allied to an emphasis upon 'social control'. Such theories served the purposes of professional 'reformers' whose work, they believed, actually helped to obscure the repressive structures of modern capitalism. The critical aspect of sociology was restricted to 'technocratic criticisms of institutional functioning' (Schwendinger, 1974, p. 288).

Surveying the early part of their period, the Schwendingers drew attention to intellectual developments such as 'defence of the role of the state, American expansionism, and antagonism towards *laissez-faire* and socialist doctrines'. They argue that these emphases were a response to conditions such as 'the increasing class conflict, the economic instability, the further development of domestic and foreign forms of imperialism, the interpenetration of corporate and state forms of monopoly capitalism, and the rise of socialist movements' (ibid, p. 162). These conditions 'sustained' new sociological ideas such as 'race conflict', 'social control', 'interest group', 'assimilation', 'survival' and 'adaptation', the authors claimed. They went on to argue that the ideological functions of sociological theory gradually became more covert as it was increasingly couched in more general and abstract language. According to the Schwendingers, the textbook by Robert Park and Ernest Burgess entitled *Introduction to the Science of Sociology* initially published in 1921, embodied the culmination of this process.

The burden of the Schwendingers's complaint is that sociology has served capitalism at the expense of democracy. This is most clearly expressed in the following passage:

'the linkage between the *professional* social analyst and the *professional* social reformer has undermined every democratic precept that has heretofore justified the direct control over political institutions by the public at large. This linkage . . . has provided the justification for removing some of the most important urban issues from politics . . . It has led to the systematic ridicule of radical proposals for genuine grass-roots administration and control over the institutions that affect the daily lives of common people' (Schwendinger, 1974, p. 288; italics in original).

The tone of the above quotation is faintly reminiscent of

Wisconsin or Kansas in the 1880s or 1890s. In fact, contrary to one implication of their own argument, the work of these authors seems to show that the populist, mid-Western style of American liberalism has certainly not been squeezed out of American social science. In fact, it has provided the spring for a stream of critical analysis which has sometimes been forced underground but which has never dried up completely. Three representatives of this approach within American liberalism, whose work spans several decades, are Thorstein Veblen, C. Wright Mills, and Alvin Gouldner. In view of the Schwendingers's critique it is worth asking whether Veblen, Mills and Gouldner have regarded Chicago sociologists as mere neutered servants of capitalism. Some interesting differences between them will shortly emerge.

> Plato's classic scheme of folly, which would have the philosophers take over the management of affairs, has been turned on its head; the men of affairs have taken over the direction of the pursuit of knowledge . . . It is a fact of the current state of things . . . Its institutional ground is the current state of private ownership . . . The fact is that businessmen hold the plenary discretion, and that business principles guide them in their management of the affairs of the higher learning; and such must continue to be the case so long as the community's workday material interests continue to be organized on a basis of business enterprise. All this does not bode well for the future of science and scholarship in the universities (Veblen, 1965a, pp. 77–8).

In *The Higher Learning in America*, Thorstein Veblen explored some of the implications of the domination of American universities by the interests and principles of capitalist enterprise. His argument was initially shaped by 'first-hand' observation of the conduct of affairs at Chicago' (ibid, p. v.), a case he found to be fairly typical. In this book Veblen argued that academics in the 'moral and social sciences' have to take account of 'not simply the vulgar, commonplace convictions of the populace' but also 'the views and presuppositions prevalent among the respectable, conservative middle class; with a particular regard to that more select body of substantial citizens who have the disposal of accumulated wealth' (ibid, pp. 183–4). In particular, added Veblen, 'A wise academic policy, conducted by an executive looking to the fiscal interests of the university, will aim not to alienate the affections of the large businessmen of a ripe age' (ibid, p. 185).

Veblen did not wish to be misunderstood. After all, he pointed out, academic researchers in the social sciences work in 'full freedom': 'That they are able to do so is a fortunate circumstance, due to the fact that their intellectual horizon is bounded by the same limits of commonplace insight and preconceptions as are the prevailing opinions of the conservative middle class' (ibid, p. 186). Veblen characterised academic social sciences as he had known it during the period between the early 1890s and the end of the First World War in the following words:

> With a view to as much precision as the case admits, it may be remarked that this branch of academic science as habitually pursued, is commonly occupied with questions of what ought to be done, rather than with theories of the genesis and causation of the present-day state of things, or with questions as to what the present-day drift of things may be, as determined by the causes at work. As it does in popular speculation, so also in this academic quasi-science, the interest centres on what ought to be done to improve conditions and to conserve those usages and conventions that have by habit been embedded in the received scheme of use and wont, and so have come to be found good and right (ibid, p. 187).

Broadly speaking, Veblen was arguing that the sociological imagination of academics was constrained by a dominant cultural climate of cautious reformism and that the limits of the latter were imposed by the demands of a regime based upon private ownership and capitalist enterprise.

This assessment may be contrasted with the views expressed half a century later by Alvin Gouldner. In *The Coming Crisis of Western Sociology* (1970) Gouldner argued that 'the liberal ideologies shared by most American sociologists were, *prior to World War II*, a source of enlightening awareness'. By Gouldner's day, however, 'in the context of the burgeoning Welfare–Warfare State, these liberal ideologies served instead to increase the centralized control of an ever-growing Federal Administrative Class and of the master institutions on behalf of which it operates' (ibid, p. 500 italics added). Like Veblen, Gouldner saw a marriage between professional self-interest and cautious reformism within narrow political limits:

> Under the banner of sympathy for the underdog, the liberal technologues of sociology have become the market researchers of the Welfare State, and the agents of a new managerial sociology . . . The liberal technologues in sociology present and experience themselves as men of good will who work with and for the Welfare State only because they want to relieve the distress of others within the limits of the 'practicable'. They say nothing about the extent to which their accommodation to this state derives from the personal bounty it provides them. It is often said, and truly, that most American sociologists today regard themselves as 'liberals', it also has to be added that the character of liberalism has changed. No longer is it the conscientious faith of an embattled minority fighting a callous establishment. Liberalism today is itself an establishment. It is a central part of the governing political apparatus (Gouldner, 1970, p. 501).

Alvin Gouldner, like his predecessors Thorstein Veblen and C. Wright Mills, was sensitive to the sorry fate of active radicals in America since the 1890s. Fired by opposition to social injustice, they had nevertheless been overwhelmed by the might of centralised bureaucracy and large-scale capital. In the wake of such defeats, Jeffersonian liberalism, democratic and individualistic, had become transformed into parochial petty-bourgeois moralism.

Mills had attacked the form of liberalism just described in a penetrating article published in 1943. The Chicago sociologists were one of his main targets. Mills cited W. I. Thomas's 'situational approach' and William Ogburn's notion of 'cultural lag' as major expressions of 'the professional ideology of social pathologists'. In his view, followers of Thomas tended to reduce social structure to 'a scatter of situations' while the concept of social change was 'generalised and applied to everything fragmentarily' (Mills, 1943, p. 177). Mills believed that the liberal ideology was well suited to social workers and judges. It expressed an idea of 'needs' and an image of 'the adjusted man' which derived from 'the norms of independent middle-class persons verbally living out Protestant ideals in the small towns of America' (ibid, p. 180).

Mills later criticised 'liberal practicality' as follows: 'A merely formal emphasis upon "the organic whole", plus a failure to consider the adequate causes – which are usually structural – plus a compulsion to examine only one situation at a time – such ideas do make it difficult to understand the structure of the *status quo*' (Mills, 1959, p. 98). In his view, liberal social science was grossly deficient in the sociological imagination. By this latter term he meant 'an absorbed realization of social relativity and the transformative power of history' (ibid, p. 14). Mills recommended the sociological approach exemplified in the works of (for example) Weber, Comte, Durkheim, Marx, Veblen, Mannheim and Schumpeter. These writers were able 'to grasp history and biography and the relation between the two within society' (ibid, p. 12). More specifically, for Mills the relevant questions were 'what is the structure of this particular society as a whole? What are its essential components and how are they related to each other? How does it differ from other varieties of social order?', 'Where does this society stand in human history? What are the mechanisms by which it is changing?' and 'What varieties of men now prevail in this society and in this period?' (ibid, p. 13).

However, in spite of his critical article of 1943, Mills readily acknowledged the vigour of the radical impulse evident in Chicago only a generation before. He aligned John Dewey alongside campaigners such as Walter Lippman, Charles Beard, Theodore Roosevelt and Herbert Croly. In his doctoral dissertation, which was subsequently published under the title *Sociology and Pragmatism: The Higher Learning in America* (1966) Mills composed a wistful obituary of progressive liberalism as it had existed before the First World War:

Everything the earlier crusading liberals, the Muckrakers, were against was *specific*: a given town's political corruption, the stock yards, a meat trust, a tobacco trust, a fake advertisement; they were against features of the big industrialization, of high capitalism. What they gave were Jeffersonian shibboleths: Was government corrupt? Civil service reform. Were there big trusts? Trust-busting. Was there an oligarchy of banks, etc.? Wilson's New Freedom – for the small capitalist, including farmers. They experimented. They were specific; they were definitely intelligent. But they were wiped out, sucked into the gyrations: the pattern of objective events, the big structural shifts to high capitalism wiped them out along with their publics and the magazines for which they wrote (Mills, 1966, p. 331 italics in original).

Mills went on to argue that big business not only largely obliterated the world of small-scale capitalism and its professional associates but also provided new bureaucratic and professional jobs for the children of the defeated 'progressive' liberals: 'Politically, they were killed by the war, and their hopes were shattered by the peace, their public by prosperity during the twenties' (ibid, p. 331).

Veblen, Mills and Gouldner obviously had much in common. All three men had an idea of intellectual craftsmanship which harks back, implicitly at least, to the masterless artisan of earlier American days. The stream of puritanism through all their writing is expressed in an insistence on the need for self-awareness (Mills, Gouldner) and the high intrinsic value of work (Veblen, Gouldner). All shared the ambition of infusing (or re-infusing) liberalism with a radical dynamic in opposition to the alienating forces of big business and the bureaucratic state. In pursuing this ambition, all three writers engaged in serious debate with theoretical approaches deriving from Europe. Veblen, not a Marxist, was thoroughly familiar with Marx's ideas. Mills had close contact with the Frankfurt School in exile during his years at Columbia University. Gouldner approved of the increasing interaction he saw between 'Academic Sociology' and 'the more Hegelian versions of Marxism' (Gouldner, 1970, p. 438).

How, then, does the Chicago School stand in relation to the critical tradition in American sociology represented by Veblen, Mills and Gouldner? Taken together, Veblen, Mills and Gouldner give us a very confused answer. They are not in agreement. Veblen's verdict, published at the end of the First World War, was evidently hostile to Chicago sociology as it had developed in the preceding quarter of a century. He found its practitioners dull and conformist. Two decades later, Mills took a much more favourable view of Dewey and his circle which included prominent Chicago sociologists such as W. I. Thomas. These men and women were active campaigners against many of the particular institutional forms taken by industrial capitalism as it became more alienating. According to Mills – who disagrees with Veblen on this point – it was only *after* the First World War that the rot really set in.

Gouldner had yet another version of history, one much more generous to the scholars of the inter-war period. As has been seen, he thought that 'the liberal ideologies shared by most American sociologists were, prior to World War II, a source of enlightening awareness' (Gouldner, 1970, p. 500). This period of relative enlightenment obviously included 'the institutionalization of Academic Sociology at the University of Chicago in the 1920s' (ibid, p. 157). Gouldner praised the 'pioneering work' on issues such as newspapers and publics carried out by the Chicago School, producing an analysis that was 'immensely rich' (Gouldner, 1976, pp. 118 and 120).

Veblen was born shortly before the Civil War. The birth of Mills occurred just before the USA entered the First World War. Gouldner was a child of the 1920s. Perhaps radical social scientists share a common human failing – that is, to recall life as having been very much better around the time you were born than it has since become. In any event, the relationship between sociology, capitalism and liberalism in Chicago remains an open issue, worthy of further exploration.

1126 and 1929

In October 1929 the Wall Street Crash occurred. Two months later Chicago University's superbly-equipped Social Science Research Building at 1126 East 59th Street was inaugurated at Chicago University. The building was paid for by a very large grant from the Laura Spelman Rockefeller Memorial. In retrospect, this event was the high point in the development of the department established by Albion Small nearly four decades before at the onset of a previous economic depression in the 1890s. It is relevant to ask: if contemporary capitalism provided the resources for academic social scientists and contemporary liberalism defined their objectives, in what respects was the academic practice of Chicago sociologists – the ways in which they thought about and carried out their work – influenced by this close interdependence with liberal culture and corporate capitalism?

Enquiry into this question will take us backwards and forwards from 1929 but some relevant evidence is contained in *Chicago: An Experiment in Social Science Research* (1929), a publication which reported upon the first five years' work of the Local Community Research Committee, a body also sponsored by the Memorial. The objects of the Committee as understood by the Memorial had been expressed as follows in 1924 by its director, Beardsley Ruml:

> The plan here was to bring together the research capacities of the university in economics, sociology, and political science and, in cooperation with public and private agencies of the city of Chicago, to undertake a systematic investigation of the Chicago community. It was felt that such a program would be beneficial both to the City and to the University – that research and instruction in social science would flourish in the presence of opportunities for access to first-hand data and experience such as the City would provide – that the public and private agencies of the City would be aided in their programs for social betterment by the careful and impartial studies which the University would make. More fundamental, it is an experiment as to the possibility of a university assuming intellectual leadership based on scientific investigation in matters affecting the welfare of the community (quoted in Bulmer, 1984a, p. 139).

That statement would certainly have raised a laugh on Chicago's North Side, where the Capone gang was busily wiping out the rival O'Banion mob. In 1927, Big Bill Thompson, exponent of a 'wide-open' Chicago, was installed for his third term as mayor. Capone covered Thompson's election expenses and supplied muscle at the polling booths. An active and high-minded superintendent of the city schools, appointed by a previous reforming mayor, was suspended and put on trial accused of being 'a stool pigeon for the King of England'. During 1928 there were sixty-two bombings in the city, many of them aimed at reform leaders.[2]

Evidence of this kind about corruption and violence at the local level has to be set alongside suggestions that 'the philanthropic foundations were key institutions in both the production and reproduction of cultural hegemony' (Fisher, 1983, p. 206) during the early decades of the twentieth century. It is likely that during a large proportion of the inter-war years, Al Capone's mob and their imitators and successors were able to maintain over a wide area of Chicago's business life a hegemony upon which the Rockefeller

Foundation and its subsidiaries made relatively little impact. Big business had to operate cheek by jowl with the criminal world, producing an inevitable cost in terms of bureaucratic efficiency and moral purity. Nevertheless, there is considerable plausibility in Donald Fisher's suggestion that the Rockefellers and some other large corporate interests 'wanted knowledge that would present their position and thereby contribute to stability and social control' (ibid, p. 208). There is equal plausibility, however, in Martin Bulmer's assertion that insofar as the foundations were directed by men like Ruml, who 'was trained as a social scientist and reflected his own professional socialization' (Bulmer, 1984b, p. 577), then they were able to exhibit 'a cultivated sense of disinterestedness and detachment' (ibid, p. 575).

Four points are relevant. First, the involvement of large-scale capital in the provision of funding for social science was the exception rather than the rule. Within many boardrooms the attitude must have been one of indifference. Second, the relationship between professional directors such as Ruml and the business interests which employed them was one of give and take on both sides. Fisher noted, for example, that Ruml's successor, Edmund E. Day, was able successfully to withstand pressure from the Rockefeller Foundation to direct the social sciences more forcefully towards specific research areas. He had argued that these disciplines 'were still in a pioneering stage and ought therefore to be excluded from the new policy' (Fisher, 1983, p. 215).

Third, the Rockefeller Foundation took great care to avoid overt involvement in any project which, to quote one of its representatives, 'in appearance or in fact, could be construed as a programme to defend or promote the private enterprise system *per se*' (ibid, p. 220). American public opinion was a power of which the large corporations had a justifiable fear. The battle for its approval had constantly to be fought or, better still, avoided. The covert use of political and economic influence was a strategy which must have looked attractive alongside the risky long-term goal of seeking 'cultural hegemony' (ibid, p. 206). Finally, in cases where the assumptions and ambitions of public opinion, social science and corporate capitalists coincided, or appeared to coincide, this was due in large part to selective appeals to a liberal tradition created by none of the three.[3]

We can now turn to *Chicago: An Experiment in Social Science*

Research (1968), edited by T. V. Smith and Leonard D. White. In this volume, the academics of Chicago presented evidence of a very busy first five years under the auspices of the Local Community Research Committee. In the course of twelve substantial chapters and two hefty appendices the authors made it clear how they wished to be regarded by the public. What picture of Chicago social science was put on display?

Three points strike home initially. First, people from different disciplines were cooperating with each other on academic projects. Academics from the departments of Sociology and Anthropology, Political Science, History, Economics and Psychology as well as the schools of Social Service Administration and Commerce and Administration served on a variety of subcommittees concerned with, for example, the registration of social statistics and research on public finance, personality and the causes of war. Second, there were many contracts with city agencies, especially in the reform fraternity. By 1929 funds had been received from local clubs of the well-heeled and high-minded such as the City Club of Chicago, the Commonwealth Club, the Rotary Club and the Chicago Women's Club. Practical research help had been given to a range of local special interests especially settlement houses and groups concerned with immigrants, blacks, social workers, the handicapped, delinquents and foundlings. Third, everyone had been very busy. As Leonard White put it: 'Contrary to a prevalent belief, "professors" do not, at least at the University of Chicago, belong to the leisure class' (Smith and White, 1968, p. 41).

Although there were nine contributors to this volume, it was dominated by Ernest W. Burgess whose three chapters on 'basic social data', 'urban areas' and 'studies of institutions' made up over one-third of the text. Burgess had in mind a two-phase programme for social science research. In the first phase the task was 'to assemble and organize the materials of special studies, to secure census statistics, to define the local communities and neighborhoods of the city, and to describe and analyse the social forces and trends in their growth'. However, 'the ultimate objective', to be achieved during a second phase, was 'the working out of a detailed and permanent plan of continuous social reporting by all the commercial, industrial and civic agencies which keep records on human behaviour in the urban environment' (ibid, p. 63). With the cooperation of the Commonwealth Edison

Company and the Chicago Zoning Commission his department had already prepared a detailed 'social research base map' of the city indicating land uses. In defining local communities this evidence was being related to information derived from interviews with key residents and a wide range of documentary materials.

Where possible, statistical sources (for example, relating to crime, migration and other demographic factors) were being used in order to trace 'the location and movement of individuals, groups and institutions in space and time' (ibid, p. 137). In the light of such information, civic and social agencies would have not only 'an objective criterion of community conditions but also, what has hitherto been almost lacking, an objective standard for the measurement of the efficiency of their own work' (ibid, p. 138). With the aid of social science research into processes of community change, urban institutions could undergo 'readjustment . . . with a minimum of stress and strain and of social loss' (ibid, p. 176).

The approach adopted by Burgess to the urban world 'outside' the university is one of the three strategies represented in the book. Burgess took for granted a happy complementarity between the social scientist's desire to understand how the city in all its complexity actually worked and the wish of agencies outside the university to turn such information to practical account in pursuing their own particular activities more effectively. In return for being let loose within the vast laboratory of the city, the social scientist would come up with useful devices such as (for example) a statistical technique for predicting with reference to twenty-one factors how likely it was that specific prisoners would be a success on parole (ibid, pp. 97, 98).

In practice, Burgess and his students found it much more difficult to study the powerful than the weak within Chicago society. For example, many of the relevant economic institutions, such as the trade unions, were 'conflict groups ever on the alert to maintain and raise their status, and . . . on their guard against unfriendly and unsympathetic investigation' (ibid, p. 153). Cooperation was most likely to come from 'the Lake Front wards of the Zone of Better Residences' which formed 'the central core of the reformers' band with its emphasis upon good government and the safeguarding of civil service.' It was far less likely to come from those who controlled 'the river wards within the Zone of Transition' which constituted 'the nucleus of the political machine bent on the exploitation of public service for private profit' (ibid, p. 135).

A second strategy, clearest in the contribution made by Charles E. Merriam, was that social scientists should work to make it easier for social improvements to be carried out by encouraging political integration, especially at the metropolitan level. The existence of a multitude of overlapping jurisdictions caused waste and division but 'in the concentration of interests and responsibility is found the key to that intelligent and discriminating public opinion which the democratic experiment presupposes' (ibid, p. 801). Researchers should not only conduct analyses but also make 'constructive suggestion of possibilities of organization and readjustment' with a view to replacing 'a policy of drift with one of intelligent foresight and planning based upon careful analysis of the social forces involved' (ibid, p. 82).

T. V. Smith came up with a third strategy. He took for granted that in dealing with community problems 'understanding' through research would eventually lead to 'control' (ibid, p. 221). However, a few pages later he brought up for consideration – but did not answer – 'the question [which] will ever recur: Who controls whom for what?' It does not take very much reading between the lines to conclude that Smith suspected that there might be strict limits to the complementarity of interests assumed by Burgess and severe restrictions on the capacity of social scientists to take effective action along the lines suggested by Merriam. In that context, 'How to turn . . . knowledge, as it accumulates, to count for the sake of community is a major problem for a social science that has matured into responsibility' (ibid, p. 224).

Smith argued that not all research into aspects of society deserved the label of social science. Industrial concerns might well employ 'students of human and social processes' who might 'uncover valuable data'. Such work 'is science when carefully done; but it is not social science, in the honorific sense here given to the term; for it aims not at general welfare, except by attribution; but rather at private gain'.

Although such work might well have socially benevolent outcomes, 'It is an appendage of business competition and must be made to produce financial gain. The social pattern involved breaks off in someone's pocket and must resume with someone's scheme for further profit' (ibid, p. 231).

In Smith's view, social science proper should cultivate not only exactitude but also 'imaginative warmth' and 'the sense of community'. In effect, his ideal social scientist was a model for the ideal citizen or community member. He or she had 'a personality enriched in sympathy' and, as a result of broad-ranging research conducted from the relatively secure base of the university, was able to achieve genuine 'disinterestedness' (ibid, pp. 221–2).

The university-based social scientist achieved 'not lack of interest' but 'wholeness of interest rather than fragmentary bias toward profit as goal'. The researcher should also be practically involved in a wide range of community activities since this would strengthen opposition to 'whatever disrupts the community and this disrupts his own personality synthesis' (ibid, pp. 231–2). Such a researcher, in the act of teaching, was producing new members of the community who shared such sympathies. Other contributors to the volume had treated social science as an instrument in the urban laboratory. To Smith social science was 'a way of life'. It offered the possibility of finding happiness 'in understanding rather than power' (ibid, p. 240) and fostered the ambition of sharing this understanding with as many members of the community as possible.[4]

The happy complementarity between social science and modern urban America envisaged by Burgess was, some of his colleagues seem to have implied, intrinsically impossible to attain. Burgess would no doubt have accepted that much technical and organisational work had still to be done in providing sociologists with the skills, experience and resources to meet the challenge 'out there'. However, Merriam and Smith went further, they indicated, from different perspectives, that the university social scientist was confronting vested interests unsympathetic to his or her enterprise located within a social and political structure which made them difficult to overcome.

Burgess had organisational flair, more so than his mentor and colleague Robert Park. More than perhaps any other factor, the energetic supervision by Burgess of several projects – such as Anderson on the hobo (Anderson, 1923), Cressey on dance halls (Cressey, 1932), Zorbaugh on the Near North Side (Zorbaugh, 1929), Thrasher on boys' gangs (Thrasher, 1927), Landesco on organised crime (Landesco, 1929) and Shaw on the jack-roller (Shaw, 1930) – has provided substance to the idea of a Chicago

School of Sociology with a distinctive methodology mixing public and private documentary sources, participant observation and interviews. There is no more famous diagram in social science than that combination of half-moon and dart board depicting the five concentric urban zones which appear during the rapid expansion of a modern American city such as Chicago. Burgess outlived many of his contemporaries. Many old students must have remembered his high-pitched, jerky voice and green eye-shade. He was an activist in the spirit of his colleague Charles Henderson, working long hours over many years. However, he did not devote a large amount of attention to analysing the issues with which this book is concerned. For our purposes it is necessary to turn to his successors and his predecessors. The activist, politically-aware approach of Merriam, who had run for mayor of Chicago in 1911, was, in some respects, to be renewed in the career of Louis Wirth. Smith's analysis was in important respects an echo of the social philosophy adopted by Albion Small. Before investigating this social philosophy more directly, Small and his colleagues must be located in a broader context. They must be seen as American liberals wrestling with inherited dilemmas and modern choices, dilemmas and choices which were quite different from those confronting their European contemporaries. To be conventional, let us begin this phase of the argument by considering the city.

Notes

1. Other highly accessible accounts that should be mentioned are in Madge, 1962; Short, 1971; Rock, 1979; Hannerz, 1980; Mellor, 1977.
2. See Dedmon, 1953, pp. 285–300, especially p. 296.
3. On these questions see also Short, 1984; Karl, 1976; Karl and Katz, 1981, and Kohler, 1978.
4. See also Smith (T. V.), 1928.

2
Dimensions of Liberalism

The wicked city

> I view great cities as pestilential to the morals, the health and the liberties of man (quoted in White and White, 1962, p. 28).

Thomas Jefferson's thundering condemnation of urban life in 1800 was echoed over three decades later by Alexis de Tocqueville who considered that the lowest classes in American cities like Philadelphia and New York were 'a rabble more dangerous even than that of European towns'. Particularly threatening, he believed, were two groups: 'the freed Negroes condemned by law and opinion to a hereditary state of degredation and wretchedness' and recent European immigrants without American citizenship who were prone to vicious and riotous behaviour.

Jefferson and Tocqueville agreed that trade and manufacture – which were good things – would generate cities which, if they grew too large, were decidedly bad. Tocqueville warned 'I regard the size of some American cities and especially the nature of their inhabitants as a real danger threatening the future of the democratic republics of the New World' (Tocqueville, 1968, pp. 343–4).

By the end of the nineteenth century future dangers had become present realities. W. H. Stead, author of *If Christ Came to Chicago!* (1894), found poverty, misery, violence, exploitation and corruption in that city. Local politicians were under the thumb of business corporations such as the profiteering railroad trusts. There were ruthless robber barons such as Charles T. Yerkes who virtually ran the city's rail system for his own private profit. These men were, in Stead's view, like the rapacious Assyrians of biblical times.

The railroads which daily injured human lives and liberties were Stead's chosen symbol of the harm caused by the way Chicago was growing. Casting about for a possible patron saint for this city, he suggested St Lawrence who likewise suffered agony while 'stretched upon a gridiron' (Stead, 1894, p. 181). However, the alternative he first considered was probably more appropriate. It was St Vitus. Like other large and rapidly expanding American cities, Chicago hummed with a restless, feverish energy ceaselessly devoted to the tasks of getting by, getting on and getting ahead. W. H. Stead was a revivalist preacher and campaigning editor who visited Chicago from England during 1893–4 (Baylen, 1964). For a while he was the biggest show in town. However, he did not tell ordinary Chicagoans much that they did not already know about their city. Stead hoped that a new regime of virtuous leading citizens would be inaugurated in Chicago. The Civic Federation founded in 1894 and run by high-minded businessmen and professionals was an attempt to pursue this strategy (Small 1895a; Small 1895c). However, it had few lasting successes.

When Stead left Chicago, the challenge of combining material prosperity with peace, social justice and personal happiness in the large manufacturing city had yet to be solved.[1] This problem was found so daunting by Jefferson and Tocqueville that they hoped it would never arise. By the 1890s, however, it was firmly on the moral, intellectual and political agenda. According to Henry Adams, who visited the great Columbian Exposition at Chicago in 1893, the people of that city were confronting 'the question whether the American people knew where they were driving' (Adams, 1961, p. 343). He argued that behind contemporary political debates a fundamental issue was being decided:

> For a hundred years, between 1793 and 1893, the American people had hesitated, vacillated, swayed forward and back, between two forces, one simply industrial, the other capitalistic, centralizing and mechanical. In 1893, the issue came on the single gold standard, and the majority at last declared itself, once for all, in favour of the capitalistic system with all its necessary machinery (ibid, p. 343).

By the early 1890s urban industrial America had well and truly arrived. It was at this point, in 1892, that a department of sociology was founded at Chicago University.

New discipline, new department, new city

Backed by the wealth of John D. Rockefeller Sr, William Rainey Harper, president of the newly-founded University of Chicago, set out in 1892 to buy talented staff for his enterprise. One product of this venture in 'hire learning' (to borrow Veblen's pun) was Albert Small (Veblen, 1965a). Small, a historian steeped in German philosophy and literature, was seduced from his position as president of Colby College in Maine by the chance to establish a strong research-centred sociology department. His new department – one of the first in the USA – began with a total of four members of staff. A strong institutional base for academic sociology was created. Chicago University was relatively free from the hostility often encountered in older foundations on the Eastern seaboard. Sociology also benefited from the flexibility of a private university in its early period of rapid growth. Furthermore:

> Chicago was a new city, built on flat ground by men adventurous in speculation and in building. Only a few Indian trails and a sickly river warped the expanding grid of streets . . . Our greatest historic event was a fire, fit symbol of a city where tearing down to make way for the new and bigger (hence better) was and is as important as building itself . . . An upstart university, founded by people *parvenu* – just in – from the East, with money made by other upstarts from the East, as a matter of course undertook an upstart program, with a faculty pirated from the East. Men with state-of-Maine accents studied the upstart city (Hughes, 1971a, p. 107).

Everett Hughes rightly stressed the newness and brashness of sociology at Chicago during its early decades. This should be balanced by recognising the continuing strength of the mid-Western tradition within that city and its hinterland. Chicago's system of public parks, bearing names like Lincoln Park and Grant Park, was on expression of local allegiance to a form of American life shaped by the old North-west frontier and the experience of civil war.

Meredith Nicolson conveyed this aspect of the city's culture in *The Valley of Democracy*, a book published in 1917 and already in its third edition two years later. He wrote:

> With all its claims to cosmopolitanism one is nevertheless conscious that Chicago is only a prairie county-seat that is continually outgrowing its bounds, but is striving to maintain its early fundamental devotion to decency and order, and develop among its millions the respect for those things that are more excellent that is so distinguishing a trait of the Folks throughout the West. Chicago's strength is the strength of the soil that was won for civilization and democracy by a great and valorous body of pioneer freeman; and the Chicago spirit is that of the men and women who plunged into the West bearing in their hearts that 'something pretty fine' (in Lincoln's phrase), which was the ideal of the founders of the republic (Nicolson, 1917, pp. 177–8).

If the taste for novelty was tempered by a strong sense of inherited ideals, traditional mid-Western confidence was confronted by the frustration and despair bred in the tenements and shacks occupied by the immigrants who poured into Chicago from Europe and the South. From their base in the famous West-side social settlement at Hull House, investigators such as Florence Kelley and Robert Hunter reported on the disease, bad housing, overcrowding and poor sanitation of districts such as Little Italy, Little Poland, Pilsen and the area around Hull House which contained members of over twenty ethnic groups including Italians, Russian and Polish Jews and Bohemians. In *Tenement Conditions in Chicago* (1901) Hunter showed that although the three districts he examined occupied less than one third of a square mile their combined population was 45 643. Only half of the families had access to water closets and 90 per cent of those were defective. Amid the excrement and garbage, rats and livestock competed for space with people. They froze during winter and then suffered Chicago's oppressive summer heat (Hunter, 1901; Philpott, 1978, pp. 26–41). Hunter deliberately passed over districts which were even worse, such as Packingtown, the scene of Upton Sinclair's *The Jungle* (1906).

European immigrants who did not succumb – or at least some of their children – were gradually able to escape the slum. Despite their dark skins, newcomers from Mexico would also eventually find the road up and out from degradation. However, this option was rarely open to Chicago's black population, sucked in from the South by the city's dynamic growth. These native American immigrants were forced to take housing which even the poorest European 'foreigner' refused. Segregation took hold early and was enforced by white residents who bombed out intruders if necessary. Where all else failed, a gradual retreat occurred. The 'colour line' shifted block by block. A ferocious and shocking race riot occurred in Nicholson's overgrown 'prairie county-seat' in 1919. A black boy crossed the colour line while bathing off the shore of one of Chicago's 'democratic' public parks on the lakefront. He was stoned and caused to drown by a local white youth. During the next few days at least thirty-eight people died and 1000 had their homes destroyed.

In the midst of this period of violent, rapid social change appeared the five-volume masterpiece, *The Polish Peasant in Europe and America*, written by W. I. Thomas and Florian Znaniecki. Published in 1918–19, it inaugurated a period of at least a decade during which it was possible to assert with good reason that Chicago sociology *was* American sociology. In retrospect the leaders of that generation have acquired the status of founding fathers. An atmosphere of awe is conveyed, wittingly or not, by their photographs on the front covers of the series, *The Heritage of Sociology*. If you place a number of the volumes in this series side by side on the desk, the bulky and granite-like faces of (for example) W. I. Thomas, Robert Park, William Ogburn and Franklin Frazier make a passable imitation of the national memorial at Mount Rushmore.

It is natural to admire the pioneer. However, undue reverence is as inappropriate as the temptation to dismiss the Chicago sociologists as mere lackeys of corporate capitalism. Apart from their dominant position in the new profession of academic sociology in America, there are three reasons for studying the Chicagoans. The first is their shared central commitment to the American Way, an ideal of living whose validity and attainability was taken for granted even if its content might often appear ambiguous. From the point of view of the present study this deep stratum of ideological conventionality, this very 'ordinariness', is a valuable charac- teristic. The second reason for studying these 'ordinary' men and women is that they lived and worked in an extraordinary time and place. Chicago in this period was extraordinary in two senses. Its pace, scale, density, variety and ceaseless noise caused deep shock and excitement to the sensitivities of small-town America, the traditional arbiter of convention. Furthermore, the clamorous and crowded city seemed to offer a privileged glimpse of how the whole world was soon going to be. A third reason for paying attention to the Chicago sociologists is, quite simply, their remarkable energy and determination in undertaking research.

In sum, the writings of the Chicago sociologists provide a rich source of materials within which to explore not only the inherent tensions of American liberalism but also the problems of adapting this tradition to the modern world. Before attacking this question directly, the particular character of American liberalism will be thrown into relief by introducing the European dimension, turning in particular to Germany.

To Germany

The German comparison is not a fanciful or arbitrary one. It is relevant partly because with the exception of W. F. Ogburn every one of the Chicago sociologists to be studied was deeply familiar with that society. Louis Wirth was born there. Albion Small married the daughter of a Junker general. Like Small, both Robert Park and W. I. Thomas studied in Germany before coming to Chicago university. Small paid a great deal of attention to developments in German social and economic theory. For example in 1909 he produced a book on 'the Cameralists', theorists of political economy who advised German princes in the seventeenth and eighteenth centuries (Small, 1909). Park, like Small, was impressed by the work of Georg Simmel. Thomas found inspiration in the 'folk psychology' of Moritz Lazarus and Moritz Steinhal. Wirth was a collaborator of Karl Mannheim. Morris Janowitz served as an intelligence officer for the Psychological Warfare Branch during the period of allied occupation of Germany after the Second World War. He has published several articles on aspects of German society, including an early piece on German reactions to Nazi atrocities.

A kind of sibling rivalry existed between Germany and the USA in the nineteenth century. They were both coming onto the world stage at about the same time, ready to elbow Britain out of the way when they could. The sense of rivalry comes through in Andrew Carnegie's highly coloured and unreliable comparison between Count von Bismarck and Abraham Lincoln, 'the greatest political genius of our era':

> Even Bismarck's reorganization of Germany dealt with far less imposing, far less gigantic forces than those which Lincoln was called upon to control. Nor has Bismarck achieved the highest degree of political success; he has not harmonised – fused into one united whole the people he has consolidated, as Lincoln did. His weapons have been those of force alone – blood and iron his cry; even in peace a master solely by brutal force. Lincoln was as generous, as conciliatory, as gentle in peace as he was in war. Bismarck excited the fears of the masses; Lincoln won their love. The one was a rude conqueror only; the other not only that, but also the guider of the highest and best aspirations of his people. With monarchical Bismarck 'might made right'; with republican Lincoln 'right made might'. That's the difference. Hence the fame of the one is to be ephemeral; that of the other immortal (Carnegie, 1886, p. 20).

Many inhabitants of Georgia or Tennessee would have given a very different account of Lincoln. However, the point is that when Carnegie wanted a country with which to compare America in order to emphasise the latter's success in embodying the liberal ideals of the Founding Fathers, he chose Germany.

In a recent study, Jurgen Kocka commented that 'the basic characteristics and chronology of capitalist industrial development' in the USA and Germany were 'remarkably similar' (Kocka, 1980, p. iii). He was not the first to see parallels. Barrington Moore noted in *Social Origins of Dictatorship and Democracy* that there were some close resemblances between the German junkers and the Southern plantation-owners. Both employed 'a highly repressive system of labour' on their large estates (Moore, 1967, p. 115).[2] Germany and the USA both underwent rapid industrial and urban growth from the 1860s onward. They overhauled or seriously challenged Britain in several sectors before the First World War. By the time this surge of expansion got under way serfdom and slavery had been abolished in both societies. Universal manhood suffrage had taken its place, several decades before it arrived in Britain.

In Germany and the USA urban-industrial growth was accompanied by resounding military victories which changed the fundamental character of the polity. The success of the North in the American Civil War set off an explosion of speculative investment in railways, machinery, land, utilities and the other ingredients of capitalist prosperity. Chicago boomed, as did her mid-Western neighbours. In a similar way, Prussian victories against Austria and the French brought huge advantages to businessmen in Berlin, Munich, Frankfurt and other German industrial centres.

Norman Stone has noted an even closer resemblance:

> The world of German heavy industry was very ugly and very successful. Protestant entrepreneurs and administrative staff, Jewish financiers like Emil Rathenau or Carl Furstenberg, and a frequently Catholic (and in Bochum or Gelsenkirchen largely Polish) work-force reproduced conditions almost ideal for the success of the very cruel heavy-industrial sweated trades of the late nineteenth century: conditions reproduced quite widely in the United States. . . . (Stone 1983, p. 164)

In spite of these similarities, industrial capitalism in Germany and the USA went along with very different forms of national development in politics and culture. According to David Blackbourn and Geoff Eley the distinctive German pattern culminating in the Third Reich did not stem from a peculiar weakness of bourgeois tendencies in that society, as is sometimes thought. Instead, it was due to the great strength and radicalism of the organised German working class (Blackbourn and Eley, 1984). Furthermore, this challenge from below was complemented by very strong pressure from above. German liberals had to cope with the demands of a traditional landowning class closely associated with central government. This pattern of a liberal bourgeoisie under attack from above and below was common in Europe. Germany was an extreme case. For this reason it provides the sharpest contrast with the American example, especially in view of the striking similarities in industrial development just noted.

It will be worthwhile to summarise the general European background very briefly. During the 1860s reforming liberal regimes in a number of societies, including Britain, Italy and France, made great progress in rationalising public institutions with a view to making the capitalist economy and the bureaucratic state more efficient. These reforms did not abolish the European aristocracies who continued to lend their enormous prestige to the governments they served. However, aristocrats retained their political influence only on the implicit condition that these governments carried out policies which suited the business and professional classes. Meanwhile, liberal politicians also tried to protect the bourgeoisie against attack from below by restricting the extension of the franchise. Freed from the hindrances imposed by 'excessive' democracy, statesmen such as Gladstone, Cavour and Delbruck reformed education, the banking system, the army, the civil service and so on.[3]

The very success of the liberal reforms helped to engender a surge in population and prosperity throughout Europe. Ironically, these pressures burst asunder the class accommodations just described upon which the liberal reforms had been based. As the food supply improved and the urban labour market expanded, the influence of the town increased at the expense of the countryside. European aristocracies underwent a profound crisis, their authority and influence weakening before being largely swept away at the time of the First World War. The morale of European liberals was also undermined. Their rational world view drew heavily upon models hammered out in the eighteenth century under the patronage of 'enlightened' aristocrats and implemented in the succeeding century through institutions whose authority was strengthened by aristocratic participation. Meanwhile, an increasingly well-educated, well-fed, well-organised and numerous working population challenged the social basis of mid-century liberal paternalism. As the franchise was extended or exploited more vigorously, 'the people' became increasingly available as a political resource. They gave support to right-wing or left-wing politicians who were willing to build up the powers of the state apparatus far beyond the wishes of their liberal rivals. As the tasks of managing the new and disruptive urban–industrial regime were being faced during the decades around the turn of the century, the old liberal moral order in Europe was rapidly disintegrating. Germany was the most dramatic instance of this widespread tendency.

European liberalism inherited an ideal which was radically at odds with late-eighteenth-century reality and progressively undermined by the mass politics coming into existence a century later. Between these epochs, commercial, professional, bureaucratic, landed and religious interests struggled with each other to hold the ring. The liberal hope of a general amalgamation between political power, material well-being and enlightenment was fulfilled neither within the circles of the powerful nor, *a fortiori*, in society at large. The point is, however comfortable and conservative European liberals might appear to be, their values committed them to a fundamentally critical stance in relation to their own societies (see also Ringer, 1979).

Back to America

Liberalism in the USA also had its troubles but they were of a very different kind. American liberalism was celebratory rather than critical. It declared that American society embodied an achieved emancipation. American citizens understood that their forefathers had thrown off the 'tyranny' of Europe and established a just, free and rational society dedicated to the pursuit of happiness. Half a century after declaring their independence Americans were told by Alexis de Tocqueville that they had actually achieved the liberal dream of uniting prosperity, enlightenment and active political citizenship within their communities (Tocqueville, 1968). Reason and freedom had, it seemed, fused to produce a regime of decency and order. Americans were inclined to agree with this description of their New World.[4]

A number of problems flowed from this very powerful tradition. One of them was: how do you criticise a society which is defined as perfect? It was difficult to make fundamental criticism in terms of the very liberal tradition which served as a legitimising ideology for American institutions. However, it was also dangerous to mount a critical attack in terms of other 'un-American' traditions such as socialism. The redoubts of class privilege within which European intellectuals might seek support or protection were not available to their American counterparts. The latter faced the full blast of native egalitarianism, often urged on by an eager press. Matthew Arnold was very sensitive to the change of cultural climate brought by crossing the Atlantic in the 1880s. He wrote 'if one were searching for the best means to efface and kill in a whole nation the discipline of respect, the feeling for what is elevated, one could not do better than take the American newspapers' (Arnold, 1888, p. 490). Confronted with the powerful batteries of public opinion, American intellectuals were largely confined within the fiercely-guarded boundaries of the national ideology.

However, American liberalism had its own internal conflicts. For example, how could the pervasive individualism of that tradition be reconciled with its equally powerful longing for the just community? From its earliest days, the American Republic was known as a society in which ordinary men and women were free from the artificial constraints of rank and privilege. They could (even should) compete as individuals. Their natural worth would obtain for them whatever success they merited. From its earliest days also, American culture valued neighbourliness. Furthermore, it bestowed upon the people at large – in other words, upon the community to which a person belonged – the authority to adjudicate on matters of right and wrong. The possibility of conflict between the rights of the community and the rights of the individual was present from the beginning. This conflict was grounded in warring impulses. As Michael Kammen puts it:

Some of the most awkward contradictions in American civilization during the nineteenth century certainly derived from men's desire to retain a family brotherhood within a social framework based upon freedom of contract. They needed to strike a balance between the absence of restraint and the ability to belong . . . In the later nineteenth century, conflicts between communalism and privatism, between social democracy and individual economic aspirations were severe (Kammen, 1980, pp. 269–70).

Another internal conflict also existed within American liberalism. It was probably intensified as the scale of social competition increased in the city. How was it possible to achieve happiness within a social order which imposed enormous pressures upon people to restrain and monitor themselves with great care in order to maximise individual achievement and contribute to a more rational and efficient society? How could you be happy if you were pushing yourself all the time? Max Lerner described a typical pattern as follows:

> The neurotic-personality-as-American may feel caught up in the conflict between the stated ideals and operative drives of his society. Because of this gap he may feel guilty, anxious, and insecure, and may seek to build himself up in the mirror of other people, or may seek the elusive inner security in the feverish effort to achieve money, power, and an outer security (Lerner, 1958, p. 694).

Lerner's observations in the 1950s recollect Tocqueville's picture over a hundred years before of the American engaged in a 'futile pursuit of that complete felicity which always escapes him' (ibid, 1968, p. 693). Thorstein Veblen's evocation of the irksomeness of labour and the appeal of conspicuous (in other words, wasteful) consumption in *The Theory of the Leisure Class* (Veblen, 1970) also drew attention to the conflict between rationality and happiness as understood in the America he knew. More recently, Richard Sennet and Jonathan Cobb have pursued related themes in *The Hidden Injuries of Class* (1972).

The two conflicts just mentioned – between the free individual and the just community and between rationality (as means) and happiness (as end) – were intensified by their association with a further problem. How could the pristine perfection of early America – remembered as being agrarian, small-scale, open and neighbourly – be recreated in the smokey jungle of the modern city? One typical view of this dilemma of American modernity was expressed by Harry Pratt Judson, the history professor who was later to succeed Harper as president of Chicago University. Judson delivered a lecture to his fellow academics on 4 July 1895 entitled 'Is our republic a failure?'

Judson's response had some paradoxical elements. On the one hand he exploited transatlantic comparisons with 'monarchical Europe' as a means of invoking the radical aspects of American liberalism (Judson, 1895, p. 37). Significantly, he put the query which formed his title into the mouth of 'A gentleman prominently connected with the diplomatic service of a European nation' (ibid, p. 28). On the other hand, when dealing with the failings of contemporary America, he appealed to that same liberal tradition as a guarantor of conservative values which would preserve Americans from the evils of the modern world. His lecture is worth examining at length.

Judson was proud to belong to a nation free of the hereditary principle, one which 'from its inception in 1776 to the present day . . . has been growing steadily more democratic and more republican'. However, [he asked] has the experiment of republican democracy in America been a failure? A 'true patriot' with a 'thoughtful mind' had to admit the existence of 'alarming evils' in public life. Two were named. One was the 'disappearance of public confidence in our legislative bodies (ibid, p. 31). For example, 'in Chicago few people would mourn if the common council were nothing more than a shadow' (ibid, p. 32). Judson scathingly condemned the jobbery, bribery and wire-pulling in city councils, state legislatures and Congress. Since 'Our legislatures are no longer deliberative bodies' (ibid, p. 33), the people were turning for protection and reform to mayors, governors and the president.

A second evil was 'the actual tyranny' abounding in the republic. Concentrations of power might be inevitable but abuse of this power should be resisted. For example, 'It is too late in the day in the history of modern society to deplore the union of capital in masses for the accomplishment of ends which can only be attained by vast financial power'. Indeed, how else could we make bridges to span seas, railways to cross continents and canals to link oceans? Wealth had to be aggregated to facilitate 'the infinity of great undertakings which engage the restless activities of our leaders of industry'. However, in the process 'the individual has withered' and employees have become 'mere cogs or pinions in the machinery' (ibid, p. 34). The villain was the 'soulless corporation' which had no regard for the public but crushed all who opposed it. Means must be found, argued Judson, to counteract this 'conscienceless tyranny' which seemed to be 'a tendency as inevitable as that of gravitation' (ibid, p. 35).

At the opposite pole were labour organisations. They had certainly given new strength to labouring men '*But*– when the union denies to any man the right to earn his living by an honest work which he chooses – when physical violence is used to enforce this denial – then there is a tyranny as utter and brutal as any ever wielded by an absolute monarch' (ibid, p. 36; italics in original). To tolerate this would be to give up the 'cherished boon' of freedom for which earlier generations had paid in blood.

Having outlined the evidence for the prosecution case, so to speak, Judson weighed the severity of the crime. The evils identified were certainly 'sapping the national strength . . . disintegrating the national conscience [and] . . . corrupting the national heart'. However, 'Can we escape them by a monarchy? Is aristocracy really the government of the best? Was the declaration of independence in truth the beginning of our woes?' The answer was, predictably, a resounding no. On the contrary, democracy and republicanism – major elements of the American system – were the necessary means of combating those social weaknesses which other systems either tolerated or encouraged. Unlike monarchy, 'Democracy is eternally inquisitive' (ibid, p. 36). In America, corruption was exposed by a free press. In Judson's view, the reserves of strength which served Americans in 1776 and 1861 would help them to meet the challenge of self-government in a large and complex industrial society.

The American Way was not in doubt. But were contemporary men and women and their modern institutions good enough to preserve and extend it?

> The real question is not – is republican government a failure? It is this – is modern civilization a failure? . . . I repeat – the real question is social. And it is gravely menacing throughout all the civilized nations. The truth is that democracy merely strips away disguises and puts us face to face with the facts . . . The whole trend of modern life – the sweep of modern progress – is towards individual freedom and individual responsibility. And that is only another way of saying democracy . . . And it is the glory of our fathers that they looked into the future with the eye of the seer. They dared at that early day to assume, for themselves and their posterity, the responsibility of self-guidance. And that responsibility now rests on us (ibid, pp. 37–8).

Judson ended his lecture on a positive note:

> I believe profoundly that in our people there is a soundness at the heart which no superficial corruption can infect . . . We shall learn how to deal with faithless and incompetent legislatures. We

shall learn how to adapt our civilization to new forms of social organization. We shall learn a more delicate sense of public honor . . . And in all our difficulties and in the stress of our most bitter strife, the thought of the men of '76 will be to us always the inspiration which we need. They cared more for honor and for self-respecting liberty than for property or for life. And inspired by that spirit our republic can never fail (ibid, pp. 39–40).

Judson's sentiments were not especially unusual or remarkable in an American context. They cannot, however, be dismissed as mere platitudes which bore little relation to the professional concerns of practising sociologists. In fact, Judson's lecture featured prominently in the first issue of the *American Journal of Sociology*.

Judson was a 'business-minded progressive Republican' (Diner, 1980, p. 19). His views expressed and reflected the close association between American academics and other rising interests within a relatively secure bourgeois establishment espousing a liberal ideology. By contrast, during the same period many German sociologists were closely associated with threatened interests within a very unstable polity which was certainly not dominated by a liberal bourgeoisie. 'I am a member of the bourgeois class' was Max Weber's ringing declaration during his inaugural lecture in Frieburg in 1895. He continued:

I feel myself to be such and have been brought up on its opinions and ideals. But it is the solemn vocation of our science to say things which people will not like to hear – alike to those above one, below one and of one's own class. When I ask myself, therefore, whether the German bourgeoisie is at present ready to be the dominant class in the nation, I cannot *at present* answer 'Yes' (Weber, 1978a, p. 264; italics in original).

Like Judson in the same year, Weber was examining the state of the nation before an audience of the propertied and privileged which included his academic colleagues. Like Judson, Weber made a contrast between the mundane, unheroic present and a more glorious recent past. It was necessary to foster the political virtues, 'the *grand* passions', among the people (ibid, p. 268; italics in original). As in Judson's case, Weber struck an imperialistic note, taking for granted the need to expand national trade and investment overseas. However, in other respects the assumptions and perspective adopted by Weber are not those of Judson.

The Chicago professor's voice was that of an American speaking to fellow-citizens, all of whom were broadly contented with what they regarded as a fundamentally sound democratic republic. Weber spoke as a troubled academic and a self-critical bourgeois in a state whose political character he disliked. Class and status antagonisms were endemic in his Germany. Weber noted, for example, that working-class leaders 'would find few signs of any community of interests with capital if they were to investigate German academic circles' (ibid, p. 266). Internally divided, the German bourgeoisie, in Weber's view, was failing to meet the challenge posed by the passing of Junker dominance. Although he hoped his generation could learn how to become 'the forerunners of a greater period' (ibid, p. 268), his verdict in 1895 was 'that the bourgeois classes, as the bearers of the interests of the nation as a *power*, seem to be declining and that there is as yet no sign that the working class is ready to take their place (pp. 266–7; italics in original).[5]

Capitalism and culture

The analysis has taken us from the USA to Germany. Now we make the return journey by way of a comparison between the writings of Georg Simmel and Thorstein Veblen. More specifically, the return journey is from Berlin to Chicago. In comparing Simmel and Veblen the object is to show that the development of modern capitalism could be analysed in very different ways. The political and cultural climates of the two cities expressed very dissimilar patterns of interpenetration between capitalism, sociology and liberalism.

Berlin, home of the young Max Weber and birthplace of Georg Simmel, was the nearest German equivalent (indeed, the nearest European equivalent) to Chicago. Both were brash newcomers which had grown with incredible speed. Chicago, an insignificant haunt of Indians in 1800, had acquired a population of 30 000 by 1850. This increased to 1 699 000 by the end of the century: the second largest urban centre in the USA. At the same three dates, the population size of Berlin was 172 000 (tenth largest city in

Europe), 419 000 (sixth largest) and 1 889 000 (third largest, behind London and Paris). Berlin, a dynamic centre for machine-building, electrochemicals, textiles and printing, followed Chicago's Columbian Exposition of 1893 with its own world fair three years later. Walter Rathenau labelled Berlin as 'Chicago on the Spree' (Masur, 1971, p. 74). Both cities were known not only for their manufacturing industry, their stockyards and their dazzling department stores but also for the restlessness of their people. Henry Vizetelly, who paid several visits to Berlin during the 1870s, complained:

> Old Berlin is huddled away into the background of the brand new splendour of the modern city . . . Ancient as Berlin claims to be, one seeks in vain for monuments which serve as an expression of the grandeur of the past . . . for streets or even houses that recall the middle ages. Such casual memorials as there might have been have found little respect in a city where the claims of the day are invariably too imperative to allow of even the smallest sacrifice to sentiment (Vizetelly, 1880, p. 67).

Despite these similarities between the German and American cities, Max Weber and his wife certainly did not give the impression of entering deeply familiar territory when they visited Chicago in 1904. Indeed, as Marianne Weber wrote, they 'felt as though they were shaken out of a state of reverie and somnolence: "Look, this is what modern reality is like"' (Weber, 1975, p. 287). Max Weber's verdict was as follows:

> Chicago is one of the most incredible cities . . . in the 'city', among the 'skyscrapers', the condition of the streets is utterly hair-raising . . . In broad daylight one can see only three blocks ahead – everything is haze and smoke . . . it is an endless human desert . . . All hell has broken loose in the 'stockyards': an unsuccessful strike, masses of Italians and Negroes as strikebreakers; daily shootings with dozens of dead on both sides . . . all in all, a strange flowering of culture . . . There is a mad pell-mell of nationalities. Up and down the streets the Greeks shine the Yankees' shoes for 5 cents. The Germans are their waiters, the Irish take care of their politics, and the Italians of their dirtiest ditch digging. With the exception of the better

residential districts, the whole tremendous city – more extensive than London! – is like a man whose skin has been peeled off and whose intestines are seen at work (ibid, p. 286).

Weber experienced Chicago as an exhilarating shock for which German experience provided no real preparation. It was, in his wife's words, a 'monstrous city', the 'crystallization of the American spirit' (ibid, p. 285).

The 'German spirit' was evidently not the same, even though some of its preoccupations seemed similar. In fact, during the decades before and after the turn of the century, intellectuals in both Chicago and Berlin became concerned with the implications for each other of art, urbanism and democracy. In Berlin writers such as Heinrich Hart discussed the nature of 'realism' and 'naturalism', drafted 'articles of faith' and looked forward to the success of the social democratic movement (Mcfarlane, 1976, pp. 107–9). In Chicago, Theodore Dreiser and Upton Sinclair investigated through fiction the relationship between the individual and the city.

Louis Sullivan revolutionised the design of tall buildings. His skyscrapers were skeletons of steel clad in concrete and glass, a demonstration of the principle that architectural form should boldly express commercial or civic function. Men like Sullivan drew upon indigenous resources, eschewing the styles of the eastern seaboard which derived inspiration from Europe. This artistic effervescence in the two cities, both of which were regarded as being in the vanguard of modernism, provided the context for the work of Simmel and Veblen. For example, Hugh Dalziel Duncan has argued that Veblen helped to make possible Sullivan's theoretical advance by clearing the ground for the 'reconsideration of art in a democratic society' (Duncan, 1965, p. 209). In particular, Veblen provided an important analysis of 'the relationship between money and art as a new kind of social rhetoric' (ibid, p. 218).

In view of their similarities, it is all the more important to stress a fundamental difference between the modern movements in Berlin and Chicago. In Berlin, intellectuals were responding to the disintegration of European liberalism.[6] This breakdown of established conventions and restrictions made space for a new phase of artistic exploration, one which imposed the need to cope with new uncertainties about meaning and consciousness. American intellectuals such as John Dewey had their own 'dark night of the soul' while attempting to reconcile the claims of science and religion. However, despite these personal traumas the American liberal tradition remained resilient and optimistic in the midst of urban–industrial expansion. There was room for considerable artistic experimentation in a period of rapid and undirected growth. Even a disaster such as the great Chicago Fire of 1871 produced scores of new commissions for innovative architects. However, the social climate was less conducive than in Berlin to the search for new frames of meaning, more sympathetic to the enterprise of trying to adapt existing cultural resources to the massive and unprecedented task of managing existence within the modern city.

Common to Dreiser and Sullivan, for example, is their perception of the American quest to realise human potential through action within an urban social order dominated by business values. Dreiser's central characters, for example, in *Sister Carrie*, are pitiable (and occasionally tragic) figures whose energies and ambitions sometimes lead them into pathways of misery. By contrast, Sullivan hoped that the architect might through his buildings create settings within which democratic social relationships might be encouraged to develop. There is little ambiguity in these representations of the world and its tensions. The human actor is either overcome by powerful social forces, as in much of Dreiser's work, or destined to shape these forces as was Sullivan's ambition (see Smith, C. R., 1984; Mayer and Wade, 1969; Duffey, 1954; Sullivan, 1956).

In Chicago, a common intellectual response to modernity was to search for unifying principles within the ramifying complexity, to interpret the urban experience in terms of inherited notions of aspiration and struggle drawn from a literary tradition encompassing both Herbert Spencer and Walt Whitman. By contrast, intellectual life in Berlin gave greater encouragement to those who relished ambiguity and sought for multi-layered complexity beyond the superficial appearance of things.

Simmel and Veblen

Georg Simmel was born in Berlin in 1858. Between 1885 and 1914 he taught at the University of Berlin. Only at the advanced age of 56 did he move away to Strasbourg, lured by a chair in philosophy. During his Berlin years, the regular salon at Simmel's private residence became renowned. Indeed, according to one commentator:

> In Simmel . . . one could feel the pulse-beat of the times most forcefully. His audience at the University of Berlin was the largest and most select. He had connections not only with the foremost philosophers and academics of his time, with Bergson, Troeltsch and Max Weber, but also with artists and poets, with Rodin, George and Rilke. He was the centre of the intellectual elite (Landmann, 1957, p. v., quoted in Frisby, 1984, pp. 36–7).

However, despite this great success in literary circles, Simmel's academic career was slow and halting. Partly because of hostility to his Jewishness and radical connections, Simmel found little favour with the university authorities in Berlin. He was confined to the lowly rank of *Privatdozent* for several years. His eventual promotion above this level, though not to a full professorship, approximately coincided with the publication in 1900 of his major work entitled *The Philosophy of Money* (Simmel, 1978).

Thorstein Veblen was born in 1857, shortly before Simmel. He was appointed in 1892 to a fellowship in economics at the newly-founded University of Chicago. His stay at the university lasted fourteen years, the longest period of time that Veblen was to remain at any single institution during his troubled academic career. During his stay at Chicago he wrote *The Theory of the Leisure Class* which appeared in 1899. This book, which in the view of Lester Ward contained 'too much truth' about American society for comfort (Ward, 1900, p. 829), soon became essential reading in fashionable society. Veblen wrote other works also, including *The Theory of Business Enterprise* (Veblen, 1965b) which appeared in 1904. His essay on 'The place of science in modern civilization' (1906) was written in Chicago as were a number of important papers on the history of economics as a discipline (for example, Veblen, 1898a; Veblen, 1899–1900). Three articles published in the *American Journal of Sociology* (Veblen, 1898b, 1898c, 1899) demonstrate that Veblen was already by that date working on the thesis later set out in his book *The Instinct of Workmanship* (Veblen, 1964), to be published in 1914. Although Veblen's bitter polemic, *The Higher Learning in America* (originally to be subtitled 'a study in utter depravity') did not appear until 1918, it is based in large measure upon the author's experiences in the University of Chicago (Veblen, 1965a).

Despite his failure to reach the heights of *academe*, by the end of the First World War Veblen's reputation was widespread. In the words of H. L. Mencken, 'Veblenism was shining in full brilliance. There were Veblenists, Veblen clubs, Veblen remedies for all the sorrows of the world. There were even, in Chicago, Veblen girls – perhaps Gibson Girls grown old and despairing (quoted in Dorfman, 1935, p. 423). Simmel and Veblen both won popular renown but remained marginal men within the academic profession. Although he came from Lutheran frontier stock, Veblen's essay entitled 'The Intellectual Preeminence of Jews in Modern Europe' (1919) is in many respects a self-portrait. John P. Diggins is justified in his comment that 'Veblen's analysis of the wandering Jew bears remarkable likeness to Georg Simmel's essay on "The Stranger"' (Diggins, 1978, p. 40; Simmel 1950a). In what are arguably the key sociological works of each writer – Veblen's *The Theory of the Leisure Class* and Simmel's *The Philosophy of Money* – both are centrally concerned with the inner meaning of market relations within contemporary capitalism and the underlying connections between these relations and other aspects of capitalist urban culture. However, their two analyses, produced in consecutive years around the turn of the century, are strikingly different.

Throughout his writings Veblen frequently returned to his central obsession: the existence, as he saw it, of a contradiction between industry and business. Complex machine technology encourages its operatives, the skilled engineers, to develop scientific habits of thought. These are organised in terms of impersonal material causes and effects. Scientific thought fostered by industry, is confronted with the pecuniary culture of managers, and bankers. Business culture is marked by instincts and assumptions which originated in the violent barbarian economy of the feudal era and the later, more peaceful, handicraft economy of the eighteenth century. The institution of property took shape among predatory warriors in barbarian times. Ownership was achieved through seizure. Property, including the ownership of women, was – and has remained (in Veblen's view) – the sign of successful exploits demonstrating superior prowess. Property gives social status because it is an indication of masculine aggressiveness.

Natural rights theorists are wrong to imply that property rights flow from the creation of value in land or a product through labour. On the contrary, insisted Veblen, such labour produces loss of prestige. The businessman's barbarian culture enjoins conspicuous consumption, including the public enjoyment of leisure. Individualistic competition of this wasteful kind wins more approval than purposeful communal cooperation. The latter propensity, which Veblen labelled the 'instinct for workmanship', is unfortunately distorted or repressed.

One product of this distortion is the perversion of contemporary taste. In Veblen's view, the 'underlying norms of taste are of very ancient growth'. He believes that 'the requirements of beauty, simply, are for the most part satisfied by inexpensive contrivances and structures which in a straightforward way suggest both the office they are to perform and the method of serving their end' (Veblen, 1970, p. 109). Compare Louis Sullivan: 'It is the pervading law of all things . . . that the life is recognizable in its expression, that form ever follows function' (quoted in Duncan, 1965, p. 322). Veblen made fun of the many ways in which this law was being broken around about him. Archaism, expensiveness and uselessness – major elements of popular canons of taste – were expressed in cast-iron rustic fences, grotesque and debilitating female fashions and, not least, the craze for classicism which reigned at the Columbian Exposition of 1893. The architecture of this world fair at Chicago showed that 'The sense of beauty in the population of this representative city of the advanced pecuniary culture is very chary of any departure from its great cultural principle of conspicuous waste' (Veblen, 1970, p. 101).

Like Veblen, Simmel identified a contradiction underlying contemporary existence. However, Simmel was concerned with a conflict in culture of tragic proportions; one which, unlike Veblen's opposition between industry and business, was not subject to remedy or alleviation. In Simmel's view, the increasing complexity of the division of labour and the ever-increasing commodification of the world of things were making still wider the gap between the interior mental world of subjective culture and the external world of objective culture. Whereas Veblen saw hope of displacing pecuniary social habits through the new forces of syndicalism and the women's movement, Simmel saw the modern world as becoming increasingly pathological. The modern consciousness was not a feudal or eighteenth-century survival but an expression of new forms of alienation endemic in urban industrial capitalism. Trade exhibitions, for example, were not intended to put on show the wasteful luxury of a leisure class (as Veblen argued) but rather to generate an aura of attractiveness which disguised the harm and wastefulness of commodity production. Simmel visited the 1896 world's fair in Berlin and commented:

> it seems as if the modern person wishes to compensate for the onesidedness of their product within the division of labour by the growing crowding together of heterogeneous impressions, by the increasingly hasty and colourful change in emotions . . . Commodity production dominated by free competition, together with the average preponderance of supply over demand must lead to a situation of giving things an enticing external appearance over and above their usefulness . . . one must attempt to excite the interest of the buyer by means of the external attraction of the object, even indeed by means of the form of its arrangement (Simmel, 1896, quoted in Frisby, 1981, p. 121).

These comments anticipated Simmel's argument in *The Philosophy of Money*. It should be noted that, according to Simmel, the alienation of the individual personality, locus of subjective culture, from objective culture rooted in the modern division of labour could not be overcome by overthrowing capitalism. He saw that socialism's desire to transform 'every action of social importance into an objective function' (Simmel, 1978, p. 296) would have the same effect. The fundamental division which Simmel was elsewhere to label the 'tragedy of culture' (Simmel, 1968) was expressed not merely in specific modes of production but also in the practice of modern science, in modern perceptions of time, in the forms of aesthetic appreciation and – most typically – in the character of money itself.

In Simmel's words, 'Money can never be enjoyed directly . . . and it is therefore excluded from any subjective relation. Money objectifies the external activities of the subject which are represented in general by economic transactions, and money has therefore developed as its content the most objective practices, the most logical, purely mathematical norms, the absolute freedom from anything personal'. Money stands between the individual and the objects which money can buy. It has a distancing function but it is also the means of overcoming the distance between the individual and the desired objects. Money, the means of exchangeability 'unites in one act the distance and the proximity of what is to be exchanged'. (Simmel, 1978, p. 128).

In contrast to Veblen, Simmel perceived the market as having completely driven out the practices and emotions of previous eras. Simmel considered it 'quite possible that the precursor of socially regulated exchange was not individual exchange but a change of ownership, which was not exchange at all but was, for instance, robbery' (ibid, p. 100). That sounds a little Veblenesque. However, Simmel went on to argue that through money 'exchange evolved a change of ownership according to criteria of objective correctness and fairness transcending the egoistical impulsiveness of theft and the no less altruistic impulsiveness of the gift' (ibid, p. 436). Unlike Veblen, Simmel did not see bankers as robber barons in lounge suits. Furthermore, modern technology did not in itself provide the means to counteract alienating tendencies. On the contrary, it increased the gap between objective and subjective culture. Veblen would not have written: 'How many workers are there today, even within large-scale industry, who are able to understand the machine with which they work, that is the mental effort invested in it?' (ibid, p. 449).

Nor was Simmel sympathetic to the views on aesthetic matters held by Veblen. He wrote: 'The attempt has often been made to derive beauty from utility, but as a rule this had led only to a philistine coarsening of beauty' (ibid, p. 74). Simmel argued that a shift from utility value to aesthetic value could occur over time: 'The more remote for the species is the utility of the object that first created an interest and a value and is now forgotten, the purer the aesthetic satisfaction derived from the mere form and appearance of the object (ibid, p. 75). Artistic styles had value in mediating the relationship between ourselves and reality. By making things less immediate and concrete they allowed us to penetrate their innermost meaning. The 'basic principle of art' was 'to bring us closer to things by placing them at a distance from us' (ibid, p. 473). Like money, art was located between our subjectivity and the external world. Both money and art were deeply implicated in the intense discomfort and yearning of the modern era:

> If that insecurity and disloyalty in relation to specific possessions which is part of the modern economy has to be paid for by the very modern feeling that the hoped for satisfaction that is connected with new acquisitions immediately grows beyond them, that the core and meaning of life always slips through one's hand, then this testifies to a deep yearning to give things a new importance, a deeper meaning, a value of their own. They have been worn away by the easy gain and loss of possessions, by the transitoriness of their existence, their enjoyability and their change. In short, the consequences and correlations of money have made them void and indifferent. Yet the lively motions in the arts, the search for new styles, for style as such, symbolism and even theosophy are all symptoms of the longing for a new and more perceptible significance of things – regardless of whether it is that each thing has its own more valuable or soulful emphasis, or gains such an emphasis through establishing a connection by release from its atomization (ibid, p. 404).

In the modern age we 'feel as if the whole meaning of our existence were so remote that we are unable to locate it and are constantly in danger of moving away from rather than closer to it' (ibid, p. 484). Towards the end of *The Philosophy of Money* Simmel brings several of his themes together in a powerful passage:

> I believe that this secret restlessness, this helpless urgency that lies below the threshold of consciousness, that drives modern man from socialism to Nietzsche, from Bocklin to impressionism, from Hegel to Schopenhauer and back again, not only originates in the bustle and excitement of modern life but that, conversely, this phenomenon is frequently the expression, symptom and eruption of this innermost condition. The lack of something definite at the centre of the soul impels us to search for momentary satisfactions in ever-new stimulations, sensations and external activities. Thus it is that we become entangled in the instability and helplessness that manifests itself in the tumult of the metropolis, as the mania for travelling, as the wild pursuit of competition and as the typically modern disloyalty with regard to

taste, style, opinions and personal relationships. The significance
of money for this kind of life follows quite logically from the
premises that all the discussions of this book have identified (ibid,
p. 484).

Where Veblen sees hope, however distant, Simmel bears witness
only to 'instability and helplessness'. David Frisby has described
Simmel's approach as 'sociological impressionism' and the writer as
'a sociological flaneur' (Frisby, 1981, p. 68). He preferred to build
up his case through a series of striking examples. He was an essayist
rather than a ponderous schoolman. Furthermore, he betrayed no
strong commitment to any of the prevailing ideologies of society.
Like Walter Benjamin, upon whom he exercised considerable
artistic influence, Simmel was interested in modes of individual
being which combat alienation. Both men wished to circumvent the
dictatorial ticking of the 'clocks and watches in Berlin' (Simmel,
1950b, p. 413) and to undermine the 'regimen [that] cities keep over
the imagination' (Benjamin, 1979a, p. 318). For Simmel, the role of
'the adventurer' offered hope and excitement (Simmel, 1959).
Benjamin found his own approach by becoming a wanderer through
the streets, trying to be, in Susan Sontag's words, 'a competent
street-map reader who knows how to stray' (Sontag, 1983, p. 10).

   Theodor Adorno, a close friend and admirer of Walter
Benjamin, commented on the work of both Simmel and Veblen.
Adorno criticised Simmel for his ideological elusiveness, tending
towards relativism (Frisby, 1981, p. 72). This was a widespread
response among members of the Frankfurt School, being shared
(for example) by Adorno's colleague Siegfried Kracauer
(Kracauer, 1963a; Frisby, 1978, p. 40). By contrast, Adorno
identified a very old and well-established point of view behind
Veblen's work. The latter was 'a puritan *malgré lui*', who saw in
culture only wasteful advertisements of power (Adorno, 1967a,
p. 83). Veblen saw 'waste', whether of time or materials, as being
the antithesis of work. Only work was the source of true happiness.
He believed that habits of thought were always behind the time,
always catching up with the implications and possibilities of
technological change. By contrast, Adorno suggested that the
modes of thought embodied in culture, including the objects of
conspicuous consumption, were anticipations of a possible future
rather than relics of the past. He recognised in capitalist luxury a

harbinger of the abundance for all and freedom from irksome effort that could be the human condition in a future, non-repressive society. From Adorno's perspective both Simmel and Veblen were interesting failures. The former's work added to the insubstantial pyrotechnics accompanying the disintegration of European liberalism. The latter, by contrast, was securely clamped within the rigid confines of the ruling bourgeois ideology in America.

Nothing occurred in America which could not be interpreted, or 'placed', in terms of the hallowed ideological repertoire handed down from the Founding Fathers, the makers of the Constitution and the victors of the Civil War. This repertoire has its internal inconsistencies, as has been seen, but this very lack of coherence gave it great survival value. According to the situation, one might stress the rights of the individual, the claims of the community, the demands of reason, the force of the popular will, the lure of the American Dream, the inevitable imperfections of humankind, and so on.

In his analyses, Veblen sought to separate and to polarise elements of American culture which are, in fact closely related. His writings may be interpreted, in large part, as an attempt to establish the existence of a dialectical contradiction whose tension and dynamic would provide the promise of radical social transformation. For example, Veblen proposed a misleading opposition between a predatory inclination and a readiness to engage in regular, purposeful and productive labour. In fact, both traits are typically found in the same individual or group. Their close relationship is nicely expressed by the notion of the American West as 'virgin land': it is land not only to be possessed by seizure but also to be cultivated for its fruits. Even more misleading is the contradiction proposed by Veblen between urban society as an arena of isolated, competing individuals and humankind as, potentially, a single cooperating community. This is a false opposition since it ignores the fact that by the time Veblen was writing, Chicagoans, like other urban Americans, thought of political life as being conducted by competing communities.

In fact, although Veblen's analysis of urban–industrialised society is acute, he was not at home in the city. In that respect his spirit was very different from that of a Benjamin or a Simmel. Veblen seems to have nurtured the hope that the new technology of the modern era would revive the instinct of workmanship and the sense of unoppressive communal solidarity. These two virtues were central to the old rural ideal of his youth. He neatly summarised this ideal in his last major work, *Absentee Ownership* (Veblen, 1967) originally published in 1923. He looked forward to the time when 'democratic commonwealths' might at last be 'neighbourly fellowships of ungraded masterless men given over to "life, liberty and the pursuit of happiness" under the ancient and altogether human rule of Live and Let Live' (Veblen, 1967, p. 28). In spite of his apparent yen to move forward to a new age, the vision of modern America carried in Veblen's mind was shaped by a strong residual nostalgia for the good old days. To a great extent, his preferred vision of the future consisted of a rearrangement of the liberal present in order to incorporate the best of the liberal past.

Notes

1. On these topics, see for example, Zueblin, 1902; Howe, 1905; Boyer, 1978; Bender, 1982; Haskell, 1977; Furner, 1975.
2. On Moore, whose concern with the prospects for human happiness and social justice overlaps with those of the Chicago sociologists considered here, see Smith, D., 1983.
3. This analysis of European liberalism has been influenced by Stone, 1983.
4. Tocqueville's analysis has been developed in an influential way by David Riesman who belonged to the sociology department at Chicago University during the 1940s and 1950s. See, for example, Riesman, 1950; Strout, 1964.
5. See Beetham, 1985.
6. For a relevant recent analysis, see Seidman, 1983.

3
Making America Work

Consider the following passage:

> Our materialism, our devotion to money-making and to having a
> good time are not things by themselves. They are the product of
> the fact that we live in a money culture; of the fact that our
> technique and technology are controlled by interest in private
> profit. There lies the serious and fundamental defect of our
> civilization, the source of the secondary and induced evils to
> which so much attention is given . . . [i.e. the] old European
> tradition with its disregard for the body, material things, and
> practical concerns . . . The development of the American type
> . . . is an expression of the fact that we have retained this [old
> European] tradition and the economic system of private gain on
> which it is based, while at the same time we have made an
> independent development of industry and technology which is
> nothing short of revolution.

Puritan contempt for mere money-making; sweeping
generalisations about the European and American types of
civilisation; an emphasis upon the contradictory imperatives
associated with the pursuit of private profit and the development of
industry and technology; confidence in the revolutionary potential
of the latter: all these may be found in Thorstein Veblen. However,
this passage is not from Veblen.

The writer being quoted is John Dewey (1930, p. 30),
philosopher and educationist. He was later to be described as 'the
guide, the mentor, and the conscience of the American people'
(Commager, 1950, p. 100). Dewey's reputation has had its ups and

downs since Commager gave him this central place in shaping 'the American mind'. However, his influence in American life during the twentieth century has been greater than that of Veblen. The latter certainly acquired a high degree of popular notoriety during the First World War when he was very active in contemporary politics. However, since that time his work has been familiar to relatively few people outside academic circles apart from members of 'the left'. By contrast, the active part played by Dewey in the development of progressive education (and, no doubt, the fact that he lived much longer) ensured that his name and his ideas became more widely known.

Veblen was marginal within American academic life during the late nineteenth and early twentieth centuries. Do we then conclude that his thought should not be regarded as 'typical'? John P. Diggins notes that 'A number of . . . American scholars . . . believed that Veblen remained too far outside the American value system to be himself of any enduring significance'. However, he immediately adds, 'Conversely, a number of European exile scholars believed Veblen remained too inside that value system to be of enduring importance' (Diggins, 1978, pp. 219–20). Writers such as Adorno argued that Veblen's concern with what is practical or efficient within the social order expressed far too narrow a conception of human potentiality. In Adorno's view, Veblen's position was 'basically pragmatic' (Adorno, 1967a, p. 77). In other words, he was fundamentally aligned with the pragmatism of 'Professor John Dewey . . . and . . . his disciples', the approach hailed by William James in 1904 as a 'new system of philosophy . . . of which Americans may be proud' (James, 1904, p. 1).

In fact, it is misleading either to dismiss Veblen as being 'un-American' or to bundle him up along with Dewey (and William James, Charles Peirce and G. H. Mead) in a package labelled 'mainstream American pragmatism'. Instead, it is helpful to see Veblen and Dewey as participants in divergent intellectual tendencies within American liberalism. A critical tension quickly became established between these tendencies and has endured for several decades. A comparison of Dewey and Veblen will introduce us to these polarities within American liberalism which were an important element of the 'climate' within which the sociologists of the Chicago School operated. These scholars were certainly thoroughly familiar with the work of both men. Veblen and Dewey spent important phases of their academic careers at Chicago University. Dewey's period of appointment (1894–1904) roughly coincided with the Veblen years (1892–1906). Each man left Chicago in the midst of controversy or scandal following disagreements with the university authorities. Dewey's laboratory school on the Chicago campus was the major cause of friction in his case. Veblen, by contrast, fell foul of the prevailing code regarding sexual conduct by married men.

In the rest of this chapter three questions are confronted: what (briefly) is pragmatism? what were the major areas of agreement and disagreement between Veblen and Dewey? and how do the tendencies within American liberalism to which they belong differ from each other?

Pragmatism

Pragmatism is a convenient label for a small group of innovative American thinkers in the late nineteenth and early twentieth centuries – especially Peirce, James, Dewey and Mead – who disagreed on many things but in general terms consented to the following propositions:

1. The best test of what is commonly referred to as the 'truth' of an idea or concept is to ask whether it 'works' in the sense of solving a specific problem confronted in a particular situation.
2. The appropriate test is an instrumental one which considers the idea's usefulness in pursuing specific enquiries. In fact, according to this view, thinking is best understood as mental effort directed at finding solutions to the problems which arise when practical activities are frustrated in some way.
3. Concepts acquire meaning in terms of the habits and practices which they bring about in the course of seeking solutions to problems of the kind just mentioned.

Underlying pragmatism was a dogged faith in the capacity of human effort – and the tendency of social change – to produce rational and benevolent outcomes. In its various forms were amalgamated bits of British evolutionary theory, German philosophy, Yankee optimism and the moral precepts expressed in the conventional pieties of small-town America. Pragmatism embodied the vital energy of American liberalism. This active, positive aspect was expressed in the conviction that knowing is wedded to doing. Direct experience of reality occurs as an adjunct to practical activity.

Some biographical details may help to illuminate the nature and origins of pragmatism.[1] The father of Charles Peirce, who came from thoroughbred Puritan stock in Massachusetts, held a chair of mathematics at Harvard University and helped to establish the National Academy of Science. His sons included, *inter alia*, a mining engineer and a mathematician (who had initially trained for the Unitarian ministry). Charles Peirce himself (born in 1839) received a thorough training in science before taking up an active career in that field and was employed by the US government in various capacities.

William James (born in 1842) was the grandson of a successful Calvinistic merchant and the son of a rather eccentric Swedenborgian. The latter had trained for the Presbyterian ministry but became disillusioned with the church. A schooling in medical science was provided for young William.

George Herbert Mead was born (in 1863) into the family of a Protestant clergyman in Massachusetts. Like Herbert Spencer, Mead spent part of his early career working for railroad companies applying scientific knowledge in a practical capacity. Although he did not care greatly for his duties as a railroad surveyor, he did not feel that his faith was strong enough to enable him to enter the ministry. Instead, he eventually took up the study of physiological psychology at Harvard.

Finally, John Dewey (born in 1859) was son and husband to two deeply religious women, his mother having been converted to Congregationalism in adulthood and his wife being an ardent freethinking Christian from genuine frontier stock in Michigan. Dewey's father came from a farming family but turned to the grocery trade as a shopkeeper. His son undertook graduate studies at Johns Hopkins, a university whcih stressed scientific learning and did not owe its foundation to any particular religious body.

Some of the dilemmas which helped to shape pragmatism are hinted at in those biographical fragments. In the late nineteenth century, the moral precepts and life habits grounded in strict Protestantism were still powerfully felt but their intellectual basis was being challenged by science. At the same time, a new range of careers in professional bureaucratic and technological occupations was opening up which demanded the systematic application of complex and highly specialised knowledge for practical purposes. The human capacity to intervene in the natural world was increasing as was confidence that the social and pyschological realms might be similarly understood and managed. The individual in the market place was losing ground to the scientist in the laboratory and the official in his or her office.

Pragmatism was no enemy of the convictions embodied in the great 'American Experiment' publicly inaugurated in 1776 and given subsequent formulation in the Constitution of the United States. As Louis Hartz put it, 'Pragmatism . . . feeds itself on the Lockian settlement' (Hartz, 1955, p. 101). It has 'rested on miles of submerged conviction' (ibid, p. 59). However, its practitioners were deeply unhappy with the heavily promoted ideology of Social Darwinism.[2] Advocates of the latter cited Darwin and Spencer to validate their claim that the laws of Nature and God decreed that power and privilege should rightfully be in the hands of those cunning and quick-witted fellows who proved themselves the fittest to survive in the jungle of unrestrained capitalism. In opposing this view, the pragmatists were sensitive to the two-way character of the traffic between the world and the mind. The pragmatists were not the only ones to mount a counter-attack. Lester Ward, an early American sociologist, stressed the human capacity to intervene rationally in the social world in order to change it. In the words of C. W. Mills:

'Social Darwinism' and instinctivist psychology were a thorn in the political flesh of liberalism. Both these inferences from evolution fitted a *laissez-faire* faith and a traditional policy of individualism. The neo-Comteanism of Ward – its utilitarian view of science, its social meliorism and telesis of progress, its foresight formulation, and its faith in education – all these were anti-Spencerian, anti-*laissez-faire*.

Now there were two features of the general instinctivist view which liberals wished to overcome or replace: they wanted to give mind, rationality, a place in nature and in the psychology of human affairs; and they wanted to see human nature as modifiable through the reconstruction of the social 'environment'. They wanted substantive rationality to prevail and to be diffused by mass education, but they wanted to deny the political implications of historical individualism. It is between these two poles that the social psychological tradition of pragmatism is worked out (Mills, 1966, p. 447).

Within pragmatism, emphases differed. Charles Peirce was deeply concerned with the procedures we may use to establish the meaning of terms (such as 'hard' or 'heavy'). He insisted that, in order to be meaningful, a sentence containing such a term should be translatable into a hypothetical form ('if x, then y') specifying the relevant human operation (x) and the relevant consequence (y) which may be observed or experienced. Such a theory of meaning was obviously unsympathetic to the metaphysical assertions surrounding religious belief. William James was deeply impressed by Peirce's approach but was unwilling to consent to the dismissal of intense religious feelings and beliefs as meaningless and invalid. As far as James was concerned, pragmatism was an approach which recognised personal religious experience as significant and 'true' in so far as it made a positive contribution to an individual's own way of life. In contrast to Peirce, James held fast to a nominalist position which asserted that while the particular and the specific were 'real', more general concepts which referred to groups or categories were 'fictions'. James was close to the individualistic pole within pragmatism.

Mead and Dewey were both closer than James and Peirce to pragmatism's 'social' pole. In Mead's view, meaning was grounded in action in the sense that it was jointly constructed within social relationships through a process recently labelled by Hans Joas as 'practical intersubjectivity' (Joas, 1985, p. 131). Facing the problem of how to resolve the apparently conflicting imperatives of religion and science, Mead did not treat the former as strictly meaningless as did Peirce. Nor did he argue that pragmatism could somehow mediate between two separate and distinct realms of meaning – scientific and religious – as did James. Instead, he sought for ways of bringing the tools of science to bear upon the interpretative capacities of human beings which include the religious dispositions explored by James.

This challenge, initially adopted by Mead in Berlin during the late 1880s, had become part of a wider mission by the time he joined Dewey in 1894 at the Department of Philosophy and Psychology in

Chicago University. This mission was to explore the ways in which democracy could and should function within a scientific urban–industrial society. Mead was for many years the treasurer of Hull House. This settlement house was established by Jane Addams in order that its residents, including educated young people with a social conscience, might 'devote themselves to the duties of good citizenship and to the arousing of the social energies which too largely lie dormant in every neighbourhood given over to industrialism' (Addams, 1960, p. 100). Intellectual discussion and practical action in welfare and politics were closely linked at Hull House. Urgent efforts were made to bring people of different class and ethnic backgrounds together in creative interplay. Mead was busy not only in Hull House but also amongst Chicago's more reform-minded professionals and business-folk, pursuing investigations in the spheres of industrial relations, education, immigration, health and urban planning.

Mead's distinctive contribution was the notion that the 'self' – seat of that individuality and its meaningful experiences so valued by James – was a product of social formation: not the precondition of society but rather its outcome. In his view, 'the field or locus of any given individual mind . . . cannot be bounded by the skin of the individual organism to which it belongs' (Mead, 1934, p. 223n). In the course of interaction which is both practical and symbolic – entailing physical cooperation as well as intersubjectivity – human beings pursue their goals and shape their culture. Mead was especially concerned that these interactions could and should take place within democratic communities committed to active experiment and open communication. The democratic community, the receptive and active self and the effective (pragmatic) application of scientific methodology were closely related to each other, in his view. Such an ideal links Mead to a number of predecessors and contemporaries, including Tocqueville and, not least, John Dewey.

During the 1880s and 1890s, John Dewey arrived at four significant sets of conclusions. The first set relates to his attempt to overleap the void separating the assumptions about the nature of knowledge embedded in religious and scientific approaches to the world. Dewey began to formulate a view of the mind as not so much a rational instrument dissecting the world as an organic form of life deeply interested in understanding, adapting to and surviving within its worldly environment. On the assumption that Nature was an expression of divine benevolence, such a view allowed empirical psychology to be considered 'the very substance of the theology of God's transactions with mankind' (Coughlan, 1975, p. 53). In this context, Dewey was able to reconcile the positivistic methods of experimental psychology with the (to him) equally attractive Hegelian notion that the knower and the known are inseparable.

Second, having located the mind (as organism) in its environment (the world), Dewey found he could also situate the world in the mind. Roughly, his argument was that if the subject matter of psychology includes human perceptions then it must admit a wide range of psychic experience including self-consciousness into its disciplinary sphere. Through the study of self-consciousness, he argued, you were in effect studying both the knower and the known. Stripped of its Hegelian metaphysics, such an approach emphasises the importance of understanding psychic processes such as imagination, judgement and memory within their proper social context.

Third, building upon his vision of the active, reasoning, imagining human organism which realises its nature by seeking to know and use its environment, Dewey went one step further and argued that 'Moral conduct is precisely that which realizes an idea, a conception' (Dewey, 1975a, p. 100). Such an ethical principle depends upon an assumption that human activity will as a matter of course tend to serve the interests and express the (benign) nature of both the actor and the broader social world to which he or she belongs. Behaviour which is not a proper exercise of function is bad and probably stems either from a failure to communicate a proper understanding of these matters to the people concerned or a failure on their part adequately to fulfil their vocation of activity:

> The moral end is always an activity. To fail in this activity is, therefore, to involve character in disintegration. It can be kept together only by constant organizing activity; only by acting upon new wants and moving towards new situations. Let this activity cease, and disorganization ensues, as surely as the body decays when life goes, instead of simply remaining inert as it was. Bad conduct is thus *unprincipled*: it has no center, no movement. The good man is 'organic'; he uses his attainments to discover new needs, and to assimilate new material. He lives from within

outwards, his character is compact, coherent; he has *integrity*. The bad man, having no controlling unity, has no consistent line of action; his motives of conduct contradict one another; he follows this maxim in relation to this person, that in relation to another; character is *demoralized*. The bad man is unstable and double-minded. He is not one person, but a group of conflicting wills (Dewey, 1975b, pp. 377–8; italics in original).

Dewey's fourth contribution during these years was his celebrated paper in 1894 on the reflex arc concept in psychology. In this paper Dewey dispensed with the sharp distinctions that were conventionally made between sensations, thoughts and acts. Analysing in detail the classic example of the child who puts its hand into the candle-flame he dismissed the old stimulus–response distinction with its assumption that behaviour is regulated 'through the intervention of an extra-experimental soul, or by mechanical push and pull' (Dewey, 1975c, p. 100). He did not accept the plausibility of a multi-phased sequence in the course of which in one phase the body acts and in a subsequent phase the mind thinks, and so on. Instead, Dewey argued that eye, arm and brain cooperate smoothly within the behaving human organism from the point where the child is 'seeing-for-reaching purposes' to the point where, fingers having been burnt in the candle-flame, looking at the candle is the 'seeing-of-a-light-that-means-pain-when-contact-occurs' (ibid, p. 98). Furthermore, Dewey argued that this human organism is able to continue to explore the world, paying careful attention to each new situation in a world of uncertainties and learning how to coordinate behaviour effectively in a widening range of practical situations.

Veblen and Dewey

In the same year that his article on the reflex arc concept was published, Dewey moved to the University of Chicago. His theories laid great emphasis upon the need to establish educational practices which would develop habits of cooperative enquiry and a readiness to adapt. In this way the democratic culture of the frontier might be transported to modern America through its classrooms. Dewey set to work to bring all this to pass. He made important contacts in the city. Wealthy Chicagoans provided finance for his laboratory school at the university. He mobilised their support behind Ella Flagg Young, his friend and disciple, who became the superintendent of Chicago's public schools (see Diner, 1980, pp. 87, 95; McCaul, 1959). He also had close ties with Jane Addams and the well-born ladies and gentlemen working among the slums around Halstead Street from their base at Hull House.

In the light of the earlier discussion it is at first sight surprising to discover that Veblen found these attempts to nourish democratic cooperation very distasteful. In his view, settlement houses were centres of élitism and snobbery, self-conscious outposts of welfare and 'civilisation' which diverted working people from the pursuit of their own best interests:

> The propaganda of culture is in great part an inculcation of new tastes, or rather of a new schedule of proprieties, which have been adapted to the upper-class scheme of life under the guidance of the leisure-class formulation of the principles of status and pecuniary decency. This new schedule of proprieties is intruded into the lower-class scheme of life from the code elaborated by an element of the population whose life lies outside the industrial process; and this intrusive schedule can hardly be expected to fit the exigencies of life for these lower classes more adequately than the schedule already in vogue among them, and especially not more adequately than the schedule which they are themselves working out under the stress of modern industrial life (Veblen, 1970, p. 224).

Veblen's implicit response to the programme being developed by Dewey as a means of strengthening the democratic community in urban industrial America was always 'yes, but . . .' On the other hand, Veblen agreed that 'man is . . . an intelligent agent . . . with a proclivity for purposeful action . . . [and] the compassing of an end' (Veblen, 1898c, pp. 188–9). On the other hand, however, Veblen also noted the conventional assumption amongst his fellow human beings that labour was 'irksome', producing 'A consistent aversion to whatever activity goes to maintain the life of the species [which] is assuredly found in no other species of animal' (ibid, p. 187). In other words, important elements of the predominant culture in a society might sanction behaviour which is *against* the society's interests, perhaps due to a kind of cultural lag. When he overcame his own sardonic pessimism, Veblen placed his faith not in education directed by the current social and political élite but in a revolution of technological and economic relations. This would produce a more progressive regime dedicated to 'mutual aid and human brotherhood' (Veblen, 1910, p. 184).

A fascinating source within which to explore some differences between Veblen and Dewey is a paper by the former entitled 'The place of science in modern civilization' (Veblen, 1906). At the heart of this paper is Veblen's distinction between the pragmatic attitude which is interested in 'knowledge of what had best be done' and the scientific attitude which is concerned with 'knowledge of what takes place' (ibid, p. 599). The former leads to 'maxims of expedient conduct' (ibid, p. 600), the latter to theories without reference to potential useful applications. Science owes its existence to the fact that whenever a human being is responding to a challenging stimulus, 'associated with the pragmatic attention there is found more or less of an irrelevant attention, or idle curiosity'. This latter attitude of idle curiosity is 'closely related to the aptitude for play' and is responsible for the large body of myths and legends found among 'the savage and lower barbarian peoples'. Such knowledge 'need have no pragmatic value for the learner of them and no intended bearing upon his conduct of practical affairs' (ibid, p. 590).

This characterisation of savage peoples is different from the version preferred by Dewey who argued that among peoples such as the Australian aborigines there developed a 'hunting psychosis or mental type' (Dewey, 1902, p. 220). The 'structural organisation or mental traits' is formed by a situation in which 'Want, effort, skill and satisfaction stand in the closest relationship to one another'. Knowledge is embodied in practical skills whose application anticipates their fruits. For example, 'The making of weapons is felt as a part of the exciting use of them' (ibid, p. 222). In Dewey's opinion, 'The transferred application of the hunting language to pursuit of truth, plot interest, business adventure and speculation, to all intense and active forms of amusement, to gambling and "the sporting life", evidences how deeply embedded in later consciousness is the hunting pattern or schema' (ibid, p. 223). Not only would Veblen wish to remove 'pursuit of truth' from that sentence but he would also argue that the predatory animus derived from the feudal rather than a more primitive phase of human development. Furthermore, while accepting the importance of practical knowledge in savage society, Veblen paid particular attention to the large body of mythical lore which sat beside it in the savage mind. In fact, he believed, the two kinds of knowledge 'may be nearly independent of each other' (Veblen, 1906, p. 591).

Veblen traced the most vigorous development of the pragmatic attitude to the medieval and early modern periods. In subsequent eras it became more widespread but not more sophisticated. 'Its highest achievements in the direction of systematic formulation consist of didactic exhortations, to thrift, prudence, equanimity, and shrewd management – a body of maxims of expedient conduct. In this field there is scarcely a degree of advance from Confucius to Samuel Smiles' (ibid, pp. 591–2). Its forms of thought were adapted to a social order based upon 'graded dignity and servitude' (ibid, p. 593), attitudes which Veblen evidently saw as being perpetuated even in the high-minded university settlements of his own day. However, as the centre of society shifted from castle and palace to workshop and laboratory – in other words, as industry and technology became more important – so pragmatic forms of thinking had to make room for a great expansion of the impersonal, objective canons of science.

Idle curiosity is, as has been seen, at the very heart of the scientific frame of mind: 'In so far as it touches the aims and animus of scientific inquiry, as seen from the point of view of the scientist, it is a wholly fortuitous and insubstantial coincidence that much of the knowledge gained under machine-made canons of research can be turned to practical account' (ibid, p. 597). In fact, the prestige of science in the modern period was so great that disciples concerned with codifying pragmatic conventional wisdom attempted to borrow its good reputation, calling themselves 'sciences' quite improperly. Veblen found this to be occurring in, for example, the social sciences which he lumped together with jurisprudence and divinity. Each was little more than 'a taxonomy of credenda' (ibid, p. 601). In *The Theory of Business Enterprise*, published only two years previously, he had argued that a similarly parasitic relationship existed between scientifically-minded operatives of modern industry and predatory businessmen who exploited and perverted the former's efforts in the course of their own pragmatic search for profit.

So, was modern science a 'good thing'? Veblen was deeply ambiguous on this point. On the one hand, he was able to trace it to social origins with which he was very sympathetic: the unwarlike savage people whose tradition survived to some extent in the lower orders during the Middle Ages; and the star-gazing dreamers of all ages. With evident satisfaction he noted the 'curious paradox that the latest and most perfect flower of the western civilization is more nearly akin to the spiritual life of the serfs and villains than it is to that of the grange or the abbey' (ibid, p. 602). He wickedly asserted that the modern scientist's 'inquiry is as "idle" as that of the Pueblo myth-maker' (ibid, p. 598). On the other hand, however, was it not possible that a 'high place' was being assigned to modern science 'idolatrously, perhaps to the detriment of the best and most intimate interests of the race' (ibid, p. 588). The authority recently acquired by science 'may not be altogether fortunate' bearing in mind that 'There are other, older grounds of finality that may conceivably be better, nobler, worthier, more profound, more beautiful' (ibid, p. 587).

Veblen's point was that in modern times the satisfactions of idle curiosity were being displaced by 'the inhumanly dispassionate sweep of the scientific quest' and 'the inhumanly ruthless fabric of technological progress' (ibid, p. 605). Imagination, spontaneity, enjoyment and 'The ancient human predilection for discovering a dramatic play of passion and intrigue in the phenomenon of nature' (ibid, p. 605) were lost upon 'the finikin sceptic in the laboratory' and 'the animated slide rule' (ibid, p. 609). Veblen finishes with this warning that science should be kept in its place:

> The race reached the human plane with little of this searching knowledge of facts; and throughout the greater part of its life-history on the human plane it has been accustomed to make its higher generalizations and to formulate its larger principles of life in other terms than those of passionless matter-of-fact. This manner of knowledge has occupied an increasing share of men's attention in the past, since it bears in a decisive manner upon the minor affairs of workday life; but it has never until now been put in the first place, as the dominant note of human culture. The

normal man, such as his inheritance has made him, has therefore good cause to be restive under its dominion (ibid, p. 609).

To summarise Veblen's position: the pragmatic approach is nothing more than a codification of inherited conventional wisdom; pragmatism has recently borrowed the prestige attached to science because of the latter's intellectual and practical successes; however, these successes initially derive from the play of idle curiosity without reference to worldly applications; recently the pressure upon science to produce usable results within modern capitalist society has transformed it into a passionless machine which threatens to ignore the importance of playful speculation and subject men and women to demands which take no account of their inherited human nature.

It is now possible to tease out the major similarities and differences between Veblen and Dewey. Both were committed to the ideals of American liberalism as expressed in the ideal of the free but cohesive small community. They were both interested in finding ways in which these democratic and humane values might be realised in the big city. For both men the engine of democracy was science. It is at this point that they began to differ.

Veblen anticipated (or, at least, hoped) that the scientific and technological development of modern manufacturing processes would undermine the economic and political position of the robber barons who had seized control as America became an urban industrial society. Effective power would be placed into the hands of the skilled and knowledgeable men and women who engineered and maintained the new manufacturing system. They would combine theoretical and practical understanding of the new mode of production with a recognition of the need to manage industry in a way which directly served the democratic communities to which they belonged.

Veblen located the pragmatic and the scientific attitudes in two potentially conflicting social groups – respectively, the predatory leisure (or business) class and the technical operatives within modern industry. The former – pragmatic and predatory – was likely to subvert the latter which were scientific and democratic. Dewey, by contrast, equated the pragmatic with the scientific and understood that the appropriate methodology of 'problem solving' incorporated the essentials of American liberalism. In other words, the very process of inquiry actually confirmed the intrinsic 'rightness' of the existing society with its built-in benevolent drift. Dewey accepted that a complex modern society had a hierarchical character but believed that its management could be produced from within democratic educational institutions. He put his faith in the schoolroom rather than the toolroom. Modern American democracy was properly expressed through the workings of an élite of scientific professionals fed from the ranks of children schooled on 'learning by doing'.

Such an approach made professionals and experts 'responsible' for American democracy without seriously confronting the social and political pressures to which they were subject or the tensions within liberalism itself. Veblen confronted both issues. He was aware that experts might become tools of the 'pragmatic' and predatory business class. As has been seen, he also attempted to develop a dialectical approach to the inner contradictions of American liberalism: between the community-minded instinct of workmanship and the egoistic pecuniary trait; between the often-frustrated rationality of the engineer and the wasteful hedonism of the business class. For Veblen, the existing urban industrial order, including the activities of Dewey and his ilk at Chicago University, represented not the expression of American democracy but its perversion.

Strategies for change

The writings of Veblen and Dewey express two possible responses to modern America. They were, respectively, criticism accompanied by a hope of progressive social transformation and accommodation accompanied by the ambition of exercising effective moral leadership through the exercise of key practical functions within the urban–industrial order.

From the stance of the inherited ideals of capitalist democracy modern urban–industrial America was vulnerable to the criticism that its development upset relations between the public and private spheres, undermined the stability of communal life and frustrated the development of individuality. Corrupt politicians were less likely to express the people's interest. Amenities which touched the lives of all citizens were in private hands. Urban dwellers were to an unprecedented degree dependent upon a market which could be suddenly and profoundly affected by the selfish policies of a few powerful speculators. The very survival of whole neighbourhoods and their way of life could be put at risk. Employees of large corporations had to adapt to bureaucratic rules which put a premium on conformity and restricted opportunity for self-advancement through inventive effort in the market-place.

Such a critique had power in a culture laden with nostalgia for a past (in many respects mythical) when an energetic and adaptable person from practically any background could acquire personal wealth accompanied by a sense of self-satisfaction. It remained a defining characteristic of 'an American' that he or she believed in that society because it provided opportunities for the individual to become prosperous and own private property.

The strategy of accommodation owed a great deal to the development of an expanding system of secondary education. Bureaucratically organised to identify, foster and measure a specific range of skills, this system began to feed an ever-growing number of alumni not only into higher education but also into various branches of business and the professions. Bureaucracy in the schools prepared future employees for bureaucracy within banks, insurance agencies, legal offices, public administration and manufacturing corporations. Under these circumstances, the rhetoric of individual opportunity continued to be plausible. Its message found apparent confirmation in the experience of upward mobility through the schools leading to personal material success. The message was reinforced by the grandiose ritual surrounding educational credentials. Academics, professionals and experts were required to make this new order work. They staffed the educational institutions, trained the bureaucrats and sold their skills to the corporations.

Criticism and accommodation are not necessarily mutually exclusive. Indeed, it could be argued that pragmatists such as Dewey have ensured that the scientific expertise in the USA is deeply impregnated with a commitment (however enfeebled) to improve the democracy, to ensure that 'our Republic' should not be 'a failure.' However, Dewey has in recent years been held responsible for justifying the development of a repressive school system serving bureaucratic capitalism (Lasch, 1965, pp. 160–1; Bowles and Gintis, 1976). He also stands accused of encouraging the 'think-tank operationalism' of the 'warfare state', crossing the bridge from being 'a servant of truth to . . . being a servant of power' (Karier, 1977, pp. 45, 47). Robert H. Wiebe has commented that 'Bureaucratic thought and pragmatism met only after John Dewey had transformed it into a theory that made individuals the plastic stuff of society' (Wiebe, 1967, p. 151).

In fact, corporate capitalism and the sciences (both natural and social) have entered into a symbiotic but conflict-ridden relationship. On the one hand, business and government have great use for the practical knowledge and enormous prestige generated by scientific endeavour associated with the university sector. On the other hand, university academics depend upon the material resources and political protection that business and government are able to offer. Universities are reluctant to undermine the sources of funds and protection. However, business and government lose out if the objectivity and reliability of scientific findings, widely held to be dependent upon free and open inquiry, are seriously put at risk. Of course there is a great deal of bluff by all concerned.[3] Furthermore, the situation is not as clearly bipolar as has just been implied. There are deep conflicts between business and government, as well as competitive relations within government, within and between business organisations and throughout academe. Another major factor is the part played by public opinion, mediated by the mass media. The press and, more recently, radio and television are an important sphere of contest among all the interests just mentioned.

Enmeshed as they were in the complexities of this modern American order as it began to take shape in the years before the First World War, Veblen and Dewey laid their bets, so to speak, on different horses. Veblen backed science as the catalyst of wholesale structural reform. Dewey backed professional men and women as the means of ensuring that a democratic ethos pervaded the existing social order. By these different means would come a happier and more just society.

As will be seen, within a framework of shared assumptions the Chicago sociologists to be studied leaned to varying degrees towards emphasising the catalytic potential of knowledge itself and the social function of intellectuals and the professions. Albion Small and William Ogburn both stressed the former: the social scientist was, above all, the discoverer and communicator of knowledge which other groups could and should apply. W. I. Thomas and Louis Wirth both concentrated to a greater extent upon the capacity for manipulative intervention by social scientists themselves at the levels of the individual and the collectivity, respectively. Distinctions should not be too sharply drawn since all the people studied were deeply interested in the interplay between knowledge and practice. Neither Robert Park nor Morris Janowitz – both of whom came (directly or indirectly) under the influence of Deweyan ideas – can easily be summarised in terms of the distinctions just made.

Notes

1. Biographical details are taken from Coughlan, 1975; Mills, 1966; Joas, 1985. See also Lewis and Smith, 1980.
2. On the influence of Darwin see, for instance, Angell, 1909; Ellwood, 1909; Garson and Maidment, 1981; Tufts, 1909.
3. On liberalism and corporate capitalism see Lustig, 1982; Hawley, 1978; McQuaid, 1978.

4
Albion Small

Preach! preach! preach!

Albion Small once wrote to a friend

> If you consent to tell the world anything about me, don't mince matters at all in telling the plain blunt truth that I spent my life insisting that there is something at the far end of the sociological rainbow, and at the same time altering my view of *what* that something will turn out to be, with every year's accounting of stock (Hayes, 1926, p. 676; italics in original).

Nearly thirty years after his appointment as head of the sociology department at Chicago University Small made this passionate appeal to his colleagues throughout America:

> Preach! Preach! Preach! wherever a listener may be found, the *functional*, the *moral*, the *human* rendering of life. Pass the word around that in the final analysis the type of people we are and the type of dealings which we practise with one another are the most important things in sight. Keep harping away on the loose connection and even the reverse connection between large bulks of our activities and this ultimate social aim (Small, 1919–20, p. 411; italics in original).

Small's early training as a Baptist minister is evident in that passage. He certainly did keep harping on and passing the word around. Although not as active in city affairs as some of his colleagues, especially Charles R. Henderson, Small was a busy member of the reforming Civic Federation of Chicago. However, Small's energies were largely devoted to the task of defining sociology and justifying its existence. This was a necessary task since his department was one of the first of its kind in the USA.[1]

Small was aided in his mission by the foundation at Chicago of the *American Journal of Sociology* under his editorship. This coup was made possible by the unexpected decision of President Harper to divert to Small some funds that were originally intended for a university extension magazine. Small edited his highly influential journal from 1895 until he retired in 1925. This office gave him a strategic position within the rapidly-growing sociological profession. However, the immensity of the task facing him in the 1890s is indicated by the fact that he was the only one of the four original members of his department who combined a traditional academic training with an interest in modern society. Of the other three, Charles R. Henderson was mainly interested in the practicalities of social reform, Marion Talbot was a specialist in 'sanitary science' and Frederick Starr was trained as a professional ethnologist. W. I. Thomas, who came to Chicago in 1895, was initially mainly concerned with anthropological investigations. The job of providing sociology as understood in Chicago University with a clear profile was very much in Small's hands.

An Introduction to the Study of Society, which Small wrote with the help of George E. Vincent was published in 1894, a year of widespread labour unrest, much of it centred on Chicago. The Civic Federation was briefly involved in a conciliation attempt during the bitter Pullman strike which pitted the Pullman Company against the American Railway Union under the leadership of the radical Eugene Debs. In the preface to his textbook, Small noted that America was 'prolific of social disturbers' (Small and Vincent, 1894, p. 20). He was anxious to distance his academic discipline from extreme social agitators but reluctant to defend rigid conservatism. He came up with the Hegelian formula: 'conventionality is the thesis, Socialism is the antithesis, Sociology is the synthesis' (ibid, p. 41). A decade later, in his *General Sociology* (1905), he was still sensitive on the issue, remarking that 'all sociologists are supposed to belong in one and the same group with the agitators' (Small, 1905, p. 375). The matter had been put quite plainly by his colleague, Charles Henderson, in 1896:

When the scholar enters the sphere of practice, he must prepare himself for the treatment given a man with a silk hat in the bull-and-bear pit on a board of trade holiday; he becomes the target for the wildest boys. If he says anything which by any chance tends to affect prices or nominations, he should not look for reverence. That is an obsolete virtue in American practical life. Nothing thinner than rhinoceros hide will do for an overcoat where conflicting interests are at stake, and arrows are flying (Henderson, 1896, p. 395).

However, these were not the only difficulties facing Small. In *General Sociology*, he reported that 'The sociologists have broken into the goodly fellowship of the social scientists, and have thus far found themselves frankly unwelcome guests' (Small, 1905, p. 21). Gradually, this resistance broke down. In the mid-1890s it was not uncommon for sociology to be 'judged . . . merely an erratic and unscientific parody of Political Economy' (Small and Vincent, 1894, p. 75). Some years later, Small recalled that:

A decade ago, at a meeting of the American Economic Association in New York, one of our most respected economists frankly declared that, if he could have his way, no sociologists would ever be admitted to a university faculty without permission of the economists. Meanwhile, some of us have found the monotony of life not a little relieved by watching the process by which this genial dogmatist has triturated himself entirely into a most extreme form of sociology (Small, 1905, p. 522).

Of all his American contemporaries, Small felt most admiration for Lester F. Ward, the author of *Dynamic Sociology* (1883). He followed Ward's classification of sociology into descriptive, statical and dynamic branches. Descriptive sociology was 'the organization of all the positive knowledge of man and society' which indicated 'the forces to be taken into calculation in all doctrines or policies of social progress' (Small and Vincent, 1894, p. 62). Statical sociology was a kind of social ethics supposedly based upon inductive methods. It entailed further examination of the results of descriptive sociology, subjecting them to 'a subsequent scientific process to exhibit the social ideals which the facts implicitly contain'. This branch of sociology produced 'systematized knowledge of the neglected economies of life' upon which could be based 'a symmetrical ideal, of the social life in which immanent potencies shall be realized' (ibid, pp. 67–8).

Dynamic sociology was 'constructive and technical'. It was concerned with 'the available resources for changing the actual into the ideal' (ibid, pp. 70–1) specifying means whereby the development of societies could be positively influenced by the application of human intelligence. In Ward's words, quoted by Small and Vincent, 'Dynamic Sociology aims at the organization of happiness' (ibid, p. 51). Small, an elegant craftsman in the art of sociability, was not so sure that human happiness could be scientifically produced. Nevertheless, the influence of Ward is clear, especially in his early years. Small's description of the work of the Civic Federation of Chicago, published in the *American Journal of Sociology* in 1895, was subtitled 'A Study in Social Dynamics'.

Ward and Small corresponded for nearly two decades. Small's letters were published after his death along with other related correspondence (Stern, 1933). The letters reveal Albion Small as an artful courtier of the admired Ward, sometimes meeting curt disregard, at other times receiving distant acknowledgement. When Small's *General Sociology* was published, Ward filled his copy of the book with comments such as 'Poor stuff', 'Bosh' and 'Plagiarism' On 18 March 1906 he wrote to his son-in-law, E. A. Ross:

> I have some curiosity to see your reviews of Small's *General Sociology* I have waded two-thirds of the way through it. I ought not to express an opinion till I have finished it, and I will only say that it is about the most provoking book I ever read. I suppose I ought to be amused instead of provoked. But a big volume stuffed with nothing but the things that you and I and the rest have been saying for years, only said over again in a verbose language which strains to avoid the particular words used by others and to palm off some other words for new ideas is certainly exasperating.

Eighty years later, a modern reader of the 700 pages of *General Sociology* will recoil, like Ross, from the book's 'cloudiness and prolixity'. However, in his reply to Ward, Ross added that 'Having no quarrel with the matter of the book I resolutely shut my eyes to the form' (Stern, 1933, p. 322).

The relevant point is that Small's approach to the discipline was, in many respects, a continuation and synthesis of existing work. Writers such as Ward and Ross were modifying the assumptions of Social Darwinianism. They argued that human beings could take rational action to improve society, possibly through the medium and coordinating agencies such as the government. Small agreed. As a sociologist, he faced hostility and misunderstanding in the rough world outside the campus. He had to put up with antagonism from fellow academics. However, he was neither brilliantly shocking, like Veblen, nor challengingly original, like Dewey. Intellectually, Small was swimming with the tide. That is one reason why he is worth studying. In the course of constructing and defending his sociology he was bringing the intellectual resources of contemporary American liberalism to bear upon the problem of understanding and shaping contemporary American capitalism.

A laboratory guide

An Introduction to the Study of Society was intended as a textbook or 'laboratory guide' (Small and Vincent, 1894, p. 15). The laboratory was American society. Its development and its condition in the 1890s were the source of most of the practical illustrations interspersed throughout the volume. Small and his collaborator gave their readers a taste of sociology in action. Only about one-fifth of the text was devoted to 'the origin and scope of sociology' (ibid, p. 21). During the rest, the sociologist as teacher took the reader as apprentice through a series of practical analyses.

General Sociology was also written as a textbook. Small presented it as 'the actual working syllabus' of a course introducing graduates to research (Small, 1905, p. vi). It represented 'in a general way, the point of view occupied by my colleagues in the Department of Sociology in the University of Chicago' (ibid, p. v). As the two titles suggest, there was a shift of primary concern away from 'society' towards 'sociology'. The first book presented analytical descriptions of the development and current state of the USA. The second showed how sociology as a discipline could contribute towards shaping the USA in the future.

Taken together, the two books reveal Small's view of what the USA was and what it could be with the help of sociology. Their tone was optimistic. In his later work this optimism had to fight a running battle with frustration and disappointment. Small's writings after 1905, especially during the last dozen years before he retired, show him engaged in a fascinating struggle to come to terms with the huge gap which remained between the USA as it was and the USA as it ought to have been, in his view.

The heart of Albion Small's sociology is found in the following passage from the 1894 text:

> In the second book of Plato's *Republic*, Socrates is represented as discussing the nature of justice. In order to illustrate a theory, he suggests the idea of tracing the gradual formation of a city or commonwealth. This he does in rapid outline, showing that social organization results from the variety of human desires, and describing the division of labour which is essential to genuinely social existence (Small and Vincent, 1894, p. 99).

Small was deeply aware of the internal tension between the desire for justice and the love of freedom within American liberalism. He sought a way of overcoming this conflict through the development of 'an effective policy of rational sociability which shall include the largest possible number of men in the fellowship of reciprocally helpful cooperation' (ibid, p. 82). He believed sociology could help US society become more rational even if it could not guarantee felicity. He could 'not lay down rules for securing human happiness, because such measure of happiness as is within our reach has to be won by practice of the arts of life, rather than by simply knowing the science of life' (Small, 1905, p. 31). However, even if happiness was not guaranteed, Americans would learn to choose freely a just way of life within which they could achieve self-realisation. Following Plato's lead, Small assumed that the task of outlining a policy of rational sociability would be made easier if sociologists made themselves familiar with the way their society had developed from its rural origins.

In a section of the 1894 text entitled 'The Natural History of a Society', the growth of 'an anonymous but not fictitious' Western settlement was outlined (Small and Vincent, 1894, p. 367). The account began with the picture of 'A rolling prairie, rich in soil [and] . . . traversed by a river . . . Of animal life there is an abundance. Rabbits make their homes in the grass; the woods shelter squirrels, raccoons, and wolves.' There are herds of antelope and buffalo, fish

in the stream and wild fowl aplenty. Between the August heat and
the January snows there is 'much delightful weather' (ibid, p. 100).
This Eden-like setting (the image is hidden but powerful) soon
acquired its Adam and Eve:

> Into this region, at the end of an early spring day, comes a 'prairie
> schooner', drawn by a pair of oxen. On the wagon seat are a man
> and a woman, husband and wife. Under the canvas cover are
> stored their family goods. A cow follows the wagon, and in a coop
> stored beneath are a cock and several hens. A dog scouts in
> erratic courses over the prairie. Encamping for a day or two of
> rest, these pioneers are attracted by the spot; they resolve to put an
> end to their wanderings, and forthwith they begin to assume
> permanent relations with the soil (ibid, p. 101).

This initial lonely settlement on the frontier in the 1840s was
followed through various stages exhibiting the 'tendency to
specialization and interdependence of parts in an increasingly
complex society' (ibid, p. 8). The 'family on the farm' became 'the
rural group', then 'the village' and, finally, the 'town and city'. The
original pioneer household, soon filled out with children and a
servant, had been equipped by society for its struggle with nature.
Unlike Adam and Eve, the newcomers had not arrived naked in the
wilderness: 'Not only their property, but the language they speak,
their knowledge and training, their power to master the region and
utilise its resources, are conditions which only associated life can
produce' (ibid, p. 101). Their lives were moulded not only by the
standards of judgement and feeling which the adults bring (and
transmit to the children) but also by 'rosy dreams' (ibid, p. 106) of
material prosperity. Equally important were the desire for
companionship and unfailing curiosity concerning the world around
them. The household divided its duties according to a division of
labour which includes passing on skills and disciplines to the young.
The death of a child left the parents doubly desolate since there
were no friends to share their grief: 'There is a higher
interdependence among men than that of economic relations' (ibid,
p. 110).

Having passed through more phases – as a rural group and as a
village – the settlement became a city. This last phase represented

modern America in Small's day. In the city, the powerful influence of entrepreneurial capitalism was expressed in the ramifying railway network and the speculative development of urban land. Specialisation, interdependence and complexity increased dramatically. Separate agencies appeared to handle policing, protection against fire, supply of water, education and so on. Communications grew – postal service, telephone exchange, trolley cars, livery stables, licensed cabs – in response to social demand and hopes of profit. Local inhabitants became prey to disasters – strikes, shortages, financial panics, unemployment – caused by the actions of people far away. Within the city differences of wealth became increasingly obvious. A large class of industrial wage-labourers grew up living meanly and in a different part of town from their rich employers.

Immigration supplied the city with colonies of Germans, Scandinavians, Irish, Italians and Poles each dominating particular neighbourhoods. Furthermore, 'One part of town, a really valuable "addition" as regards location, was early opened by its equality-loving owner to negro purchasers. The white population shunned the place, which never brings the price that other conditions would easily have given to it' (ibid, p. 154). The city was divided by residential segregation expressing differences of ethnicity, race and economic class. However, there were also religious, political, educational and dramatic associations and a host of other specialised groups within the city. To some degree they were cross-cutting and 'by virtue of having many members in common are bound together in a bewildering way' (ibid, p. 156).

As in the village, public opinion was a powerful force within the city. Public opinion was shaped by the influential views of authorities such as editors, ministers, teachers, political managers, businessmen and labour leaders. The latter, in turn, took care not to get too far out of step with the ingrained views of the common people. Differences of opinion between urban groups 'constantly modify each other' and in some cases resulted in 'laws which roughly represent the resultants of antagonistic views' (ibid, p. 161). There were, in fact, a host of legal regulations which restrict individual liberty. Such laws were not able to eradicate the crime, corruption and poverty endemic within the big city, those 'vicious elements, which, by reason of the very complexity, compactness and interdependence of urban life, subtly penetrate the whole social fabric and so much more threaten individual and family life' (ibid, pp. 164–5).

Finally, two other characteristics distinguished modern urban America from its rural origins. First:

> In the village, every citizen knows every other. As the community grows, such general acquaintanceship becomes more and more difficult until finally it is impossible. In the city, even neighbors may be strangers. Intellectual sympathies and other ties are stronger than mere proximity, when life is more intense and varied. The fact that the population is separated into groups which know little or nothing of each other is a conspicuous characteristic of the urban life. The city in this respect is a combination of villages, each with its own 'society'. The territorial and social separation of rich and poor is equally significant in connection with this fact. Isolation of classes each from the other is, in itself, easily explained and, at the same time, largely accounts for the mutual misconceptions which result in further estrangement, and often in suspicion and hatred on one side and distrust and intolerance on the other (ibid, p. 159).

Second, social and psychic estrangement were accompanied by a lack of understanding and interest with regard to public affairs on the part of most citizens. Apart from the occasional short-lived reform movement backed by a surge of popular feeling, most honest and upright leading citizens preferred to keep clear of municipal politics. They left the administration to 'men less capable and too often less upright'. Shrewd and unscrupulous professional politicians made themselves into machine bosses in cahoots with saloon-keepers who could help to bring in the votes of the foreign population. Spoils, favours and secret deals were the substance of this form of politics which was based upon the pursuit of 'self-interest . . . as opposed to the public good' (ibid, p. 162).

This 'natural history' had two purposes. The first purpose was to encourage students to carry out their own detailed empirical research. Possible 'subjects for investigation' were listed under headings such as 'Distribution of population: (a) territorial grouping according to wealth; (b) according to nationality'; 'Grouping of population: (a) neighborhood; (b) nationality; (c) religion; (d) education; (e) wealth, etc.'; 'Physical conditions: (a) unifying influences; (b) class antagonisms; (c) race antagonisms, etc.' and 'Abnormal conditions: defects and failures of institutions and activities . . ., especially faults of municipal government'. The 'sociological maps' being produced at Hull House were recommended as models for further maps of city districts which could 'show by colors: (a) the distribution of nationalities; (b) the average weekly wages; (c) location of churches, schools, jails, police stations, saloons, gambling houses, brothels, etc.' (ibid, pp. 165–6).

The second purpose was to illustrate a model of how societies work which gave equal emphasis to two sets of factors. The first included the 'essential conditions of . . . existence' (ibid, p. 170) such as material resources and the composition of the population. The other set of factors included motivating human wants such as the desire to realise the capacity for, respectively, physical functioning ('health'), using material resources ('wealth'), engaging in social activity ('sociability'), using the intellect ('knowledge'), aesthetic appreciation ('beauty') and satisfying the urgings of conscience ('righteousness'). In the course of attempting to satisfy these wants within the limiting physical and demographical conditions of existence, human beings became enmeshed in relations not just of economic exchange but also of psychical interdependence. Human beings belonged to a complex 'psychical system' – 'all knowledge of language, all power to communicate ideas, all education and training' – without which 'Cooperation becomes impossible, social bonds are destroyed; every man loses his relation to the whole; power over nature is lost; [and] . . . death of the society, if not of all its individual members, follows' (ibid, p. 181).

Responding to the motivations, opportunities and limitations just described, men and women participated in a range of primary bonds focused upon the family. They also belonged to 'social aggregates' – many of them 'spontaneous' and 'voluntary' – based upon psychic and other bonds deriving from (for example) common nationality or birthplace or a shared trade, religion or political allegiance. Such aggregates expressed 'the Manifoldness of the individual' (ibid, p. 10). They most fully 'serve . . . the interests of compact social structure' when, like university settlements, they forged bonds between 'rich and poor, educated and ignorant' (ibid, p. 207).

Interwoven within such aggregates in the social fabric were 'social organs' which took responsibility for functions such as 'sustaining', 'transporting' and 'regulating' members of the society. With respect both to social aggregates and to the functioning organs of society, two issues were raised. To what extent did they exhibit effective discipline and coordination? In what respects was the society exhibiting pathological symptoms?

Contemporary America furnished many examples of social ill-health, including 'extremes of poverty . . . idleness of rich and poor . . . gambling and speculation . . . bribery and corruption . . . stealing, fraud, and pandering to vice . . . [and] oppression of the economically weak' (ibid, p. 289). These 'social diseases' were responsible for 'The present widespread unrest among all classes' (ibid, p. 283). They were, in Small's view, the result of psychical causes whose roots were to be found in the spheres of 'social consciousness', 'social intelligence and feeling', 'morality and law' (ibid, pp. 11–12). His approach to these issues was more fully set out in *General Sociology*, to which we now turn.

Against individualism

Small considered that sociology was 'the science of the social process'. He envisaged a large-scale enquiry by sociologists into 'the whole of human experience' in order to wrest from the world its deepest purposes. Such an enquiry would 'reveal the last discoverable grounds upon which to base conclusions about the rational conduct of life':

Nothing is ever described properly unless it is described with reference to an end which it is supposed to be fitted to serve or to the process in which it occurs. This is conspicuously the case with the fact of human association . . . We must . . . reach some kind of a conception of what this vast unity that we call human society is for; then we must be able to trace the effects which different kinds of action have in the line of promoting or retarding this total purpose of society. We have in this knowledge a basis for practical morality (Small, 1905, pp. 34–5).

Starting from these assumptions, Small saw no reason why

sociology should not help to overcome the 'conflict of interests in modern society' (ibid, p. 372). Small believed that the notion of an 'irrepressible conflict between capital and labor' was as implausible as 'a theory of health that pitted the stomach against the muscles' (ibid, p. 374). He condemned the tendency for vested interests in American society to make individualistic demands and then battle it out with opponents under the banner of fighting for their rights. Such contests were decided by relative resources and not by the relative validity of the claims for consideration made by each side. In Small's view, the quintessential modern conflict was between 'the knowledge interest . . . and all the other interests combined' (ibid, p. 387) or, to put it another way, 'between individualistic feeling and corporate reason' (ibid, p. 388).

American society needed 'authoritative social principles' which would act as 'a tribunal' concerned with the general welfare. This tribunal would, in effect, revive the claim, originally made by kings, to look after the higher interests of all members of the society:

> The history of democracy may be said to have shown two things: first, that democracy escapes anarchy by incorporating in disguised form the essential strength of monarchy; second, democracy achieves progress, in spite of its contained contradictions, by gradual socialization of the conflicting interests (ibid, p. 389).

Sociologists should take up the task of socialising conflicting interests by explaining to people that their innate desire for (and interest in) health, wealth, sociability, knowledge, beauty and righteousness (or 'rightness', ibid, p. 392) could be more fully realised. This would be achieved if they adjusted their own selfish, irrational and shortsighted demands to take account of the benign purposes immanent in society as a whole. These purposes would be fulfilled more quickly to the benefit of all if vested interests had done with wasteful conflict and devoted themselves to intelligent and enlightened cooperation. The difficulties of doing all this were enormous because, in Small's view:

> Society is ethically bankrupt . . . Speaking generally our ethical capital consists of a heterogeneous collection of provincial moralities . . . By means of them society keeps in motion, but in

spite of enormous waste consumed upon the frictions which retard the motion (ibid, p. 657).

Small wanted to encourage Americans to attain the degree of collective self-consciousness that their forefathers had achieved in the late eighteenth-century. By a painful process of political bargaining and internal argument, the colonists had become aware that their broadest interests as a society would be best served by seeking the ends – which initially 'few wanted' (ibid, p. 537) – of independence and nationhood. Small had carried out detailed empirical research of his own on the Continental Congress when preparing his doctorate in history. He obviously admired the way that the members of the Congress had 'studied the situation, so far as they were able, in all its bearings. They tried to take into account everything that concerned their welfare in the largest sense . . . [and] accordingly adopted a program that controlled them for the following seven years' (ibid, p. 713).

America in 1905 was 'a case of social childhood', faced with the job of further realising and maturing 'the completest conception of civilization that has yet been formed' (ibid, p. 375). The original principles and institutions of America were correctly conceived: 'Our American problem is not, in the first instance, that of reconstructing institutions. It is the problem of the spirit which we shall show in working the institutions that we have' (ibid, p. 380). Henry Pratt Judson would have applauded this point. Small's programme was: let us build upon what we have. For example, 'there is opportunity for every man in America' but 'More opportunity can come about only by adjustment of the interests of all the individuals' (ibid, p. 376), in other words by eliminating social waste and acknowledging broader social ends.

Contemporary Americans were confronting 'the most prodigious technical problems which any people ever had to solve – i.e. in the largest sense of the term "technical"'. It was vital that these problems were not treated in a fragmented manner: 'we need to work upon general surveys of the situation' (ibid, p. 715). Contemporary difficulties were an expression 'of the poverty of our concept *democracy*' (ibid, p. 716; italics in original).

In Small's view, America's problems were not primarily to do with economic production but with the way resources were distributed and used. As a consequence, he applauded the changes that were being made in challenging and revising 'crudities in prevalent conceptions of property rights . . . There is intolerable maladjustment, and the social pain goads us to find and remove its cause' (ibid, p. 716).

Coming, as they did, just thirteen pages from the end of this ponderous tome Small's critical remarks on existing conceptions of property rights were a sting in the tail. However, Ross's comment in 1904 on Small's intellectual approach is relevant here: 'It does not appeal to me as reasonable that the authorities of the University of Chicago would interest themselves in heading off the diffusion of such general ideas as sociologists deal in. They can see in them no concrete menace to property or to the Standard Oil monopoly' (Stern, 1933, p. 320). Small dealt in general principles rather than detailed practical applications. In this respect, he was unlike his colleague, Charles Henderson, who crowned a lifetime of active campaigning for reform in Chicago by working himself to exhaustion and an early grave during the unemployment crisis of 1915.

Nevertheless, the progress of American politics during the decade following the publication of *General Sociology* cannot have provided Small with much comfort. Progressivism, a movement peopled with men and women from a background similar to himself, proved to be not so much the shaping of a unified and organised force for change as one aspect of 'the rise of modern, weak-party, issue focused politics' (Rogers, 1982, p. 117). The programme of Herbert Croly, whose Hamiltonian views on democracy and nationality (Croly, 1964) were similar in a number of respects to those of Small, was given short shrift by the electorate. In 1912 they chose Woodrow Wilson's 'New Freedom' rather than Theodore Roosevelt's 'New Nationalism'.

By 1914, Small was adopting Veblenesque language. In 'The social gradations of capital' he made distinctions between 'tool-capital' which is used solely by its owner, 'management-capital' whose exploitation depends on the cooperation of others in association with the legal owner, and 'finance-capital' which 'might be just as productive as it is, if the owner had never lived' (Small, 1914, p. 739). Small's view was that:

first, the function of economic management would be relatively impotent without the support of social cooperation; second, this social cooperation morally entitles the cooperating laborers and the cooperating society to a share in controlling the terms under which the management capitalist shall work, and a larger and much more influential share than our present economic system has either realized in practice or admitted in theory (ibid, p. 732).

As for finance-capital, possession of it is 'a purely conventional arrangement . . . by the agreement of civil society' (ibid, p. 739). It could almost have been Veblen writing when later in this same article Small poured scorn upon 'the inbred sophistry of traditionalism' (ibid, p. 734) and castigated 'the amateurish provisionality of our distributive system' (ibid, p. 738). Like Veblen, Small was bemused by 'the gravitation of industrial custom' (ibid, p. 737) and the effects of 'generations of stultifying habit' (ibid, p. 747). Hope was to be found in 'the modern temper [which] is no longer conformity to models, but inclination to understand and obey or control laws of cause and effect' (ibid, p. 751). He looked forward to the time when 'our economic machinery gets into stable equilibrium with the implications of human needs' (ibid, p. 752).

Soon after the First World War, Small published some notes on American democracy which he had composed in 1914. He found that the developing system of vocational education, largely constructed in the name of Deweyite principles, was failing to introduce 'deliberate training for community cooperation'. Instead, it was becoming 'a program of equipping individuals for more efficient competition in the half-conscious economic struggle' (Small, 1919–20, p. 276). Things were moving in the wrong direction.

Small admitted that 'American civilization has turned out to be bigger, more unwieldy, less amenable to the control of anyone's preconceptions, than could have been anticipated' (ibid, p. 406). He then produced a brilliant image of the society he knew:

American civilization has been very much like a Chicago park of a fine summer day. Hundreds, perhaps thousands, of families have gone to it for an outing. All were moved by the same ground motive – relief from physical discomfort and enjoyment of physical comfort. All have to observe certain police regulations, but with trifling exceptions each has followed his own bent. There has been no system in the pleasure-seeking. There has been greedy grabbing of the most favourable spots for games or picnicking. A great deal of physical relaxation, a great deal of amusement, a great deal of incommoding one another, a great deal of irritation, some quarrelling, some injuries, much bodily weariness, and at the close of the day a liberal allowance of wondering whether after all it had paid, would be a fair summary of the day's account. From time to time the park commissioners have attempted to modify the regulations and to improve the accommodation of the parks in the interest of a larger ratio of satisfaction to effort. To the outsider there is still in the sight presented by these parks of a midsummer Saturday or Sunday much to suggest the query of an aristocratic Englishman when taken to a similar resort and told of the number that visited it – 'Why should anyone *want* to come here?' (ibid, p. 408).

This was a long way from Eden. In fact, it was in just such a park, bordering the lake front, that Chicago's terrible race riot began in 1919, the very year these words were published.

The note of disillusionment was even clearer in the following year when Small published his thoughts on Christianity and industry. He expressed his dislike of the system of corporate property embodied in the institution of the trust. These arrangements were only efficient from the point of view of the companies involved. They embodied a 'deathless superpersonal selfishness' which was beyond the control of 'mere natural persons'. Small then produced a telling comparison: 'So far as the *desideratum* of equal rights is concerned, our corporation-dominated property system is to the property system of the pre-corporation centuries as the extemporized dictatorship of Lenin is to the traditional dictatorship of the Romanoffs' (ibid, 1920, p. 693).

In 1925 Small weighed his natural optimism in the balance against a wealth of disconfirming evidence. By this time he was adamant that Americans should 'strengthen every rational attempt to restrict the exercise of the capitalistic spirit'. He recalled that thirty years earlier he had supported municipal ownership of natural monopolies. Since then he had discovered by following the history of the Chicago street railways that if you 'Mix the something-for-nothing spirit with party politics' then 'capitalism is not restrained but stimulated'. Thirty years earlier he had 'believed ardently in trade unionism'. However, since then he had found that organised labour exhibited 'all the evils of the something-for-nothing spirit' (ibid, pp. 46–61). In effect, his rational enquiries into society had revealed the enormous difficulty of promoting the programme of social improvement to which he had dedicated his professional life. He was reduced to recommending a policy of 'patches' or minor but obtainable reforms. The problem was that 'no devices are in sight to which we can pin our faith as feasible and comprehensive substitutes for capitalism, either on its subjective side as the acquisitive spirit, or on the objective side as an economic technique' (ibid, p. 460).

Small's career as a sociologist had been devoted to the task of discovering ways in which his discipline could contribute to the reform of modern American capitalism. His ambition was that this economic system should help to realise the visionary objectives of the Founding Fathers and not, as was happening, frustrate them. He was forced to admit that the mission had been a failure. However, he refused to relinquish the ambition. As late as 1925 he was demanding restrictions on the level of dividends and the distribution of a proportion of capitalist profits to working people and to industrial enterprises needed in the public interest:

> Since I have more than once expressed beliefs about desirable social changes which were at once ridiculed as the day dreams of a closet philosopher, or denounced as dangerous fanaticisms, only to see them absorbed a little later into the most commonplace practice, I do not doubt that the extravagance of the present prophecy will become a matter of course in a not distant future (ibid, p. 461).

Ultimately, even to this dedicated rationalist, this trenchant critic of corporate capitalism, the weight of empirical evidence was less persuasive than his belief in the validity of the American Dream.

Note

1. On Small and the early Chicago sociology department, see Diner, 1975; Dibble, 1975; Barnes, 1926; Hayes, 1926; Bulmer, 1984.

5

W. I. Thomas

From coercion to cooperation

William Isaac Thomas was born in 1863, almost a decade after
Albion Small. Like Small, Thomas had a father with a religious
vocation. Like Thorstein Veblen, he came from a farming
background. Like G. H. Mead, he attended Oberlin College.
Thomas shared with Dewey and Veblen a deep interest in the
origins of modern civilisation in 'savage' societies. Like Robert
Park, he was fascinated by the issues of immigration and race.
However, like Veblen, Mead, Dewey and Park, W. I. Thomas was
also a deeply individualistic thinker. He shared other men's
obsessions but he would not suffer himself to be the visible captive
of any one else's intellectual system.[1]

Looking back in 1928 to his time at Chicago University Thomas
argued that his interests were in fields 'marginal' to sociology and
not in 'the historical and methodological approach of Professor
Small and the remedial and correctional interests of Professor
Henderson' (Baker, 1974, p. 249). He had found Dewey to be
'essentially a mystic and a metaphysician' and believed 'it would be
more correct to say that he came under my influence than that I
came under his' (ibid, p. 245). More generally, he 'never became
influenced by philosophy as offering an explanation of reality' (ibid,
p. 248). In fact, as will be seen, he had much in common with
Dewey and Small.

W. I. Thomas was forced to leave his post at Chicago in 1919 after
a scandal in his private life. Before that time he had produced four
major works: *Sex and Society* (1907) which included a number of his
papers published since 1896; *Source Book for Social Origins*

(1909a), a wide-ranging collection of which he was contributing editor; his best-known work *The Polish Peasant in Europe and America* (1918–19) in which he collaborated with Florian Znaniecki; and *Old World Traits Transplanted* (1921) in which he develops certain themes from *The Polish Peasant*. The last-named volume was primarily his work despite being originally published under the names of Robert Park and Herbert A. Miller because of the controversy surrounding Thomas's departure from Chicago.

The grandfather of W. I. Thomas was, in the latter's own words, 'a Pennsylvanian Dutchman, rich in land but with peasant attitudes' (Baker, 1974, p. 246). This aspect of his ancestry helps to explain Thomas's interest in the European peasantry although many years later he gave as his opinion that 'The Poles are very repulsive people on the whole'. This fragment of unsociological prejudice was swept aside because in Poland 'there had been a movement for "enlightenment" and freedom' which had generated 'many documents and masses of material on the peasant' (Thomas, quoted in Bulmer, 1984, p. 47). Polish society had for long periods of time existed either with a weak or non-existent state or under the dominion of a foreign and oppressive state. Poland possessed an educated and patriotic upper class. Some of its members had sought to persuade the mass of their countrymen to join in a national revival. In fact, many of these features evoked aspects of the heroic myth of the birth of the American Republic and its early period of nationhood.

A powerful latent preoccupation runs through not only *The Polish Peasant in Europe and America* (1918–19) but also its sequel *Old World Traits Transplanted* (1969). This preoccupation was shared by Albion Small. Both men wanted to help to complete the work of building democratic civilisation which was supposedly commenced in the American Revolution of 1776. Thomas must have been sensitive to the parallels between aspects of national development in Poland and America.

Compare some key passages in *The Polish Peasant* and Tocqueville's *Democracy in America*. The following quotations contain, in a simplified form, a central argument running through three successive chapters in Tocqueville's work entitled, respectively, 'How the Americans combat the effects of individualism by free institutions', 'On the Use which the Americans make of Associations in Civil Life' and 'On the

Connections between Associations and Newspapers'. Tocqueville was praising the Americans for expressing their political liberty through active participation in the affairs of the local community and even beyond:

> Citizens who are bound to take part in public affairs must turn from their private interests and occasionally take a look at something other than themselves. As soon as common affairs are treated in common each man notices that he is not as independent of his fellows as he used to suppose and that to get their help he must offer his aid to them (Tocqueville, 1968, p. 657).

> The Americans have used liberty to combat the individualism born of equality, and they have won (ibid, p. 658).

> The more government takes the place of associations, the more will individuals lose the idea of forming associations and need the government to come to their help. That is a vicious circle of cause and effect . . . The morals and intelligence of a democratic people would be in as much danger as its commerce and industry if ever a government wholly usurped the place of private associations (ibid, pp. 664–5).

> In a democracy an association cannot be powerful unless it is numerous. Those composing it must therefore be spread over a wide area, and each of them is anchored to the place in which he lives by the modesty of his fortune and a crowd of small necessary cares . . . So hardly any democratic association can carry on without a newspaper . . . Newspapers make associations, and associations make newspapers (ibid, p. 668).

The following passage from *The Polish Peasant* described social life in the wake of the breakdown of the isolation of peasant communities in modern Poland:

> The social system which develops . . . naturally tends to reconcile by modifying them, the two originally contradictory principles – the traditional absorption of the individual by the group and the new self-assertion of the individual against or independently of the group. The method which, after various trials, proves the most efficient in fulfilling this difficult task is the method of

conscious cooperation. Closed social groups are freely formed for the common pursuit of definite positive interests which each individual can more efficiently satisfy in this way than if he worked alone. These organized groups are scattered all over the country in various peasant communities but know about one another through the press . . . The peasant begins consciously to cooperate in those activities by which national unity is maintained and national culture developed. This fact has a particular importance for Poland where for a whole century national life had to be preserved by voluntary cooperation, not only without the help of the state but even against the state, and where at this moment the same method of voluntary cooperation is being used in reconstructing a national state system (Thomas and Znaniecki, 1927, pp. 1305–6).

Thomas and Znaniecki were obviously not implying that Poland before its modern national revival was in all or even in most respects the same kind of society as America before the Revolution. However, the mechanisms of social transformation in Poland which Thomas emphasised bear an uncanny resemblance to the instruments of American democracy delineated by Tocqueville.

Albion Small would have been delighted if the social process in the USA in the early twentieth century had developed in a similar manner to that in contemporary Poland as reported by Thomas and Znaniecki:

The content of the national ideals . . . is sufficiently developed to become in favourable circumstances the supreme principle of both individual behavior and social organization . . . [T]he social activities which we have studied . . . either have their source in national aspirations and their ultimate purpose determined by the national ideal or at least are continually subjected to criticisms and appreciation from the national viewpoint . . . On the one hand the national ideal is exalted above everything else. Any preference shown, in the case of a conflict, to any other kind of interest is branded as national treason . . . On the other hand, the national idea is interpreted as including everything else. It includes individual happiness . . . It includes economic security . . . Intellectual values are included in the national idea . . . The acceptance and pursuit of the national idea is further identified with virtue in general (Thomas and Znaniecki, 1927, pp. 1458–60).

Reflecting upon the national revival in Poland, Thomas and his collaborator had no doubt that 'The significance of such a historical experiment for sociology' was

> evident, for it contributes more than anything to the solution of *the most essential problem of modern times* – how to pass from the type of national organization in which public services are enacted and public order enforced by coercion to a different type, in which not only a small minority, but the majority which is now culturally passive will voluntarily contribute to social order and cultural progress' (ibid, p. 1306; italics added).

Like Small, Thomas was looking backwards and forwards. In the glorious past there was an exemplary eighteenth-century revolution. In the challenging future there lay the task of constructing a truly democratic America.

Like Small, Thomas drew upon European materials. Small's European borrowing was mainly theoretical. In particular, he discovered in recent German economic thought the principle that 'there are no economic questions which are not at last moral questions' (Small, 1914, p. 724). Furthermore, social life 'must be concerted, cooperative construction' (Small, 1919, p. 274). Thomas drew similar conclusions from his empirical investigations in Poland and neighbouring European societies. For example, in the course of national reconstruction in Poland there developed a variety of cooperative ventures such as agricultural associations for buying machinery, raising loans and selling farm products. He commented that 'active interest and direct personal participation are required of every member. Thus, though founded on an economic basis, these institutions are *social organizations*, not merely business enterprises' (Thomas and Znaniecki, 1927, p. 1401; italics in original). As Small and Vincent put it, 'there is a higher interdependence among men than that of economic relations' (Small and Vincent, 1894, p. 110). Cooperative organisations were contributing economically and morally to the search in Poland for a solution to 'the most essential problem in modern times'.

Thomas and Small

Before discussing in more detail Thomas's analyses of peasant societies and the immigrant some more similarities and, equally significant, a number of differences of approach between Small and Thomas will be noticed.

First, neither man could accept that a stable and durable social order might persist at the expense of opportunities for human self-realisation. On this question, their assessments of the state of early twentieth-century America were similar in important respects. In 1908, Thomas commented: 'There is at present a great disturbance of consciousness and failure of ideals among ourselves, indicated by the manipulation of the many by the few in industrial life, by the failure of many, indeed of most, to command the leisure and the access to copies which would develop their characteristic powers' (Thomas, 1908, p. 736). Continuing, he argued that a combination of internal and external threats faced America in the early twentieth century including the likelihood that a challenge from Japan and China to the power of white men would be supported by black people. Thomas's approach to this situation was positive and optimistic: 'While we are working under strain, I cannot think that we are in danger of making a failure. Psychology teaches us that what a situation dominated by habit or inadequate ideas needs is a shock; and this, at any rate, is coming from the Orient'. The Japanese challenge would, he believed, stimulate 'a radical revision of our western civilization' (ibid, p. 739).

Second, both Thomas and Small were as interested in 'what ought to be' as they were in 'what is'. Small held to the ambition of discovering 'what ought to be' through a scientific investigation of the social world. This investigation would reveal the purposes intrinsic to human desires and social institutions, the rational ends embedded in their constitution even if they were frustrated and only half-realised. His response to the world's kaleidoscopic nature was to seek an encompassing general interest. However, while Small sought unity and totality, Thomas relished diversity and the possibilities of comparison. His approach was to explain a wide range of human activities and beliefs, including diverse notions of 'what ought to be', in terms of their contribution to the human capacity to survive and exercise control within given environments. In other words, societies would evolve appropriate moralities which would prove their own worth by their contribution to group survival.

In practice, Thomas and Small concentrated upon the same central issues. One was the decline of the moral order of the close-knit primary group, whether in the form of the Polish peasant family or the homestead community on the frontier. Another was the need for a moral order in the big city based upon 'conscious and rational technique' and an 'objective attitude towards social reality' (Thomas and Znaniecki, 1927, p. 1). Small's evident nostalgia for the lost rural Eden suggests that he would have agreed with Thomas that the declining importance of the primary-group in the metropolis was rightly felt as 'a rather dangerous effect of social evolution' (ibid, p. 1118). The following passage from *The Polish Peasant* would not have been out of place in Small's *General Sociology*:

> Innumerable human interests all over the world are still on a stage where their pursuit is chiefly dependent on the direct social response and recognition of the primary-group which constitutes the individual's immediate environment. It is, therefore, most important, both for theoretic and for practical purposes, to study the social process by which these interests become independent, economic, political, moral, intellectual, religious, aesthetic aims, pursued for their own sake, and social groups become rationally organized for the purpose of an efficient common pursuit of these aims. Our civilization, when not taken at its highest manifestations but in its totality, is still in the midst of the same process of change which began half a century ago among the Polish peasants; it is on average much more advanced, much more distant from the exclusive predominance of the primary-group type, but it is still very far from a thorough-going teleological systematization of values and a rational control of attitudes (ibid, pp. 1118–19).

Within this broad framework of agreement there were differences of emphasis between Small and Thomas. Small hoped that he and his colleagues would implant their knowledge of 'what ought to be' within society as a guide to future development. The strategic point, as far as he was concerned, was the political centre. For example, national party policies would be shaped under the influence of 'general surveys of the situation' whose 'significant features' would be charted by 'a quota of thinkers who will help us to take our bearings from these chief landmarks' (Small, 1905, p. 715). The sociologist would become the exemplary representative of the 'knowledge interest', a key shaper and constituent of the ideal society.

By contrast, Thomas emphasised the contribution that sociologists and social psychologists could make at the level of the individual. He wanted to encourage each person, as far as possible, to control his or her own 'life-organization' (Thomas and Znaniecki, 1927, p. 1906). Society should 'remove obstacles preventing spontaneous personal development' and 'give positive help, to furnish every individual with proper methods for spontaneous personal development' (ibid, pp. 1906–7). These contrasting emphases were related to a fourth difference between the two men.

As has been seen, Small was deeply troubled by the wrongs that were committed in the name of American individualism. He aspired to the creation in America of a just society even at some cost to 'freedom' as it was defined and exploited by robber barons. By contrast, Thomas was more concerned with another conflict, one which focused attention on the personality. This was the tension between the search for rationality or efficiency and the pursuit of individual happiness. The two conflicts just mentioned were, as indicated in the first section of this book, endemic to American liberalism.

Thomas's underlying concern with the dimensions of individual happiness repeatedly surfaces during the discussion at the end of the 'methodological note' of the problems raised by *The Polish Peasant*. For example, Thomas and Znaniecki argued that 'the question of the antisocial individual assumes no longer the form of the right of the society to protection, but that of the antisocial individual to be made useful' (ibid, pp. 79–80). Furthermore, the lack of stimulating jobs 'necessarily affects human happiness profoundly' (ibid, p. 80). Raising explicitly 'the problem of social happiness', they claimed that their own sociological method 'gives the most reliable way of studying it' (ibid, p. 84). Finally, tackling 'the problem of an ideal organization of culture' they argued that 'the systematic study of various cultures' was 'the only way to solve' the 'widest and oldest sociological problem'. That problem was as follows: 'Is there one perfect form of organization that would unify the widest individualization and the strongest social cohesion, that would harmonize the highest efficiency with the greatest happiness?' (ibid, pp. 85–6).

A further difference between Small and Thomas relates to their responses to the intellectual and social implications of pragmatism. As has been seen, in Small's later career disillusionment with the capitalistic spirit set in. It perverted and frustrated the best inclinations of human nature. In his writing he began to resemble Veblen on occasion. Small's major criticism was that the pursuit of efficiency should not win approval for a society if its property system was unjust. In the 'methodological note' a different criticism was made by Thomas and Znaniecki regarding the application of a pragmatic approach, especially in scientific investigation. They accepted that 'we must have an empirical and exact social science ready for eventual application' but added that 'Such a science can be constituted only if we treat it as an end in itself, not as a means to something else'. Their view was that since it was impossible to tell how a science would develop or the world would take shape 'The only practically justifiable attitude toward science is absolute liberty and disinterested help'.

There was a catch, however, 'As one of the pragmatists has expressed it . . . sooner or later science must pay her debts, and the longer the delay the greater the interest required' (Thomas and Znaniecki, 1927, pp. 15–16). Like Veblen, Thomas and Znaniecki recognised that modern science was an alliance between idle curiosity and the pragmatic attitude. Veblen thought that the pressure for practical results from capitalist interests was perverting science, making it less fulfilling as an activity and more threatening in its results. By contrast, Thomas was more prepared to accept the Faustian contract between science and the world. The activity of scientific investigation could still be fulfilling and enjoyable as long as the world was prepared to wait for the *eventual* application of its results.

Miss Helen Culver, heiress to the fortune which established Hull House, was evidently prepared to wait. It was in 1908, a whole decade before the publication of *The Polish Peasant*, that she had bestowed upon Thomas $50 000 for research on immigrant problems. Subsequently, she paid for substitute teaching while Thomas made innumerable visits to Europe. As a consequence

Thomas was able to put into practice what Small had only recommended and Henderson had only partially sought to do: he devoted himself wholeheartedly to detailed, empirical research into the social relationships and mentalities of individuals and human groups undergoing painful changes.

The theoretical approach which Thomas brought to his work on the European peasantry and their experience of immigration was influenced by his heavy involvement in the reform activities centred on Hull House. He was very interested in the work of the Juvenile Protective Association and the Immigrants' Protective League. He also served on the Chicago Vice Commission established in 1910, supported campaigns for the rights of immigrants and became involved in schemes to advance the education of American blacks. One benefit of these activities was the opportunity to gather materials about particular individuals, especially life histories, for use in his research. A disadvantage was that his very public advocacy of advanced views on moral and racial issues was to weaken support for him in Chicago at a time of personal crisis. However, that is to anticipate the story.

G. H. Mead and John Dewey were also active and influential at Hull House. As a consequence, the pragmatism which Thomas encountered in these crucial years was deeply imbued with the spirit of reform. Under the influence of this pragmatic approach with its socially radical tinge Thomas moved away from his early academic preoccupation with exposing the inadequacies of prevailing biological conception of human behaviour (for example, Thomas, 1895; Thomas, 1897; Thomas, 1898; Thomas, 1899a; Thomas, 1899b). Instead, he began to fashion the approach set out in his 'Standpoint for the interpretation of savage society' (Thomas, 1909b).

Four key ideas were control, attention, habit and crisis. *Control* of the environment in order to ensure survival was 'the object, realized or unrealized, of all purposive activity' (ibid, p. 154). For example, language was 'a powerful instrument of control, because through it knowledge, tradition, standpoints, ideals, stimulations, copies are transmitted and increased'. Our moral sense of what is 'laudable and virtuous' refers to actions which 'can all be stated from the control standpoint', in other words they have survival value. Not least, 'Liberty is favorable to control, because with it the individual has opportunity to develop ideas and follow his own bent which he would not develop under repression'. Above all, 'The human mind is preeminently the organ of manipulation, of adjustment, of control' (ibid, pp. 155–6).

Control is secured by the application of *attention*, in other words the subjective orientation to the world which takes note of opportunities for manipulation. When control is achieved, attention relaxes into *habit*. When control is threatened in a new situation to which existing habits are not well adapted, the resulting *crisis* stimulates renewed attention and the search for new techniques of control. In this process, mental and social capacities develop: 'the mind itself is the product of crisis. Crisis also produces the specialized occupations . . . who have or profess special skill in dealing with crises'. The resemblance to the organism/environment approach of John Dewey is evident.

The Polish Peasant

The Polish Peasant runs to 2250 pages. Well over a third of the text is devoted to a series of personal letters between Polish immigrants of peasant background and members of their families still in Poland. When you add the extensive quotation of letters and reports intended for publication in a Polish-language journal, church records, materials from Polish-American societies and written evidence from social work organisations and legal agencies, the total proportion of text given over to the presentation of documents is approximately 60 per cent of the whole. Not surprisingly, a great deal of attention has been paid to the appropriateness of the authors' apparent reliance upon such evidence in order to make their case. At a conference devoted to *The Polish Peasant* held in New York in 1938 under the auspices of the Social Science Research Council it was agreed that the authors' 'conceptual scheme was not and cannot be derived logically from the documents, nor proved by them, although the documents are greatly illuminated when interpreted by the scheme'. However, Read Bain, who made these comments, added that in its use of 'human document material' and its commitment to empirical research '*The Polish Peasant* is a monumental instance of the revolt against "armchair sociology" which began about 1900' (Blumer, 1979, pp. 191–2).

The comparison with Albion Small's work has suggested that

although Thomas was indeed out of the armchair he was still, conceptually speaking, in the same living room. Broadly speaking, Small's problems were his problems, the main differences being Thomas's warmer response to pragmatism as an intellectual approach and his greater interest in the dynamics of the personality. Thomas's conclusion about the situation of the peasantry in Poland and Polish immigrants in America were presumably shaped in the course of reflections stimulated by extensive personal travel and involvement both in Europe and Chicago. His Polish collaborator, Znaniecki, was a knowledgeable and sympathetic source of information, partly because of his experience in running a bureau for the protection of emigrants.

Morris Janowitz has persuasively described Thomas's approach as offering 'a synthesis of the anthropologist's or ethnographer's participant observations, the case-study method of the social worker, and the content-analysis procedures of the traditional humanistic disciplines' (Thomas, 1966, p. xxiii). In the event, it was perhaps incautious of Thomas and Znaniecki to claim that in the search for 'abstract laws', personal life records were 'the *perfect* type of sociological material' (Thomas and Znaniecki, p. 1832; italics in original). However, with the reservations just made, the verdict of the 1938 conference, influenced as it was by a trenchant critique carried out by Herbert Blumer, may surely stand.

The Polish Peasant was staggeringly ambitious and remains impressive. Within a single intellectual framework were contained a comparison between processes of change in late nineteenth-century and early twentieth-century Poland and America. In each case attention was focused upon the interplay between transformations at the level of personality and at the level of social organisation. With respect to both societies urgent contemporary problems were related to broader societal developments which were considered within a historical and comparative context. Where appropriate, strategies were suggested for dealing with such problems. The implications were considered of alternative patterns of possible future development for Polish and American society. Suggestions were made concerning the objects and procedures of sociology and social psychology and both were distinguished from current practice. Finally, there was a check-list of problems, simultaneously theoretical and practical, which were considered as ripe for investigation in the course of extensive comparative research.

Leaving aside the long life-record of the immigrant Wladek Wiszniewski, a minor epic in its own right, *The Polish Peasant* was constructed in a way which, perhaps deliberately, suggests incompleteness, tension and further work to be done. Part One and Part Two were concerned with peasant life in Poland. They discussed, in turn, 'primary group organization', 'social disorganization' and 'social reorganization'. Part Three was concerned with Polish immigrants in America. It was concerned with 'organization of the immigrant' and, subsequently, the 'disorganization of the immigrant'. The 'missing' chapters, not yet able to be written, would obviously have to be concerned with the 'reorganization of the immigrant'. Some proposals in this respect were made in *Old World Traits Transformed*.

According to Thomas and Znaniecki, sociology was the study of social organisation, in other words, the rules embodied in institutions which are intended to regulate human behaviour. By contrast, the closely-related discipline of social psychology was concerned with 'the subjective side of social culture' (Thomas and Znaniecki, 1927, p. 31) and included the study of various forms of individual organisation or 'life-organization' (ibid, p. 1843). The term 'life-organization' referred to the embodiment of particular sets of values and attitudes in 'consciously followed rules' of personal behaviour (ibid, p. 1852). The term 'attitude' was used to refer to 'subjective social-psychological elements of social reality'. The term 'value' referred to 'objective, social elements which impose themselves upon the individual as given and provoke his reaction' (ibid, p. 1131). Social disorganisation took the form of 'a decrease of the influence of existing social rules upon individual members of the group' (ibid, p. 1128). This may well be the result of shifts in individual attitudes.

According to this analysis, the occurrence of social disorganisation does not necessarily imply individual disorganisation or 'demoralization' (ibid, p. 1129) on the part of all members of the collectivity. Some might undergo this process. Others might not. A collectivity whose institutions had been disorganised might become reorganised or reconstructed. In other words, new institutions and new rules develop which gave fuller rein for action informed by the attitudes which had become dominant. A key part was played by innovators who did not undergo individual disorganisation at the time of social disorganisation. They identified the appropriate spheres of action within which new institutions might be constructed.

In fact, social stability represented 'a dynamic equilibrium of processes of disorganization and reorganization' (ibid, p. 1130). In conditions of widespread social disorganisation such as were associated with the development of a modern urban industrial society, a great deal depended upon whether a sufficient degree of reorganisation could be effected sufficiently quickly. In Poland, effective leadership from among the peasantry developed. It was able to supplement the decaying family-group and rural community with new institutions as already described. By contrast, in the USA the parochial associations, mutual insurance clubs and other Polish–American organisations – all provincial, separatist and exclusive in spirit – were unable to prevent rapid demoralisation among Polish immigrants. This took such forms as loss of economic independence, break-up of families, delinquency and immorality. Those who escaped these sorry conditions were unlikely to avoid the strains of increasing individualisation and isolation. This overall argument was buttressed by analysis of the changing linkages between the regulation of personality, the structure of the primary group and national institutions in America and (in much more detail) Poland.

The quest for control

In America, as in Poland, the problem was not 'how to suppress the new attitudes, but how to find for them institutional expression, how to utilize them for socially productive purposes, instead of permitting them to remain in a status where they express themselves merely in individual revolt and social revolution' (ibid, p. 1121). How to face that problem for the good of American democracy was the main outstanding item on Thomas's intellectual agenda following this research project. Indications of his preliminary thoughts may be found in three places: in the examination of the 'special task of the social technician' (ibid, p. 71); in the discussion of 'typical lines of genesis' of 'social personalities' (ibid, p. 1839); and in the exploration in *Old World Traits Transformed* of what is 'required in a democracy' (Thomas *et al.*, 1969, p. 260). These will be discussed in reverse order.

Modern Americans found themselves in 'a system of relationships, political and economic, over which . . . they have no control', being effectively 'disenfranchised'. At the same time they were 'importing large numbers of aliens . . . in the main below our cultural level' (Thomas *et al.*, 1969, pp. 261–2). The danger was that the persistence of a vast cultural gap between the existing Americans and the newcomers would produce 'a state of chaos unless we abandoned the idea of democracy and secured efficiency by reverting to the "ordering and forbidding" type of state'. To protect the democratic aspect of American culture it was necessary to 'make the immigrants a working part in our system of life . . . Self-preservation makes this necessary; the fact that they bring valuable additions to our culture makes it desirable' (ibid, p. 264).

Assimilation required a sympathetic approach to immigrant heritages and a search for points of similarity between their attitudes and 'American ways of thinking' (ibid, p. 265). Instead of 'Americanization through . . . suppression and repudiation' (ibid, p. 281) Thomas recommended a process of mutual learning so that the established and the newcomers could build up means of communication and understanding. Democracy depended upon the ability of 'all to share vicariously the inner life of each' (ibid, p. 271). It also required that the individual should experience a sense of participation in the community and control over his or her own life. This last point was taken up in the 'methodological note' and the discussion of individual life-organisation. A key part was played by 'social technicians'.

The social technician was to play a vital role in American democracy. His or her task was to influence 'active practical situations' (Thomas and Znaniecki, 1927, p. 68). Such situations (or practical problems) were to a significant degree shaped by the definitions of the individuals involved, particularly their perceptions of the social means available to satisfy their desires for new experience, recognition, personal mastery and security. Aided by the findings of sociology and social psychology and aware of the individual's dependence on society as 'the only medium within which any of his schemes or wishes can be gratified' (ibid, p. 73), the social technician could get to work. The task was to 'prepare, with the help of both science and practical observation, thorough schemes and plans of action for all the various types of situation which may be found in a given line of social activity' (ibid, p. 71).

Such schemes were to include the object of developing in individuals 'the ability to control their own activities by conscious reflection' (ibid, p. 72). This was an increasingly important factor as the externally imposed control of traditional primary groups grew weaker.

If we borrow a comparison made by Plato in *The Republic* when describing his 'Guardians', the firm but benevolent social technician evoked by Thomas may be compared to 'a good watchdog' (Plato, 1955, p. 110). In fact, Thomas, whose first degree was in the classics, may well have been as powerfully influenced by this ancient model as was Small who explicitly referred to Plato's work when sketching his 'natural history of a society'. The ninth part of *The Republic*, entitled 'Imperfect societies', is especially relevant. Here Plato contrasts various types of imperfect individual – tyrannic, democratic, oligarchic and 'timarchic' – corresponding to types of society. For example, the democratic individual is subject to 'an invasion of pretentious fallacies' leading to 'a triumphal torchlight procession of insolence, license, extravagance, and shamelessness' (ibid, p. 333). By contrast, the 'timarchic' individual (or Spartan military type) is 'ready to listen, but quite incapable of expressing himself. . . . He will be polite to his equals and obey his superior readily'. He lacks 'A properly trained mind' (ibid, pp. 319–20). Having contrasted the types of character and their relative degrees of happiness, Plato turns to the happiest individual of all. This is the philosopher who has 'a character in which self-control and fair-mindedness are combined'. Plato argues that within society 'wisdom and control should, if possible, come from within; failing that it must be imposed from without, in order that, being subject to the same guidance, we may all be brothers and equals' (ibid, p. 368).

Returning to Thomas, the parallels are immediately obvious. He argued that the types of social personality evident in modern society reflected different approaches to individual control. The 'Philistine' had a fixed set of attitudes which were not subject to critical reflection. The 'Bohemian' was the opposite of rigid and remains uncritically 'open to any and all influences'. Both types were being produced on a large scale by the sterile and frustrating conditions of modern organised life. However, a third type existed. The 'creative individual' had a character which was 'settled and organized' but capable of evolving in the course of regulated and planned 'productive activity' along the 'line of his preconceived development' (ibid, p. 1854). Through 'sublimation', potentially harmful attitudes could be made 'useful'. They should be directed towards the more 'sacred' spheres of life: a potential murderer may thus become a butcher by occupation, or even a surgeon (ibid, pp. 1868–9). By contrast, attempts at utter suppression of desires by society produced, where successful, the 'limited, stable, self-satisfied Philistine' and, where unsuccessful, the 'inconsistent, nonconformist, Bohemian type' (ibid, p. 1871).

The increasing specialisation of occupational groups was producing two effects noticed by Thomas. On the one hand, each individual was shaped in his or her attitudes from several different directions, the overall effect being 'a complete lack of organization'. A single personality might comprise several 'disconnected, often radically conflicting characters'. One consequence was 'a new style of Philistinism – the Philistinism of the dissociated personality, amounting to a sort of stabilized Bohemianism' (ibid, p. 1888). On the other hand, however, the social demand for efficiency was beginning to encourage increased social cooperation between specialised agencies. This was accompanied by a stress on the effectiveness of results rather than the conventionality of means. It was becoming 'more necessary . . . to leave to every individual as much freedom as is compatible with efficient cooperation'. Perhaps, then it was indeed possible to overcome the tension between the pressure for social efficiency and the pursuit of individual happiness: 'The individual must be trained not for conformity, but for efficiency, not for stability but for creative evolution' (ibid, p. 1906).

Aftermath

What became of the authors of these words? Before the final volumes of *The Polish Peasant* had been published W. I. Thomas had been forced to resign from his post at Chicago University. In 1918, he was arrested by the FBI at a hotel in Chicago where he was in the company of a Mrs Granger, the wife of an army officer serving in France. Thomas was charged with false hotel registration, disorderly conduct and violation of the Mann Act. The prosecution was unsuccessful but there was extensive publicity. There were suspicions that the whole affair may have been designed to embarrass Thomas's wife who was active in the peace movement during the First World War. Albion Small reportedly wept but did not act effectively to save Thomas. His colleague's radical opinions and colourful life-style presumably did not help his case in the eyes of the 'large businessmen of a ripe age' (Veblen, 1965a, p. 185) who exercised influence in the university's higher councils. The *coup de grâce* was delivered by Henry Pratt Judson, who had become the university's president by this time. Judson no doubt recalled complaints against Thomas such as the letter he had received in 1906 denouncing a lecture on women given by the sociologist as being 'a vicious attack upon the social system of America' (quoted in Matthews, 1977, p. 102). In effect, Thomas the 'creative individual' was labelled a dangerous 'Bohemian' by those whom he, in turn, might well have labelled 'Philistines'.

And Florian Znaniecki? He returned to Poland by 1920. Had he, in fact, experienced the receptive welcome from native Americans which Thomas had recommended, especially to 'the foreign intellectual, who is . . . the type of immigrant best fitted to make a cultural contribution' (Thomas *et al.*, 1969, p. 107)? The following evidence is relevant.

In 1920 an article written by 'A European' appeared in *Atlantic Monthly*. It was entitled 'Intellectual America'. Its anonymous author was a Pole trained in philosophy who came to America at 'the first opportunity which presented itself, in the form of some work to be done for Professor *X*, a prominent American sociologist whom I met in Poland'. Just before the First World War, the author of this article 'came here and settled in one of the most important American university centres, within a short distance of a big city' (ibid, p. 193). The author found a 'continually rising wave of narrow nationalism', a 'growing mistrust and aversion to "foreigners"' (ibid, p. 198). Americanisation meant 'that the immigrant should simply leave all he brought with him as worthless stuff' (ibid, p. 197). The Polish author was dismayed by 'the lack of social freedom, the oppression of the individual by all kinds of traditional or recently created social norms'. In fact, he added, 'I feel more bound in the expression of my opinions here than I felt under Russian occupation at Warsaw' (ibid, p. 196). There is a striking similarity between this comparison and Small's comment, made in the same year, that the 'corporation-dominated property system' of the USA recalled 'the extemporized dictatorship of Lenin' (Small, 1920, p. 693). At least two sociologists working in Chicago had encountered quite fundamental conflicts between their liberalism and the institutions of modern capitalist America.[2]

Notes

1. On Thomas, see Thomas, 1966 (introduction by Morris Janowitz); Baker, 1974; Deegan and Burger, 1961; Young, 1972–3; Diner, 1975; Bulmer, 1984.
2. Znaniecki later continued his career as a sociologist in the USA. See Znaniecki, 1969.

6
Robert Park

Sociology and the real world

Robert Park, Albion Small and W. I. Thomas represented three different ways in which sociology and the 'real world' could be related to each other. Albion Small intended that sociology should develop a body of rational lore regarding the means to improve American democracy and, by implication, human society in general. His task and that of his colleagues was, he believed, to persuade Americans of the usefulness of this new discipline which could help to reintroduce the principle of justice within American capitalism, especially its property system. Small retired a frustrated man, defeated by the selfish irrationality embedded in the prevailing mores.

W. I. Thomas adopted a reverse strategy. He did not stay indoors, devoting himself to fashioning a new academic discipline which would eventually, so to speak, be wheeled out for presentation to the real world. Instead, Thomas plunged himself straightaway into the midst of that world, wresting from it empirical evidence to be carried back to his study for examination with a social scientist's eye. As has been seen, in his case direct confrontation with the prevailing mores brought personal tragedy and professional ruin. After his departure from Chicago University he continued to write and publish but never again held a regular university post.

Robert Park's career followed yet a third pattern, one alternating between bouts of intense involvement in 'real life' and periods of academic withdrawal which allowed him to mull over his experiences. Park was born in 1864, a year later than Thomas.

111

Although Park's place of birth was Luzerne County, Pennsylvania, the family moved to Minnesota when his father came home from service in the Union Army. After a period of economic struggle, Park's father became so successful in business that he was able to leave his son a substantial legacy when he died in 1911. Park avoided drawing upon this private income until it was needed to support his wife and children after his appointment at Chicago University on a very meagre salary. When he went to take the job at Chicago in 1913 Park was already 49 years old. He had arrived in the sociology department by a rather circuitous route.[1]

After his studies in philosophy and German at the University of Michigan, where his teachers included the young John Dewey, Park spent twelve years as a newspaperman. He began as a cub on the *Minneapolis Journal*, carried out crime reporting and investigative journalism on the *New York Journal* and eventually ended up as the drama critic for the *Chicago Journal*. Having discovered by his mid-thirties that journalism was a young man's game, Park spent the next few years studying at Harvard, Berlin, Strassburg and Heidelberg. His academic interests in this period included philosophy and psychology (which he studied under William James), sociology (as taught by Georg Simmel, another ex-journalist), political economy and geography.

Having completed his dissertation on 'the crowd and the public', Park turned down an offer from Albion Small, an acquaintance of his father, to do some part-time sociology teaching at Chicago. Instead he worked as a researcher, publicity officer and ghost writer. He was employed initially by the Congo Reform Association and subsequently by Booker T. Washington who was based at Tuskegee. Washington was then at the height of his national influence. Tuskegee was the base from which he advocated a programme of vocational education as a means of inculcating self-discipline in Southern blacks and assimilating them to the mainstream of American life. During the best part of a decade Park had ample opportunity to travel and become thoroughly familiar with the daily life of Southern blacks, especially the upper levels of this society. It was during his time working for Washington that Park met W. I. Thomas who in 1912 persuaded Park that he should come and teach at Chicago.

During the quarter of a century since leaving the University of Michigan, Park had acquired considerable knowledge of the newspaper world and life in the American South. He had also developed a fascination with large modern cities combined with a strong aversion (reminiscent of Veblen) to moralistic philanthropists and 'do-gooders' drawn from the leisure class. These interests, inclinations and prejudices were modulations of Park's strong sense of pride in his national heritage. Like Small and Thomas, he accepted without question the rightness of the American Way with its commitment to equality, freedom, justice and happiness within a democratic society.

Park took some care to avoid excessive personal dependence upon the material fruits of American capitalism. He was neither a big spender nor a fancy dresser. Thomas offered to buy him a new suit when he first came to Chicago. In fact, although Park took upon himself a large amount of teaching and began collaborating with Ernest Burgess on a major new sociology textbook, he did not receive a full-time appointment until 1919. As has been mentioned, he was able to rely upon his father's legacy. His financial independence insulated Park from the pressure to seek promotion assiduously or to get his name in print at all costs. Furthermore, as Fred Matthews has pointed out, Park was fortunate during the 1920s in being able to 'make use of the foundations in their "soft" period' (Matthews, 1977, p. 113). In other words, financial aid from bodies such as the Laura Spelman Rockefeller Memorial Fund was still readily available for projects which could be justified in terms of their contribution to the development of scientific understanding even though they might have no practical social applications except perhaps 'indirectly' or 'eventually'. This climate, which had been so favourable to Thomas's work on the Polish peasant, was not to survive the Depression at the end of the 1920s.

Park shared Small's concern for Christian principles and attended church regularly during his Chicago years. One of his last papers was on the work of Christian missions in helping to 'create a moral solidarity among the nations and peoples' (Park, 1950, p. 339). However, Park balanced these religious concerns with a strong sense of realism. In a piece on social planning and human nature, he argued that despite their Utopian aspirations for 'a perfect city and an ideal state', writers such as Plato had been divorced from the real world, their impact being restricted to the shaping of public opinion. Park preferred Aristotle and Machiavelli to Plato:

With the exception, perhaps, of Aristotle's politics it was not until the publication of Machiavelli's *The Prince* that literature affords an example of a man who thought realistically and in the modern manner in the field of politics and social science, seeking to describe, not the sort of state men should desire, but rather how, human nature being what it is, such political society as existed could hope to survive in the world in which it found itself (Park, 1955, p. 43).

Following his practical education on the reporter's beat and in the South, Park was very cautious about the scope for social scientists to induce planned change. In fact, he had persisting reservations about the relative desirability of the new world being brought into being by 'progress' as compared with the old world being left behind. For example, despite his liking for Ibsen, he was no great advocate of the women's movement.

Park's approach to life displayed an interesting combination of restlessness and conservatism. In his youth, he had been given to Whitmanesque enthusiasm for the possibilities of a world of natural fulfilment untrammelled by convention. Later, however, he was very sensitive to the contribution made by social etiquette to the management of relations between individuals and groups, especially in hierarchical or caste societies such as Japan and the American South. Park was aware of the revolutionary potential of the crowd, its capacity to break down old orders and liberate human energies. However, he believed that the tensions and conflicts of a modern urban society could only be reconciled with democracy if the crowd was transformed into a public which accepted rules of rational discussion and tolerated differences of opinion and attitude.

Park depended less upon the academic world for recognition, response and security than did either Small or Thomas. However, he did find within it enormous opportunities to satisfy the promptings of his gargantuan desire for knowledge about the way the world worked. As co-director with Ernest Burgess of scores of student research projects, he had command of a multitude of eyes, ears and intelligences which were in many respects an extension of himself. Less intellectually original than Thomas, less conscious than Small of a duty to guide mankind, Park – more than either of them – was driven by unalloyed curiosity. The objects of this curiosity were dictated by his intense interest in the way the American Experiment was working out.

The big picture

On his arrival at Chicago shortly before the First World War Park must have presented an intriguing and contradictory character to those who got to know him: conservative yet restless, armed with a self-protective puritanism yet driven by enormous curiosity, attracted by the vital energy of the crowd yet committed to the rational procedures of the democratic public, soaked in the individualistic values of late nineteenth-century Minnesota yet mourning their destructive potential, a regular church-going Christian yet scornful of do-gooders.

During his time in Chicago, especially in the earliest years, American sociology benefited from a combination of favourable circumstances: Park's driving curiosity undiverted by any evangelical reform impulse, his *savoir-faire* and self-confidence flowing from long involvement with the 'real world', his willingness to assume academic responsibilities in return for a pittance, his persistence in repeatedly exploring a limited set of chosen themes, his exploitation of the loose rein allowed by the foundations in the 1920s, and (not least) his access to the skills and energies of Ernest Burgess and a generation of keen young researchers. As a consequence of such factors, Park was able to give substance to the discipline whose foundations in Chicago had been laid by Small and Thomas.

Like Albion Small and W. I. Thomas, Robert Park was keen to understand 'the big picture', the underlying factors shaping the individual and the world. Park was more ambitious than either of his colleagues in the scope of his enquiries. Small usually restricted himself to general observations. Thomas tended to focus upon the social psychological dynamics of the individual. Park, however, gave generous amounts of attention to a wide range of interlocking issues: the workings of reason, imagination and desire within the individual; the interplay of individuals within groups or communities; the tensions and accommodations between communities within the city; the operation of institutions such as the press, the law and social agencies within American society; and the competition between racial groups in Europe and (especially) the Pacific.[2]

Park was aware of two major challenges confronting America during the first half of the twentieth century. One was the problem already encountered in the discussion of Small and Thomas: 'the most characteristic trait of *homo Americanus* is an inveterate individualism . . . reinforced by the conditions of life on the frontier. But with the growth of great cities, with the vast division of labor which has come in with the machine industry, and with movement and change that has come about with the multiplication of the means of transportation and the communication, the old forms of social control represented by the family, the neighborhood, and the local community have been undermined and their influence greatly diminished' (Park, 1952, p. 59).

However, there was another challenge. It concerned the competitive relations between the multi-ethnic American polity and its rivals in Europe and Asia. Were these rivals more socially efficient or politically effective than the USA in handling nationalist or ethnic feeling? How would their example affect Americans? Writing in 1913, Park noted 'The aim of the contending nationalities in Austria–Hungary at the present time seems to be a federation . . . based upon the autonomy of the different nations composing the empire'. He added that in a similar way in the American South 'the races seem to be tending in the direction of a bi-racial organization of society, in which the Negro is gradually gaining a limited autonomy. What the outcome of this movement may be it is not safe to predict' (Park, 1950, p. 220).

In his book *The Immigrant Press and its Control* (1922), Park warned native Americans of the dangers of enforcing 'uniformity of language and ideas' in the USA. He found it conceivable that 'if it should come to be regarded as a mark of disloyalty or inferiority to speak a foreign language, we should reproduce in a mild form the racial animosities and conflicts which are resulting in the breaking up of the continental imperiums, Austria–Hungary, Russia and Germany' (Park, 1922, p. 67). However, the newcomers had to adapt also. During the First World War it had appeared that 'Some of our immigrant peoples did not regard this country as a nation. It was merely a place in which people lived, like the Austrian Empire – a geographical expression' (ibid, p. 419).

Germans in America had been told by one prominent compatriot to resist attempts to 'do away with our German cultural type . . . in the smudge kitchen of a national melting pot' (Goebel, 1914, pp. 11–13, quoted in Park, 1922, p. 62). Despite propaganda efforts by foreign agents, such appeals lost their attraction for German–Americans in the course of the First World War. However, as late as 1941 Park was noting that the capacity of the German totalitarian regime to animate 'with a common will and a common purpose vast armies and a whole people' (Park, 1955, p. 138) was not matched in a democratic society which tolerated divided opinions.

More troubling still was the perceived threat from the Pacific, especially Japan. In 1924 the Exclusion Law had 'created in our West Coast a barrier to immigration that is distinctly racial . . . It is as if we had said: Europe, of which after all America is a mere western projection, ends here. The Pacific Coast is our racial frontier' (Park, 1950, p. 139). Their success in the First World War had shown that 'The Japanese are an organized and morally efficient nation. They have the racial pride and the national egotism which rests on the consciousness of this efficiency'. Park had serious doubts about both the wisdom and the effectiveness of exclusion as a way of coping with 'the rising tide of the oriental invasion' (ibid, p. 228).

Considering these matters, Park must have sympathised strongly with Small's view that 'American civilization has turned out to be bigger, more unwieldy, less amenable to the control of anyone's preconceptions than could have been anticipated' (Small, 1919, p. 406). Indeed, that sentence identifies the problem at the heart of Park's writing, the issue with which he struggled to cope in formulating his approach to sociology. While Small sought ways to implant a dedication to justice in modern America and Thomas puzzled over the means to bring happiness back into the world, Park was engaged on his own intellectual quest. It was to discover what was gained and what was lost in the hurricane-like transition from the brute simplicities of small-town prairie life to the dangerous complexities associated with the big city, a new gigantic America and a crowded, jealous world.

Words like 'justice' and 'happiness' were rare in Park's writings. His tone was rather sardonic. If he called something 'romantic' it was not a term of praise. 'Civilized' was a double-edged epithetic, likely to mean that the person or group concerned had lost something precious – perhaps a culture – rather than gained the key to life's mysteries. Park had a fatalistic, gloomy side to him which makes it all the more intriguing to discover that in his youth he 'gained an intimate acquaintance with Norwegian peasants' (Baker, 1974, p. 252) partly through his Norwegian nurse who made him thoroughly familiar with the Norse legends which were also Veblen's childhood staple. Other, more truly American, legends were also woven into Park's early experience. He claimed to have a clear recollection of the death of Lincoln, an event which took place when he was under 2 years old (Matthews, 1977, p. 3). As a loyal American, Park was unlikely to deny the positive character of the liberating, emancipating impulse which, to use a phrase he borrowed from Walter Bagehot, broke 'the cake of custom' (Park, 1952, p. 227). Nevertheless, he was keenly aware of its negative aspects. Like William James, he could see that in many respects 'Progress is a terrible thing' (Park, 1952, p. 60).

Following his arrival, Park evidently soaked up very quickly the prevailing spirit in Albion Small's sociology department. Professor Small must have been pleased to read, at about the time of his own retirement, Park's implicit nod in his direction: 'Only gradually [wrote Park in 1925], as he succeeds in accommodating himself to the life of the larger group, incorporating into the specific purposes and ambitions of his own life the larger and calmer purposes of the society in which he lives, does the individual man find himself quite at home in the community of which he is a part' (ibid, p. 57).

Park fitted easily into grooves already well worn in the Chicago sociology department. Like Small and Thomas he was strongly influenced by two powerful intellectual currents: the assumption that through a combination of learning through experience and the application of rationality individuals and groups could shape their own future in many respects; and the view that social development was a result of inexorable natural laws of selection, adaptation and transmission which favoured those individuals and groups most fitted to survive. The former position, which emphasised the intellectual and imaginative capacities of human beings, was favoured by the theorists of pragmatism. Advocates of the latter position, which was buttressed with reference to biological factors, typically drew upon the work of Malthus, Darwin and Spencer.

Small and Vincent's *Introduction to the Science of Society* had been full of biological analogies. Book III was entitled 'Social

Anatomy' and included discussion of 'social organs'. In Book IV, on 'Social Physiology and Pathology', was to be found a chapter on 'The Pathology of Social Organs – Characteristics of Social Disease'. However, a special place within this framework was found for 'psychical force' as expressed in individual and social consciousness and in the 'psycho-physical communicating apparatus' including education and the press. Within this system the individual was 'a communicating cell' (Small and Vincent, 1894, pp. 9–11).

Two years later, in his discussion of the 'scope and method of folk-psychology', Thomas was arguing that differences in temperament in individuals and races were due to 'chemical constitution' (Thomas, 1895, p. 442). However, tackling a similar theme in 1905 he made a different argument, suggesting that 'what have sometimes been regarded as biological differences separating social groups are not really so, and that characteristic expressions of mind are dependent on social environment' (Thomas, 1905, p. 452). Discarding his biologistic tendencies, Thomas developed a Dewey-like schema emphasising the interplay between control, habit, crisis and attention. Park readily adopted this schema in his turn. Nevertheless, in spite of this vote of confidence in pragmatism, Park was less willing than Thomas to relinquish either the biological view of race or the Social-Darwinist view of history with which it was often associated.

In some respects, Park's emphasis upon ecological processes represented the revival of a declining Social-Darwinist point of view. In the early 1890s, three decades before Park was giving currency to the term 'human ecology', Small and Vincent noted that 'The distribution of population over the area of a given society is engaging the careful attention of sociologists' (Small and Vincent, 1894, p. 283). As has been seen, they also encouraged their student readers to engage in the kind of urban map-making which was to become a prominent feature of the Chicago department under Park and Burgess. The 1894 textbook had been presented as a 'laboratory guide' (ibid, p. 15). In an article published the following year, Small referred to Chicago as a 'vast sociological laboratory' (Small, 1895c, p. 582), a phrase echoed in Park's own evocation in 1929 of 'The city as a social laboratory' (Park, 1950, p. 73).

Intellectual influences

The index of the three-volume collection of Park's papers, edited by Everett Hughes and others, provides a rough-and-ready guide to the contemporaries and predecessors whose work influenced him. Some of the tensions and conflicts mentioned earlier are reflected in the list. It is interesting to notice that Max Weber is credited with one reference and Sigmund Freud with three. Karl Marx and Aristotle are each mentioned four times. Higher up the list come Bronislaw Malinowski and Thomas Malthus (five each), Georg Simmel (seven) and G. H. Mead (eight). Oswald Spengler (ten) who anticipated the 'decline of the west' (Spengler, 1923) is balanced against Graham Wallas (ten) who, in contrast, envisaged the emergence of a 'Great Society' (Wallas, 1914) in which rational reconstruction could create the conditions for human happiness. Walter Lippman (eleven) and C. H. Cooley (eleven) are followed by Emile Durkheim (twelve) and Gustave Le Bon (twelve) – all concerned in different ways with human nature, individual and collective consciousness and the conditions of social order.

The pragmatists William James (fourteen) and John Dewey (sixteen) are cheek by jowl with Charles Darwin (fourteen) and Walter Bagehot (sixteen). The work of the last-named on the application of the principles of natural selection and inheritance to political society particularly attracted Park's attention. References to Herbert Spencer (sixteen) who stressed the part played by competition in social evolution are complemented by acknowledgement of the contribution made by Auguste Comte (sixteen). The latter envisaged the emergence of a consensus within the social organism based upon the findings of positivistic sociology.

None of the above-mentioned are referred to by Park even half as frequently as the two men whose names come right at the top of the list. They are W. I. Thomas (thirty-three) and W. G. Sumner, author of *Folkways* (forty references). Before exploring the implications of this last finding, it is worth noting how infrequently, comparatively speaking, Georg Simmel is mentioned in Park's papers. At first sight this fact is surprising since it is sometimes assumed that Park introduced a Simmelian viewpoint into American sociology.

It is true that the German philosopher and sociologist was quite heavily quoted in Park and Burgess's *Introduction to the Science of*

Sociology, published in 1921. However, too much should not be made of this fact. The textbook followed the pattern of Thomas's *Source Book for Social Origins* in the sense that editorial introductory material was interspersed with extracts from a wide range of specialist authors. In Simmel's writings could be found general formulations concerning the nature of social interaction, conflict, subordination and superordination. They contributed usefully to the stock of formulae and theorems urgently required by a new discipline in need of scientific credentials. Simmel's work was the source for eight of the seventy-five extracts included in the Park and Burgess textbook, the largest single contribution but still scarcely more than 10 per cent of the total count.

Simmel placed the question of individual freedom at the centre of his thought. Fred Matthews suggests that Simmel's popularity in America at this period was due to the fact that 'it incorporated sociological insights without forcing a violent break with American confidence in the benevolent effect of a market-place of liberated individual atoms' (Matthews, 1977, p. 50). However, as was seen in the first part of this present study, the cultural context and social implications of Simmel's thought were very un-American.

In spite of the apparent compatibility of his ideas with intellectual tendencies in Chicago, Simmel did not share some basic assumptions of his transatlantic admirers. Small, Thomas and Park were all interested in finding a way to build a rational social order through which human individuality might be fully expressed. All three felt a certain moral repugnance for those who chose not to contribute to this task. For example, Park regarded the hobo as 'a belated frontiersman' (Park, 1952, p. 95) whose freedom was wasted because of his 'lack of a vocation' (ibid, p. 93). By contrast, Simmel would have seen the positive side to this life of restless locomotion. He treated individuality as a treasure to be preserved by those who had sufficient personal luck and *finesse*. It had to be protected carefully within the interstices of a modern institutional order whose relentless development inevitably threatened it with extinction. As Charles Axelrod points out (Axelrod, 1977) Simmel shared Nietzche's low estimation of humanity *en masse*.

To the extent that Park drew upon Simmel, he Americanised him. For example, Park referred to Simmel's essay on 'the stranger' when delineating his own concept of 'the marginal man' (Park, 1950, p. 354; Simmel, 1950a). The cultural or racial hybrid of whom

Park wrote resents his marginality and aspires to the full group membership from which he is excluded. By contrast, Simmel's 'stranger' is a wanderer who still relishes or yearns for the freedom of coming and going as he pleases. A recent study of Simmel's influence within American sociology pointed out that 'the ambiguities, dualistic conceptions, and dialectical aspects of Simmel's thinking have often been screened out by those trained in American modes of thought' (Levine *et al.*, 1976, p. 1128).

Important clues to the impact made upon Park by W. G. Sumner and W. I. Thomas can be gathered from a critique of their methods which he originally published in 1931, two years before his retirement. Park argued that Thomas and Znaniecki's *The Polish Peasant* and Sumner's *Folkways*, a wide-ranging analytical and descriptive survey of 'usages, manners, customs, mores and morals' (to quote its subtitle), were both amongst 'the two or three most important books in the field of sociology by American authors' (Park, 1955, p. 243). *Folkways*, published in 1899, contained the results of well over ten years' work by Sumner exploring the habits and customs (or folkways) which arose in societies in an unplanned way through 'efforts to satisfy needs' (Sumner, 1940, p. v). In Park's words, Sumner was seeking 'in a broad, disinterested, and empirical study of human nature, a sound basis for all practical efforts to direct the course of current events, to control political action, and to improve social life generally' (Park, 1955, p. 249).

Folkways lay between inherited and instinctive ways of behaving on the one hand and, on the other, 'those rational constructions of human wit and forethought, erected upon a foundation of custom and habit, that we call "institutions"' (ibid, p. 248). A sub-class of folkways were the mores which at specific times and places, define 'what is right and proper' (ibid, p. 246). Like all folkways, they arose out of and were oriented towards human activity. They could only be understood sociologically with reference to the broader cultural context. Park concluded that although *Folkways* lacked 'coordination and structure' (ibid, p. 243) Sumner's work had laid 'a foundation for more realistic, more objective, and more systematic studies' (ibid, p. 252).

The Polish Peasant complemented *Folkways*, in Park's view. The former was a sociological study of the mores, the latter a social psychological study mainly concerned with attitudes. In this context, the chief contribution of *The Polish Peasant* was 'not a body of fact, but a system of concepts' (ibid, p. 265). Sumner paid great attention to the influence of 'the struggle for existence' and 'societal selection' in accounting for the part played by folkways and mores. In contrast to the message of hope derived by Thomas from the Polish national revival with its transformation of popular consciousness, Sumner issued the following general warning:

The Renaissance in Italy shows that although moral traditions may be narrow and mistaken, any morality is better than moral anarchy. Moral traditions are guides which no one can afford to neglect. They are in the mores and they are lost in every great revolution of the mores. Then the men are morally lost (Sumner, 1940, p. 539).

In discussing Sumner and Thomas, Park was indirectly identifying tensions within his own approach: pragmatism versus Social Darwinism, optimism versus pessimism, reason versus tradition, emancipatory individualism versus communal solidarity.

Faces, races, places

Robert Park's name has become synonymous with the study of the city. This is misleading or, rather, it is a narrow view of things. Park would probably have been happier being described as a student of human nature. As he wrote:

in the city all the secret ambitions and all the suppressed desires find somewhere an expression. The city magnifies, spreads out, and advertises human nature in all its various manifestation. It is this that makes the city interesting, even fascinating. It is this however, that makes it of all places the one in which to discover the secrets of human hearts, and to study human nature and society (Park, 1952, p. 87).

The city as a social organism was only one item on Park's research agenda. Equally important items included the dynamics of personality, the nature of race in the national and international arenas, and the role of the press.

In Park's view, social structure was a consequence of human

activity and not *vice versa*. The key realm of activity was not 'unconscious competition and cooperation' but rather 'conscious participation in a common purpose and a common life', made possible through speech and the existence of shared symbols. In this sense 'It is not . . . a division of labor, but the fact of social control that characterizes human society' (Park, 1955, p. 17). In a passage strongly reminiscent of Mead or Cooley, Park insisted that man 'lives in his imagination, and, through his imagination, in the minds of other men'. Through suggestion and imitation 'men invade one another's lives and participate one with another in their efforts to direct, control and give expression to their own conflicting impulses' (ibid, p. 18).

Park drew a picture of men and women as actors striving for social recognition. Their public behaviour was interpreted and ultimately controlled by others. Each individual's public face became a 'mask', an earlier meaning of the very word 'person'. These masks represented our conceptions of ourselves and our roles. Our mask became 'part of our personality . . . We come into the world as individuals, achieve character, and become persons' (ibid, p. 19), our acts subject to self-control and social control. The collective actions of a group typically crystallised as its institutions, its habits became the folkways. As this happened, group organisation and morale were complemented by the form and content of individual morality.

However, secularisation of society – for example, the disruption of tradition by migration, urban growth and new forms of industry – brought with it internal divisions, differences of interest and rising individualism. The established mores were challenged by an emerging order characterised by public debate and political activity. Park suggested that in these circumstances political unrest, collective action and even, in some cases, revolutionary movements developed which weakened old mores and institutions and established new ones. Through this process issues arising out of the mores were, in time, brought back and incorporated into the mores. The process just described was accompanied by major changes in human nature since the dynamics of personality and society were closely linked in (often conflictual) interdependence.

In the long run these changes in human nature were bringing more freedom and sophistication. However, this liberating process was accompanied by a rising tide of race prejudice. This prejudice was a reflex of 'the group mind' stimulated by 'unrestricted competition of peoples with different standards of living' (Park, 1950, p. 229). Before social relations and human interests could be successfully adjusted to produce more cooperation and less conflict the problem had to be more fully understood. Park argued that each race inherited temperamental qualities which were the foundation of interest and attention. These intrinsic characteristics predisposed it to select certain 'elements in the cultural environment' and 'seek and find its vocation' in a specific region of the larger social organisation. At the same time, this 'inner core of significant attitudes and values' was 'modified by social experience' as shaped by the external environment (ibid, pp. 281–2). Racial temperament and social tradition were intimately related. In the course of global change accompanied by migration and miscegenation, the complex of 'biologically inherited qualities' of each race was likely to be broken up, initiating changes in mores, traditions and institutions.

This was happening, above all, in the USA. By the mid-1920s Park was pointing out that second-generation immigrants were losing their ancestral traditions. They were inheriting a 'generalized' and 'rationalized' civilisation based on a set of techniques rather than a local, unique and individual culture based upon a set of mores. He commented: 'This is a nondescript age in which we live. The old isolations within which the older cultures grew up have broken down' (Park, p. 32). Behind these cultural changes, which brought 'Nothing inspiring or uplifting', were inexorable economic and technological developments. The one hopeful note Park sounded was that there would be ample opportunity for empirical study of 'the whole cultural process' (ibid, p. 35). He was soon doing this, examining racial frontiers globally and in the USA.

On America's 'racial frontier on the Pacific' the 'race relations cycle – contact, competition, accommodation and eventual assimilation' was 'apparently progressive and irreversible' (ibid, p. 139). This cycle occurred in the context of 'vital interdependence' which characterised 'all living things, plant and animal alike' (ibid, p. 139). The world's race consciousness after the First World War was almost unprecedented. However, race differences, the consequence of geographical isolation, were subject to the impact of widening communication between groups as the world economy became more complex. Huge migrations were stimulated, apparently as part of a 'general tendency to restore the equilibrium between population and food supply, labor and capital, in a world economy' (ibid, p. 143). At the same time, there was widespread resistance to colonialism as subject peoples sought independence and the Japanese government demanded equality of treatment for its nationals in the USA.

The physical, moral and social distance between races was being reduced, not least through the impact of American films abroad. In a fascinating passage, Park suggested that, in some respects, the American experience and the American Dream have become global:

> This is today the most romantic period in the history of the whole world; not even the discovery of America has influenced man's imagination more . . . and it is in men's minds and in their intimate personal experiences that the most profound and significant changes in the world are taking place today. It is in the obscure, dream-haunted recesses of our inner lives that the future of the world is taking shape . . . If America was once in any exclusive sense the melting pot of races, it is no longer. The melting pot is the world (ibid, p. 147–9).

Park recognised that the same forces which produced cultures with their strong sense of belonging to a localised 'we-group' also generated prejudice. Despite his enthusiasm for the liberating aspects of civilisation, Park also greatly valued the stability associated with a regional or racial culture with well-established mores. Park could not condone prejudice but he argued that it was a social attitude which, in the very nature of things, became embodied in the habits of individuals. In some manifestations prejudice was 'merely the resistance of the social order to change' (ibid, p. 233). In fact, he argued, in the American context it was better to speak of 'racial antagonism' rather than 'prejudice'; 'There is probably less racial prejudice in America than elsewhere, but there is more racial conflict and more racial antagonism'. This conflict was a sign of 'progress', of the fact that 'The Negro is rising in America' (ibid, p. 233).

The dilemma just mentioned was acutely relevant to this situation. In Park's view, the demise of slavery overturned a plantation hierarchy in which human interests and passions had been in relatively stable equilibrium. Gradually, new forms were developing in the South which preserved social distance but permitted blacks to advance in occupational status: 'The races no longer look up and down; they look across'. This rather romantic view of a South which Park had known best only through the eyes of the black élite was contrasted with the fate of northern migrants. As ex-slaves went north to the city they entered an unfamiliar world as strangers. They met fear and hatred in a social environment that lacked 'the etiquette which makes intercourse and cooperation among the races in the South possible' (ibid, p. 243).

The comforts of paradox

The American cities to which the Southern blacks made their way were becoming crowded with immigrants from Europe, Latin America and Asia. Such cities, impersonal and rational, were 'the natural habitat of civilized man' (Park, 1952, p. 14). Ecological processes of competition, specialisation and segregation produced a characteristic distribution of population and functions within the city. These processes were expressed in differential land values, variations in land use and the segregation of the population in 'natural social areas' (ibid, p. 170) such as immigrant colonies and racial ghettos. Social mobility of individuals and groups was typically accompanied by geographical mobility. As a consequence, within the city there were distinctive 'Bohemias', 'rooming-house areas' and 'apartment-house areas' as well as the central business district with its periphery of slums (ibid, p. 171).

The interdependent communities into which a city like Chicago was divided were organised ecologically, economically, politically and culturally. Within each community, the restless and romantic urges which expressed themselves in competitive individualism were restrained to some extent by the requirements of cooperation. It was vitally important, in Park's view, that individual efficiency or success should not be at the expense of 'communal efficiency' (ibid, p. 68). Each community within the city was part of a larger, more inclusive one. Furthermore, there were several major counter-attractions which diverted energies from the needs of the local residential community. The city offered individuals the chance to 'live at the same time in several different worlds (ibid, p. 20). These worlds included 'moral regions' (ibid, p. 49) which catered for a wide range of tastes, passions and vices. They also included the worlds of work. This was highly significant because within the city, character was formed at least as much by vocation or occupation as it was by local and family ties. In his early paper entitled 'The City: Suggestions for the Investigation of Human Behavior in the Urban Environment' (1916), Park had noticed the tension between vocational specialisation and the interests of neighbourhood-based communities.

A decade later Park returned to this issue. He noted that the Russian system of soviets gave professional people a deep interest in the local community in sharp contrast with the American metropolis whose neighbourhoods were the province of the juvenile gang and the machine politician. Some efforts were being made by (for example) social settlements to 'reconstruct and quicken the life of city neighborhoods and to bring them in touch with the larger interests of the community' (Park, 1955, p. 19). The magnitude of this task was increased by the fact that the moral order of the primary group was weakening. Social control was increasingly being undertaken by the legal system rather than the mores. Park did not welcome this development: 'it probably is fair to say that the relative security of society can be estimated by the number of its unwritten as compared with its formal and written laws' (ibid, p. 49).

Park was forced to take comfort in the workings of paradox. Modern America was being shaped by two apparently contradictory forces: increasing race-consciousness and galloping individualism. With regard to each, there were tendencies at work which gave some hope that a stable moral order might develop balancing competition with cooperation. For example, Park came to the conclusion that 'in the case of the Jew, the Negro, and the Japanese . . . their conflict with America had been grave enough to create in each a new sense of racial identity, and to give the sort of solidarity that grows out of a common cause'. They had improved their 'group efficiency'. Their communities 'may be regarded as models for our own' since they are conducive to 'a new parochialism'. It was typical of Park's deep ambivalence towards the onward sweep of civilisation at the expense of culture that he should welcome these tendencies: 'Our problem is to encourage men to seek God in their own village and to see the social problem in their own neighborhood' (ibid, p. 72).

The mobile urban world gave shape to another paradox, complementary to the one just mentioned. The city encouraged human diversity within its complex division of labour. Diversity of experience made communication necessary. Communication cultivated and depended upon shared understandings. Individualism thus led towards consensus. The basis of consensus was rationality: 'A rational mind is simply one that is capable of making its private impulses public and intelligible' (ibid, p. 175). Ironically, however, the very self-consciousness stimulated by diversity of experience produced personal reserve, a need for social distance which, in turn, created an obstacle to communication. Park was undaunted by this observation. Returning to the point where his theoretical approach began, he recalled that the very sense of self, of being a person, was, to a considerable degree, socially controlled: 'The individual whose conception of himself is not at all determined by the conception that other persons have of him is probably insane' (ibid, p. 177).

The press and the public mind

Inhabitants of the city were subject to constant alarms and agitation which produced 'a chronic condition of crisis' (ibid, p. 31). Within urban society, the atmosphere of crisis disrupted habits and stimulated heightened attention. Where was this attention directed? Park was deeply aware of the tendency for attention to be dissipated, not least in leisure whose improvident use was, he suspected, the cause of 'the greatest wastes in American life' (ibid, p. 68). The most powerful agency for focusing attention upon specific objects or issues was the newspaper. Park explored this institution in his book *The Immigrant Press and its Control* (1922) which was a companion volume to *Old World Traits Transformed*.

With the invaluable aid of his assistant Winifred Rauschenbusch, Park presented a wealth of material on scores of foreign-language newspapers. The work was divided into four parts. The first part discussed the origins of the foreign-language press in America, paying particular attention to the role of emerging national consciousness in the latter days of the Austro-Hungarian empire and the patriotic significance of the national language: Armenian, Greek, Polish, Czech or whatever.

In the second part, Park analysed the content of the foreign-language press, distinguishing between an old-fashioned provincial press and a more radical cosmopolitan press. The latter was preoccupied with the issues of class and war, sometimes taking an ambiguous line of the issue of assimilation with the host society. At one point, Park quoted the English editorial side-by-side with the Polish editorial from the same newspaper. The first proclaimed the paper's adherence to 'true, loyal and unwavering Americanism'. The second was critical of 'any Americanization motive, for we resent forcible and silly efforts in that direction' (Park, 1922, p. 211). One of Park's central findings was that despite efforts by journalists and editors to use the press as a medium of radical or subversive propaganda, newspapers had in fact provided a wide range of knowledge, entertainment and intellectual stimulation for its readers.

In the third part, Park presented a 'natural history' of the immigrant press, detailing 'the struggle for existence' (ibid, p. 309) which results in 'the survival of the fittest' (ibid, p. 328). A substitute for the informal gossip channels of the small community, newspapers joined with the telegraph and the telephone in converting the world into 'a vast whispering gallery' (ibid, p. 328). In fact, 'The newspaper may be said to perform, for the public and the "public mind", the function of attention in the individual' (ibid, p. 329).

Part four was concerned with the control of the press. Park was well aware of the power of capitalist interests in this area. Discussing the contention that the capitalist advertiser represented 'a menace to democracy' (ibid, p. 365), he argued that the interests and wishes of the general public and commerce were interdependent: 'The businessman is bound to advertise in the paper which has the largest circulation, and the paper which has the largest circulation will at least tend to be the paper that most effectively reflects the interests, defines the attitudes and the opinions of the largest public' (ibid, p. 366). A successful newspaper was the result of an 'unstable equilibrium' of interests within which a 'working balance has been built up very gradually' (ibid, p. 464). Above all, 'People will not read a paper with which they continuously disagree. In the long run, the newspaper expresses, rather than creates, public opinion' (ibid, p. 466).

Park was by no means naive. In another context he wrote: 'The vital part of an army, as of a community, is its morale and morale may be weakened or sustained by a well directed press bureau . . . One way to educate community is through the press' (Park, 1955, pp. 148–9). Did this imply (to revise a previous statement) that 'in the long run, the newspaper expresses, *because it creates*, public opinion'? Park appreciated perfectly well the way propaganda worked, having spent several years not only as a journalist but also as (in effect) a lobbyist and public relations officer. Park's sociological analysis of the American press displayed a strong belief in the ultimate rightness of the people's judgement, a belief so deeply entrenched that in some respects it shaped rather than reflected his observation of the world.

Questions, not answers

It is likely that most students of sociology became aware of Robert Park through his co-authorship of *Introduction to the Science of Sociology*, the 'green bible' which first appeared in 1921. It was not so much a 'new testament' as a reworking of aspects of two 'old testaments'. One was Small and Vincent's *Introduction to the Study of Society* with which it shared the concept of a first chapter outlining the development of sociology followed by the presentation of material relating to conflict and accommodation in the course of social change. The other was W. I. Thomas's *Source Book for Social Origins* (1908) which provided the idea of presenting a wide range of readings accompanied by editorial introductions. The new textbook had chapters on human nature, society and the group, social contacts, social interaction, competition, conflict, accommodation, assimilation, social control and collective behaviour. It apparently aimed to be encyclopaedic and it was certainly eclectic.

It is difficult to believe that its abstractions and generalities made much of a contribution to the protection of corporate capitalism, as implied by Herman and Julie Schwendinger (1974), any more than Small's sweeping criticisms damaged that regime. The Schwendingers identify Park and Burgess as part of a movement characterised by psychological reductionism and a concern with social control. That is misleading. In fact, a great deal of the text concerned racial and national conflict and the conditions under which popular uprisings occur. The final chapter, which was on collective behaviour, ended with a discussion of revolution.

Park, the leading light in this project, was no smooth front man for the big corporations. Nor was he a brain-washed puppet. In his early decades, he had sought excitement and adventure, exploiting the opportunities for varied experience offered in a society undergoing the enormous transformations associated with rapid capitalist development. Later, as a university man, he was sensible enough to keep his mouth shut on issues that seriously threatened the corporations. The experiences of Veblen and Thomas (and others) provided ample 'encouragement' for this strategy. In any case, his discussions of the press imply that Park regarded the power of the people as being, in the end, more than a match for the power of private property. There is an obsessive concern in Park's writings with the forces making and breaking the moral solidarity of 'the public'. This was no accident. Although it could not be tactfully stated in such terms, the force of an 'educated' American public opinion was the only conceivable countervailing power against the business corporations.

Park is a crucial figure in the development of American sociology not because he provided clear answers and explanations regarding the development of American society but because he did not. Instead, he kept asking questions. They were specific, researchable questions like 'Where within the city is the population declining? Where is it expanding?' (Park, 1952, p. 18) and so on. Park was not locked up in his library as was Small (metaphorically, at least) nor digging away, like Thomas, in some far-away central European archive. Park was on hand, readily available to the keen and useful student, making suggestions and responding to them. He considered that he had been 'most successful . . . in my introductions to other men's books – books which represent the problems I am most interested in' (Baker, 1974, p. 260). If the name of Robert Park was remembered and inspired loyalty it was not because there was a creed of 'Parkism' supported by 'Parkists'. It was because in the absence of an integrated sociological theory the discipline was organised around practice. In Chicago that practice was inspired by the driving enthusiasm of Robert Park.

Notes

1. On Park, see Matthews, 1977; Park, 1967; Faris, 1967; Carey, 1975; Bulmer, 1984; Ballis Lal, 1986; Frazier and Gaziano, 1979. For an important influence on his thinking, see James, 1917a.
2. Many of Park's papers are collected in Hughes *et al.*, 1950–5, in three volumes entitled respectively, *Race and Culture* (Park, 1950), *Human Communities* (Park, 1952) and *Society* (Park, 1955). In my discussion of Park I refer to the following papers (date of original publication given in brackets): from *Race and Culture* 'Racial Assimilation in Secondary Groups with Particular Reference to the Negro' (1913); 'Race Prejudice and Japanese-American Relations' (1917); 'Culture and Cultural Trends' (1925); 'Our Racial Frontier on the Pacific' (1926); 'The Bases of Race Prejudice' (1928) and 'Missions and the Modern World' (1944). From *Human Communities*: 'Community Organization and Juvenile Delinquency' (1925); 'The Mind of the Hobo: Reflections on the Relations between Mentality and Locomotion' (1925); 'Community Organization and the Romantic Temper' (1925); 'Urban Community as a Spatial and Moral Order' (1925); 'The City as a Social Laboratory' (1929) and 'The City as a Natural Phenomenon' (1939). From *Society*: 'Human Nature and Collective Behavior' (1927); 'The Sociological Methods of William Graham Sumner and of William I. Thomas and Florian Znaniecki' (1931) 'Social Planning and Human Nature' (1935) and 'Morale and the News' (1941).

7

From Park to Parsons

The rebellion against Chicago

Robert Park retired from the Chicago sociology department in 1934. Soon after he left, Chicago lost its position of dominance within the profession. The special influence of Albion Small's brain-child, the *American Journal of Sociology*, was undermined during the annual meeting of the American Sociological Society at New York in December 1935. The members decided by a majority of about 2 to 1 that the *American Journal of Sociology*, which was under the control of Chicagoans, should no longer be the official journal of the society. In its place a new journal entitled the *American Sociological Review* was established. This rebellion was led by men from Washington, Yale, Baylor, Oberlin and Pittsburgh. During the same meeting almost complete success was achieved by the rebels in capturing the main executive positions of the society. In the opinion of L. L. Bernard, at the head of the rebels, 'the department of Chicago under its leader at the time had become arrogant'. Furthermore, it 'was suspected of making the interests of the American Sociological Society subsidiary to those of the Chicago department' (Odum, 1951, p. 410). In the decades immediately following this movement against Chicago, 'Columbia and Harvard emerged as the new dual papacy of American sociology' (Kuklick, 1973, p. 8).

In her anatomical dissection of this 'rebellion' Patricia Madoo Lengerman shows that the enormous influence of the Chicago sociologists within the profession had been the cause of discontent for about half a decade before the blows just described were finally struck (Lengerman, 1979). Drawing upon previous interpretations

134

(for example, Kuklick, 1973) she identifies three reasons for this movement. They are: the increasing size and complexity of the American sociological profession; the challenge of new theoretical and methodological emphases; and the new opportunities and pressures brought about during the era of the Depression and the New Deal. This framework provides useful guidelines for the following analysis.

By the time Park retired from Chicago, graduate departments of sociology were in existence not only at Columbia University, Chicago's old rival, but also at (for example) Duke, Vanderbilt, Pittsburg, Michigan State and Harvard. With the exception of Columbia, where Franklin H. Giddings had been teaching sociology since 1893, the departments just-named were all recent creations. One of Giddings's old students, Stuart Chapin of Minnesota University, calculated that graduate training in sociology was being provided in 1933 at a total of thirty-two American universities and colleges by approximately 130 faculty members in all. That same year 258 doctoral dissertations by sociology students were in process as recorded in the *American Journal of Sociology*. Fifty-one of the students concerned were registered at Chicago, forty-nine at Columbia with the New York School of Education (twenty-two) and Wisconsin (eighteen), leading a long field of smaller fry. The likely annual turnover of faculty staff leading to possible vacancies for newly qualified sociologists was calculated by Chapin as being about 5 per cent. Was this not clear evidence of 'overproduction?' he asked (Chapin, 1934, p. 508).

Ellsworth Faris, chairman of the Chicago department replied to these points. He noted that of the 106 sociology doctorates awarded by Chicago up to that time about 60 per cent had found employment in administration, business, research posts and teaching either abroad or in departments other than sociology. Furthermore, over 60 per cent of Chicago's current doctoral candidates were already assured of employment upon completion of their degrees. The bullish spirit of Faris is conveyed in his observation that there were 575 colleges in the USA, of which 164 had over a thousand students. Many of these students, he insisted, 'ought to have sociological instruction' (Faris, 1934, p. 510).

Despite Faris's apparent confidence, the appearance of this exchange in the *American Journal of Sociology* reveals the anxious preoccupation of sociologists during the mid-1930s with their place, individually and as a group, within American society. Many of them were the products of the expansion in secondary and higher education that had occurred in the late nineteenth and early twentieth centuries. Were they going to be left high and dry by the Depression with its doleful consequences such as 'the . . . decline in the financial resources of universities, the drop in their enrolment, the closing up of small colleges, and the termination of research enterprises' (Chapin, 1934, p. 507)?

The situation before and after the 1935 'rebellion' could easily be analysed in terms of the ecological approach with which Chicago is conventionally associated: expansion of the population of sociologists; competition for resources; conflict between sections of the population associated with different institutional and territorial bases (for example, in the mid-West, the east and the south-west); a tendency towards differentiation (for instance, as ecologists, interactionists, quantifiers or functionalists); and the displacement of an old dominant centre by a series of competitors. Henrietta Kuklick has suggested that interwoven with the 'academic *realpolitik*' of 'generational conflicts and university power-blocs' (Kuklick, 1973, p. 3) was an 'identity crisis' (ibid, p. 5) accompanied by a shift from an established paradigm to a new one. From an examination of articles written in the *American Journal of Sociology* and the *American Sociological Review* she identified two opponents to 'the Chicago ecological-interactionist paradigm' (ibid, p. 9). They were the 'operationalism' of the highly statistically-minded George A. Lundberg based at Columbia University and the functionalism of Robert K. Merton (also of Columbia) and, especially, Talcott Parsons (of Harvard). Kuklick suggests that although operationalism with its emphasis upon statistical methodologies 'seemed very important in the late 1930s and early 1940s' (ibid, p. 8) it failed to establish itself as a distinctive theoretical approach. By contrast, the impact of the new paradigm of functionalism was 'revolutionary' (ibid, p. 9).

From ecology to functionalism

The passage from 'ecological-interactionism' to functionalism is worth examining briefly. Human ecology as applied by Park during his years at Chicago was at best a loose framework of ideas oriented to both measurement and meaning which drew upon the borrowed prestige of the natural sciences. A collection of concepts such as competition, invasion, succession and symbiosis were taken from plant and animal biology and applied to human collectivities. Park's student and collaborator, R. D. McKenzie, was more thoroughly identified with this approach than Park himself. It was only after he had retired from Chicago that Park tried to turn a loose ecological 'approach' into a theory of human ecology. By that time the major ecological studies of the classic Chicago tradition – Anderson, Thrasher, Zorbaugh and so on – had already been completed. Despite the efforts of Park, Burgess and McKenzie, Louis Wirth was justified in writing in 1938 that 'In the rich literature on the city we look in vain for a theory of urbanism presenting in a systematic fashion the available knowledge concerning the city as a social entity' (Wirth, 1964, p. 67).

Ironically, one of the first coherent accounts of human ecology was provided in 1938 by Milla Alihan. This fact is ironic because, in the same breath, she dealt human ecology a powerful critical blow. Alihan regarded this 'essentially American' approach as being committed to 'action in place of reflection; facts in preference to theory' (Alihan, 1938, pp. 1, 3). In her view human ecologists 'undertook to explain the social complex by fastening upon its salient manifestations, such as the growth of cities, the spread of industry, the extensions of railways and highways, the mosaic of nationalities and races, the movements and distribution of people and utilities'. As a result, 'their universe of discourse became limited to externalities, and the interpretation of social life hinged upon its most concrete aspects'. They were 'reducing social behavior to a common denominator of the tangible and the measurable' (ibid, p. 6). Although Park benignly accepted many of Alihan's criticisms, his own writings were in fact not as rigidly confined as her remarks would imply.

It is true that in 'The urban community as a spatial pattern and a moral order' Park stated that 'In so far as a social structure can be defined in terms of position, social change may be described in terms of movement; and society exhibits, in one of its aspects, characteristics that can be measured and described in mathematical formulas' (Park, 1952, p. 166). More generally, a range of structures and processes could be expressed in statistical form with reference to their spatial aspects. However, Park also stated his belief that 'In the case of human relations . . . the individual men and women who enter into these different combinations . . . are notoriously subject to change. They are so far from representing homogeneous units that any thoroughgoing mathematical treatment of them seems impossible' (ibid, p. 173).

In fact, Park was not 'merely' an ecologist. On the one hand, he found it helpful to think about social relations in terms of the adaptation of economic, occupational, ethnic and racial groups to their 'environment' which includes each other. In his view, competition for position and resources tended to resolve itself into cooperation or symbiosis between the occupants of functionally interdependent ecological niches or 'natural areas'. The state of symbiosis within human communities was repeatedly undermined and re-established, its basis constantly shifting. On the other hand, Park was well aware that human beings shared an economic, political and cultural life. They had the capacity to shape their material and social environment. They were subject to moral regulation enforceable through opinion and law. 'Society' – the realm of the cultural, political and moral – reacted back upon the ecological realm of 'community'.

How did the approach associated with Talcott Parsons differ from the one developed by Park? Kuklick suggested a number of differences between the paradigms of the Chicago School and Parsons. One was the relative neglect of the work of Sigmund Freud by the former, including Park. This issue will be taken up shortly. Another was the different ways in which social 'equilibrium' was conceived. Park and the Chicagoans considered this state to be dynamic, a shifting balance of contending forces which were not only active within a society but also acting upon it from outside in the course of social change. By contrast, equilibrium within a Parsonian functionalist framework was the outcome of continuous system adjustments governed by the influence of an abiding normative consensus. In its early decades at least, the Parsonian framework did not seem capable of explaining social change.

Differences between the two approaches were emphasised by Morris Janowitz in his introduction to the abridged student edition of Park and Burgess's *Introduction to the Science of Sociology* (1970). He commented that critics had recently 'raised the question whether sociology was not unduly concerned with "consensus" and static analysis. Therefore, [he added] I hope that this student edition will accurately convey the notion that the study of conflict and social control was at the very heart of the work of Park and Burgess' (ibid, p. xii). More recently, Norman Wiley has compared 'American sociology's two historically dominant theories, the interwar Chicago school and post World War II functionalism' (Wiley, 1985, 183). His analysis is worth quoting:

> [They] were both [he argued] prosperity theories needing the updraft of economic growth and social mobility to make them seem plausible. But Parsonian functionalism added value consensus which was not part of the Chicago school's bundle, loose as that was. Had the Park and Burgess school been around in the protest sixties, they would have taken to it like a duck to water. All aspects of the cultural revolution – rock music, drugs, communes, sexual liberation, and student protest – would have been exhaustively studied, looking not for functions [or dysfunctions] but processes. And the highly political side of the sixties, with sharp racial conflict and a massive antiwar movement, would have been of great theoretical interest to them as well. They needed prosperity to push their processes, and the seventies might have been their meat (ibid, p. 183).

The relative open-handedness of bodies such as the Laura Spelman Rockefeller Memorial in the 1920s certainly made possible a vigorous and wide-ranging research programme. However, it is not evident that the Chicagoans 'needed prosperity to push their processes'. They were as much interested in losers as they were in winners. As has been seen in earlier chapters, ecological and interactionist approaches linked to a deep curiosity about the shaping of the modern city and modern America were already crystallising in the Chicago department's earliest years, during the fierce depression of the 1890s.

Nor is it accurate to assume that value consensus was 'not part of the Chicago school's bundle'. Park was very sensitive to the way in which moral solidarity was placed under threat by the whirling tides of migration and, in some circumstances, recreated in the enclave of the urban neighbourhood. Value consensus, and the consequences of its absence or presence, was very much part of Park's 'bundle'. He was deeply interested in the conditions under which a strong ethically-based collective consciousness or identity might emerge at a higher level than the neighbourhood, uniting different classes and ethnic groups within the nation.

In fact, the preoccupation with national morale provided a common focus in the 1940s for Robert Park, Talcott Parsons, Louis Wirth and Morris Janowitz. The first-named, at the end of his career, was concerned with the effects upon national morale of, respectively, the German totalitarian propaganda machine and the democratic press of America (for example, in his articles in 1941 on 'News and the Power of the Press' and 'Morale and the News', both reprinted in Park). That same year Parsons was very active within the Harvard Faculty Defense Group as vice-chairman of the committee on morale. The previous year he had insisted in a memorandum prepared for the Council on Democracy that in order to realise America's national destiny on the world's stage it was necessary to solve the 'national morale problem'. This had to be done by 'promoting attachment [to] a basic desirable common orientation' and fostering 'solidarity at a group level'. Like Park, Parsons was sensitive to 'minority group phenomena' in the USA which were ripe for 'exploitation by Nazi propaganda' (Parsons quoted by Buxton, 1985, pp. 96, 98).

In 1941 Louis Wirth also devoted an article to the problem of 'Morale and Minority Groups', arguing that 'The existence of such groups calls attention to the fact that our society has not yet been fully knit together into a single, integrated, national unit' (ibid, p. 1941, p. 415). A few years later, the young Morris Janowitz was exploring 'Trends in Werhrmaht Morale' (Gurfein and Janowitz, 1946), attempting, among other things, to explain the 'extraordinary tenacity of the German army' (Shils and Janowitz, 1975, p. 345) in the face of almost certain defeat.

Talcott Parsons and Chicago

Edward Shils, who collaborated with Louis Wirth at Chicago in the 1930s, has recently described the following scene:

> One day in the summer of 1936 Louis Wirth came down into the room in the Social Science Building which . . . I shared. He was accompanied by Talcott Parsons. The first thing that struck me

about Parsons was the look of refinement on his face, which was not common among sociologists. He looked well-bred, and gave the impression of pacific concentration of mind. Most sociologists looked very ill-assorted. They were no longer clergymen; they were not businessmen; they were gawky, awkward country boys, however old they were. Parsons looked a little like a genteel easterner, although, like many sociologists, he too came from the Middle West, having been born in Ohio (Shils, 1981, p. 191).

Shils added that Parsons 'was very conscious of his mission to bring intellectual order into sociology . . . By 1936 he was well on the road to completion of the first stage of his journey and he knew that he had travelled a great distance'. In the following year, Parsons gave some lectures at Chicago based on the 'huge typescript' of his *The Structure of Social Action* (1937). Parsons

spoke very slowly in a low, dry monotone, as from a vision. He spoke with some pride and with confident modesty of his intellectual accomplishment in demonstrating, with great meticulousness and rigor, the structure of traditions behind Durkheim, Weber, Pareto and Alfred Marshall' (Shils, 1981, p. 191).

The publication of *The Structure of Social Action* was the first major landmark in a process of theory development beginning with the specification by Parsons of a 'theory of action' which placed great emphasis upon the 'normative orientation' (Parsons, 1937, p. 44) of the actor. In his attempt to discover the bases of social order, Parsons went on to incorporate a structural–functional approach, influenced by Durkheim, Malinowski and the biological work of W. B. Cannon. Roles and institutions were to be interpreted with reference to their dynamic contribution towards maintaining the social systems of which they were a part. In *The Social System* (Parsons, 1951) and *Working Papers in the Theory of Action* (Parsons, 1953) key aspects of personality, culture and social systems were analysed in terms of 'pattern variables' (affectivity *vs* affective neutrality, diffuseness *vs* specificity, universalism *vs* particularism, achievement *vs* ascription) and 'functional imperatives' (adaptation, goal-attainment, latency and integration). By the 1960s (for example, in *Societies: Evolutionary and Comparative Perspectives* [Parsons, 1966]), the structural–functional approach had been refined by positing a form of cybernetic control within self-equilibrium social systems. Such systems were subject to change through the working-out of evolutionary processes of differentiation and adaptation affecting the relevant subsystems responsible for realising the various functional imperatives.[1]

Louis Wirth reviewed *The Structure of Social Action* for the *American Sociological Review* in 1939. Although he found its treatment of European theorists, especially Weber, to be 'intensive and intelligent' (Wirth, 1939, p. 404), Wirth directed his fire upon the claim made by Parsons that his 'voluntaristic theory of action' was 'a new development . . . In view of the writings of men like Dewey and Mead, to cite two Americans, the claim of novelty of this theory would be difficult to maintain' (ibid, pp. 401–2). In fact, Parsons had quite disregarded the contributions made by pragmatism and its close associate, symbolic interactionism. In later years he admitted that certain aspects of his own approach had been anticipated by American thinkers. For example, the internalisation of norms and personality characteristics through the influence of social interaction was an idea which 'appeared with great clarity in the work of a group of American social psychologists, notably G. H. Mead and W. I. Thomas' (Parsons, 1970, p. 839). Furthermore, his scheme of four 'primary functional subsystems . . . involving cultural, social, psychological and behaviorally organic systems . . . converged with the scheme of W. I. Thomas' (ibid, p. 860) (that is, his scheme of the four wishes – for experience, response, recognition and security).

Parsons was born in 1902. His father, a Congregationalist minister with deep interests in the Social Gospel movement, had become head of a small Ohio college. Parsons himself initially intended to follow a career in medicine. This interplay of religion, science, social reform and mid-Western provincialism was, as we have seen, characteristic of the cultural ambience in which Chicago sociology had developed around the turn of the century. Furthermore, in making his pilgrimage to Europe, especially Germany, as a young scholar in the mid-1920s Parsons followed a trail which has been well-trodden before. Perhaps unsurprisingly, Parsons developed aspirations for his (eventually) chosen profession of sociology which were very reminiscent of Albion Small and his colleagues.

Like Thomas and Park, Parsons tended to think of institutions as practical embodiments of human values. As he wrote in 1935: 'There is in every society a more or less coherent underlying system of common ultimate values . . . institutions are primarily an expression of these attitudes in certain particular relations to action' (Parsons quoted in Buxton, 1985, p. 81). It was the responsibility of sociologists, at the head of other professional groups and related members of the intelligentsia, to look after the cultural tradition from which the moral imperatives guiding correct action were derived. Like Small, Parsons had little confidence in the capacity of American capitalists to exercise their power in the interests of the society as a whole: 'one of the important reasons why the business class failed . . . is that its primary role has been defined in "self-oriented" terms, thus exposing it too readily to the charge that power would not be exercised as "responsibility" but as exploitation' (Parsons, 1951, p. 319).

Social scientists had a duty to serve the larger interest, to exercise 'an office held on behalf of the larger impersonal whole' (Parsons, 1930–35, p. 673). It was part of their professional vocation. In Parsons's view, 'by contrast with business . . . the professions are marked by "disinterestedness"' (Parsons, 1964, p. 35) not only with respect to particular clients but also with regard to values and norms embodied in the social system. The experience of the 1920s and 1930s revealed the potential for disorder within capitalist democracy in the USA. The professions in American society could help to restore conditions of more effective social control by contributing to 'a revivification of values and their effective embodiment in institutions' (quoted in Buxton, 1985, p. 23).

These ideals were shared by the early Chicago sociologists. For example, it is likely that Parsons would have agreed with Ellsworth Faris who wrote in 1934 that 'The spirit of individualism and fierce competition is out of line with modern acceptance of social responsibility, emphasized indeed by familiar developments in the attempt to meet the present crisis, but antedating any political event of recent times'. Continuing, Faris asserted:

America is not interested in helping any young man or any group of young men to get ahead. America is interested in giving the highest training possible to its gifted youth only if this training is socially valuable. Having given this training, America has the right to expect the youth to make his plans with reference to his obligation to the nation (Faris, 1934, p. 512).

If Robert Park did not devote a great deal of space to the shape of society 'as it should be' it was due partly to his fascination with society as it was, partly to his fatalistic sense of how mighty were the (often discouraging) social tendencies he observed. However, a hankering for a rational, moral and integrated social order expressing the best interests of all is evident in much of his work. The social system described in the theoretical work of Parsons is the *telos* which Park, like Small and Thomas, sought to discover in the hearts and minds of Americans.

Parting of the ways

Between the publication of *The Structure of Social Action* and *The Social System* Talcott Parsons developed a relatively coherent theoretical approach which encompassed personality, culture and the social system. During the same period, in their own much more empirical investigations Park's successors at Chicago were failing to encompass a comparable range of topics within a single integrated approach. We have already seen that Park's writings contained a plethora of internal tensions and unresolved ambiguities. However, his work expressed a unity in the sense that the various subjects he investigated – urban mentalities, the South, Pacific cultures, newspapers and so on – all converged upon the American city and its neighbourhoods. It seemed that here, closely intermingled, were the most meaningful experiences and the most vital social forces of the modern world. Capitalism was an urban-based phenomenon, invading the countryside with its combine harvesters and mail-order catalogues. Democracy was made concrete, very imperfectly, through political machines which won their votes by working the neighbourhoods. Evidence of human nature and of the tidal flows of the world's economy were both equally to be found in the American city, in Chicago itself.

However, the Depression and the New Deal were important phases in a movement of influence away from the ward and the municipality as competing centres of power at the state and federal levels grew stronger. Although the machine in Chicago itself displayed unusual tenacity, the highly local spirit of this form of politics increasingly had to come to terms with the ambitions and interests of government planners whose sphere of operation was the metropolitan region or the nation as a whole. Social scientists and the students they were training were bound to be specially sensitive to these trends since they offered an expanding field of employment at a time when private business was running into considerable trouble. Between 1929 and 1933 the combined expenditure of federal, state and local government rose from 11.9 per cent of national income to 26.6 per cent. Despite fluctuations the higher level of proportionate spending was maintained subsequently, rising even higher over time (Janowitz, 1978, p. 186). The Second World War decisively confirmed this trend and also had the effect of inextricably involving the USA as a world power in the complex politics of Europe and Asia. As the state expanded its role, it had need for social scientists.

Park had been able to study not only the complex modulations of individual experience but also the ecology of social power within the limits of the American city. Like Thomas, he moved easily and frequently between the study of social control and consideration of psychological control at the level of the individual. These dual emphases were present in much of the work supervised by Burgess and himself, such as Clifford R. Shaw's *The Jack-Roller* (1966). However, Park's successors found that investigation of the problems and mechanisms of social control took them away from ordinary individuals and the dense tissues of their local environment and towards the study of regional and national aggregates. These tended to be analysed in statistical form rather than with reference to individual experience. The Chicago sociology department accepted the importance of statistical analysis of social trends when it recruited William F. Ogburn from Columbia University in 1927. He subsequently chaired the department between 1936 and 1951.

In reaction against the twin threats of the statistician and the abstract theorist of 'the social system', Chicago sociologists such as Everett C. Hughes, Howard Becker and Herbert Blumer concentrated their attention on various aspects of the social construction of the 'self' in the context of human interaction. What became known as 'symbolic interactionism' thus stressed one particular aspect of a complex intellectual inheritance drawing upon (for example) Dewey, Mead, Thomas and Park. The business of claiming and denying particular ancestors has been the occasion of considerable debate.[2] Of the sociologists trained in Chicago since the Second World War who have specialised in studies of the self, one of the most impressive is Erving Goffman. He is notable for his preoccupation with the various ways in which controls are exercised in social encounters by participants who are each undertaking a 'conscious performance of the self' (Goffman, 1971, p. 320).

An inevitable criticism of the writers just mentioned is that the perspectives they adopt do not provide explanations of the ways in which the settings of individual or small-group behaviour and perception are related to the encompassing structures of the polity and economy. In the rest of this book I am mainly concerned with three Chicago sociologists – Louis Wirth, William Ogburn and Morris Janowitz – with a deep interest in the structures just mentioned. They have all been concerned to understand the problems of achieving effective social control, a term they understood to refer to the institutional means of realising the 'higher interests' of American society.

The three writers just mentioned traced a kind of arc. Wirth began his career as a sociologist soaked in the ethnographic tradition of local studies. His book *The Ghetto* (Wirth, 1928) was a notable contribution to this tradition with its emphasis upon the interplay between a distinctive local culture and the personality types it produced. However, in his later work Wirth became equally involved with the dynamics of social planning at the regional and national levels. In contrast to Park's interest in the cultures of the little worlds growing up in the ecological niches of the city, Wirth evoked a pervasive 'urbanism' characterised by 'superficiality . . . anonymity, and the transitory character of . . . social relationships' (Wirth, 1964, p. 71). The focus also shifted from sustaining cultures to constraining, narrowing ideologies.

Wirth's colleague, William Ogburn, was mainly concerned with social change, a process he measured with reference to the whole society or specific institutions within it such as the American family or aspects of technological organisation. The only individual to which he paid any degree of attention was 'the great man' as a potential cause of social change (Ogburn, 1926). His interest in culture was directed at the level of the region, especially the South. With Morris Janowitz, Chicago sociology made a decisive return to the interplay between the dynamics of personality, neighbourhood and city while retaining and deepening the interest in the power and efficiency of political, economic and (especially in the case of Janowitz) military structures.

The tide from Europe

One bridge back to the traditional concerns of the Chicago ethnographers was the work of Sigmund Freud. The interest of Janowitz in this approach was evident in his early work on the dynamics of prejudice, undertaken shortly after the end of the Second World War in collaboration with Bruno Bettelheim (Bettelheim and Janowitz, 1975a). Talcott Parsons had developed an interest in Freud's work during the 1930s and 1940s. Before discussing the particular significance of the reception of Freudian approaches in American social science, that movement should be placed in a larger context.[3]

Earlier in this book, a comparison was made between the patterns of development of liberalism in Europe (especially Germany) and the USA during the late nineteenth and early twentieth centuries. I contrasted the confident vision of Henry Pratt Judson, urging his fellows to live up to established American liberal ideals, with the troubled voice of Max Weber, critical of his class and his state. Weber behaved as a 'responsible' bourgeois liberal concerned to advance the interests of the German nation. The *Verein für Sozialpolitik* (Institute for Social Policy) to which he belonged and which sought to advance these objects was much admired by Albion Small. However, if Small and his colleagues had to encounter the indifference of American public opinion and the sensitivity of business people, Weber and his associates had to reckon with the Prussian state on the one hand and anti-Liberal mass political movements on the other. By the outbreak of the First World War, the municipal councils were the last redoubt of German liberals: 'once a beach-head for the liberal conquest of German politics, by 1914 the city had become a fortress in which Liberals sought to defend their privileges and their cherished procedures against an increasingly hostile world' (Sheehan, 1971, p. 137).

Weber, Simmel and the rest of the German academic world experienced defeat in a war which had been presented to their compatriots as a battle between German *kultur* and the baser, materialistic 'civilisation' of Germany's enemies. Military defeat was followed by an attempted workers' revolution. Simmel died in the last months of the war, Weber two months after the subsequent German Revolution had been put down by troops. During the 1920s, Karl Mannheim, an immigrant from Hungary, tried to sustain the mission of liberalism in German society. As a student, he had attended Georg Simmel's lectures and subsequently he worked closely with Alfred Weber, brother to Max. Mannheim envisaged a reconstructed liberal order. Intellectuals, as 'outsiders' on the margins of several intersecting cultural and social groups, could help to rebuild a sense of common purpose. It is an apt comment on the viability of his program that Mannheim, Professor of Sociology at Frankfurt, was forced to flee from Germany in 1933. The incoming National Socialist government had little sympathy for newly-naturalised Hungarian Jewish sociologists.

The tide of American academics seeking enlightenment at the centres of Germanic culture was followed by a flow in the opposite direction culminating in the flight of persecuted groups, especially Jews, during the 1930s as the last embers of Weimar liberalism were extinguished. Between 1932 and 1937 Louis Wirth helped to get every member of his own family out of Germany, most of them going to the USA. Wirth himself had emigrated to America in his mid-teens at the beginning of the First World War. Ideas as well as men and women were imported from Germany as they were also from the remnants of the Austro-Hungarian Empire. Wirth undertook a translation of Mannheim's work, *Ideology and Utopia* (Mannheim, 1936). A translation by Parsons of Max Weber's *The Protestant Ethic and the Spirit of Capitalism* appeared in 1930. As in the case of Robert Park's adoption of some aspects of Simmel's approach, the original American importers of German social science did not always emphasise or even recognise its radical potential. For example, C. Wright Mills drew heavily upon Weber when forging a critical perspective which enabled him to expose the threats to human dignity and freedom in modern American capitalism.

Freud and Marx

The most challenging intellectual imports were associated with the names of Karl Marx and Sigmund Freud. Marxism and Freudianism were difficult to deal with because they exposed certain inner conflicts in American liberalism. For example, by stressing the high destiny of the proletariat Marxism appealed to the American regard for social justice and the people's rights. Marxism and liberalism united in a longing for the just community. Freudianism appealed to the American belief in the practical application of reason and science through the significance it attached to the therapeutic function of the psychoanalyst. If Marx touched a nerve on the issue of justice, Freud spoke to the American desire for happiness. However, Marxism taught that justice could only be achieved at the expense of the strong liberal commitment to possessive individualism. Freudianism was consistent with individualism but it saw the human psyche as being prey to neurotic conflict stemming from non-rational drives, especially frustrated sexual energies. Such conflicts often found expression in the sphere of the unconscious. In part, the Freudian message was that the rational pursuit of happiness was being undertaken by beings whose non-rational drives were likely to lead them towards misery.

As both Gisella Hinkle (1957) and Ernest Burgess (1939) agree, there was at least a decade of resistance to Freud's ideas in the USA. However, from the end of the First World War Freudianism was plundered by social scientists in a fairly piecemeal way, for example through the adoption of terms such as 'sublimation' (Burgess, 1939, p. 38). W. I. Thomas and others remained largely content, however, with the models of personality they had already developed under the influence of the pragmatists. From the mid-1930s a more whole-hearted acceptance was under way, signalled (for example) by the devotion of a whole issue of the *American Journal of Sociology* in 1939 to Freud's contribution to the social sciences.

By contrast, Marx has always remained something of an illegal immigrant, regarded with a lingering suspicion. It was, in fact, possible to adopt a relatively rational view of Marxism as long as the context was either theoretical or the condition of a foreign society. Albion Small paid a great deal of attention to Marx's writings in the course of examining the dynamics of class conflict. Small arrived at a reasonably balanced, if no doubt contentious, conclusion:

in spite of the fact that I am as genuinely convinced as Marx that there are centers of deadly infection in capitalism, certain of Marx's attempts at diagnosis have seemed to me to be so plainly to misrepresent capitalism that they have slowed up and confused my own attempts to find out what is the matter (Small, 1925, p. 440).

During the early years of the revolutionary regime in Russia, John Dewey remained a relatively sympathetic observer, though he changed his views later. Dewey fully understood the desirability of being cautious in the expression of radical views. In a piece on academic freedom published in 1902 he commented:

One might . . . be scientifically convinced of the transitional character of the existing capitalistic control of industrial affairs and . . . that many and grave evils are incident to it [but the whole argument can be stated in such a way] as to rasp the feelings of everyone exercising the capitalistic function. [It should be stated] as a case of objective social evolution (Dewey, 1902, p. 7; quoted in Carey, 1975, p. 58).

It is not surprising that Small did not go further in expressing in print his disillusionment with contemporary capitalism even though in the view of commentators such as H. E. Barnes and Ernest Becker he could have produced an analysis which would have rivalled the work of Veblen (Barnes, 1926, p. 25; Becker, 1971, p. 64). His only attempt to set out his ideas at any length in print was in his *Between Eras* [subtitled 'From Capitalism to Democracy'] which appeared in 1913. According to H. E. Barnes, this book provided 'as relentless a criticism of our conventional unmitigated capitalism as can be found in Veblen's *Theory of the Leisure Class*, *The Theory of Business Enterprise* and *Absentee Ownership*, Tawney's *Acquisitive Society*, or the Webbs' *Decay of Capitalist Civilization*' (Barnes, 1926, p. 25).

Danger arose when, whether or not Marx was mentioned, practical criticisms were made of capitalist institutions in the USA. For example, the economist Edward Bemis, a disciple of Richard T. Ely, had been dismissed from Chicago University in 1894 following a series of attacks on *laissez-faire* institutions. He had advocated increased trade-union power, government intervention in economic matters and measures against the railroad companies during the Pullman strike (Diner, 1980, pp. 47–8; Small, 1895b). Over four decades later, enormous pressures were still being brought to bear upon academics who overstepped the mark. Take the case of Edwin Sutherland who had been awarded his degree at Chicago in 1913. When Sutherland was preparing for publication of his influential study *White Collar Crime* (Sutherland, 1983), both his university (Indiana) and his publisher (Dryden Press) took exception to the fact that he had identified individuals and specific corporations allegedly involved in illegal activities. None of these details appeared in the censored version which was finally published.

One point of entry for Marxian approaches was the writings of members of what later became known as the Frankfurt School.[4] Originally based at the Institute for Social Research, founded at Frankfurt in 1924, many of the school's adherents left Germany in 1931 and by the mid-1930s they were established in the USA at Columbia University. Writers such as Theodor Adorno and Max Horkheimer drew heavily upon both Marx and Freud, a fusion encouraged by the fact that Marx and Freud were each concerned with the interplay of repression and liberation (in the spheres of, respectively, society and personality). In 1944 Horkheimer helped to establish a programme of empirical research on prejudice under the auspices of the American Jewish Committee. One of the resulting studies was published as *The Authoritarian Personality* (Adorno *et al.*, 1950). Another was *Dynamics of Prejudice* (1950) by Bruno Bettelheim and Morris Janowitz. Before considering in more detail the work of Janowitz, including his attitude towards competing approaches, it is time to turn to the writings of Louis Wirth and William Ogburn.

Notes

1. On Parsons, see Buxton, 1985; Hamilton, 1983; Rocher, 1974.
2. See, for example, Lewis and Smith, 1980; Denzin, 1984; Kuklick, 1984.
3. On the interplay between American and European intellectual traditions, see (for example) Bramson, 1961; Herbst, 1965; Fleming and Bailyn, 1969; Hawthorn,

1976; Moreno and Frey, 1985; Rytina and Loomis, 1970; Simich and Tilman, 1980.
4. On the Frankfurt school, see Jay, 1973; Held, 1980; Bottomore 1984.

8
Louis Wirth

First generation, second generation

In 1897 Louis Wirth was born into the Jewish community in the village of Gemunden, near Koblenz in Germany. He emigrated to the USA at the age of 14 and attended high school in Omaha, Nebraska. Then he headed for Chicago. Unlike the scholars treated in the second part of this book, Wirth initially became involved with Chicago sociology not in the guise of a pioneer but as an apprentice learning from established masters. Wirth was still in his teens when Robert Park's paper 'The City: Suggestions for the Investigation of Human Behavior in the Urban Environment' appeared in 1915. By the time Wirth received his first degree from the University of Chicago in 1919, Thomas and Znaniecki had published *The Polish Peasant in Europe and America*. Wirth was awarded his doctorate at Chicago in 1926, the year of Albion Small's death.[1]

Wirth took up a full-time appointment at Chicago in 1931 and remained at the university until his death in 1952. Wirth was 34 when he became an associate professor at Chicago. Albion Small (born 1854) and Robert Park (born 1864) had been, respectively, in their late thirties and late forties when they underwent metamorphosis and became academic sociologists. Thomas (born 1863) had been slightly younger than Wirth when he joined the Chicago faculty in 1895. But Thomas had transformed himself from a professor of English into a sociology student only a couple of years previously. By contrast, Wirth had undergone a decade of sociological training.

Wirth was as committed to active social reform as Thomas. Like Small he was fascinated by European social theory. From Park, who did much to make his doctoral work on the Jewish ghetto in Frankfurt and Chicago a 'pleasant adventure' (Wirth, 1928, p. xi), Wirth inherited his deep interest in urban life and human ecology. However, Wirth – as first-generation American and second-generation Chicago sociologist – had undergone experiences denied to any of his mentors. He was a graduate of the secular *Volksschule* and the rabbi's religious Sunday classes in Gemunden. He had experienced the shock of transplantation from the Rhineland to the mid-West. He was familiar at first hand with the troubles of an often marginal and sometimes persecuted people. Furthermore, a deep sense of the increasingly oppressive threat to liberal ideas and practices experienced by intellectuals in continental Europe was woven closely into the texture of Wirth's life and career, more so than it could possibly be in the case of his native-born colleagues in Chicago. It was not, after all, until 1924 that Wirth, at the age of 27, forsook his German nationality and became an American citizen.

In a sense, Wirth was Germany's 'revenge' for Albion Small. Whereas Small had gone to Berlin and carried off a daughter from the von Massow family, Wirth came to Chicago and married a social worker whose family came from Paducah, Kentucky. In his writing, Small had incorporated aspects of the work of German writers like Schaffle and Ratzenhofer within a sociological approach that stood four-square on the assumptions of American liberalism. By contrast, Wirth brought across the Atlantic the work of Karl Mannheim, a product of the intellectual culture prevailing at the tail-end of Weimar Germany. Whereas Small had given his American heritage a European gloss, Wirth Americanised a distinctively European product. In the process of translating Mannheim's work (with the considerable aid of Edward Shils), Wirth contributed to 'a shift from the theoretical frame influenced by Marxism, historicism, and Idealism, towards empiricism, psychologism, and pragmatism' (Kettler *et al.*, 1984, p. 164).

The Ghetto

Wirth's first major work, *The Ghetto* (1928), recalls *The Polish Peasant* in its effective exploitation of the possibilities of comparison between Europe and America. However, the comparison was approached from different directions in the two cases. Thomas set out from Chicago to discover the central

European *origins* of Polish–American culture in Chicago, Wirth explored in Chicago the American *destiny* of Jewish emigrants from Europe. The intriguing complementary of the two studies is suggested by the following passage:

> The relationship between the Poles and the Jews in Chicago is of especial interest. These two groups detest each other thoroughly, but they live side by side on the West Side, and even more generally on the North-west Side. They have a profound feeling of disrespect and contempt for each other, bred by their contiguity and by historical friction in the pale; but they trade with each other on Milwaukee Avenue and on Maxwell Street. A study of numerous cases shows that not only do many Jews open their businesses on Milwaukee Street and Division Street because they know that the Poles are the predominant population in these neighborhoods but the Poles come from all over the city to trade on Maxwell Street because the know that there they can find the familiar street-stands owned by Jews. These two immigrant groups, having lived side by side in Poland and Galicia, are used to each other's business methods. They have accommodated themselves one to another, and this accommodation persists in America. The Pole is not accustomed to a 'one-price store'. When he goes shopping it is not a satisfactory experience unless he can haggle with the seller and 'Jew him down' on prices (Wirth, 1928, p. 229).

Wirth was influenced by Werner Sombart's analysis, *The Jews and Modern Capitalism* (Sombart, 1913), in spite of its often hostile tone. Wirth agreed that the mobility, adaptability and flexibility of Jews fitted them, historically, to be successful organisers, traders and fixers. The ghetto, typically found on the outskirts of European cities, sustained a symbiotic relationship of physical closeness and social distance between Jew and Gentile. Jews who ventured beyond the ghetto experienced the 'problem of a divided consciousness' as they left 'the warmth of the familial and tribal hearth' (Wirth, 1928, p. 2809). This problem was one recurrent aspect of the natural history of the ghetto whose various phases were traced by Wirth.

The ghetto in medieval European cities was originally a voluntary arrangement, sometimes buttressed by the special protection of the local political power. By the fifteenth century it had become compulsory, a mark of degradation rather than privilege. When Jews emigrated to America, the ghetto was recreated as old neighbours found each other again in the New World. Old divisions persisted between Sephardic Jews and Ashkenazim, between city-dwellers from Western Europe and village people from Eastern Europe, and so on. In Chicago, Jews on the North and South sides assimilated more readily than Jews on the West side, location of the Chicago ghetto. As Jews moved out of the ghetto with its bustling trade and political graft towards neighbourhoods of second settlement (such as Lawndale) they found that the ghetto, eventually travelled with them. They tended to acquire Jewish neighbours making the same upward journey. Condemned by traditional Jews for their assimilationist tendencies, these second-generation settlers found that the Gentile world refused to let them forget their Jewishness. Suffering the worst of both worlds, some made the reverse journey back to the old ghetto.

The promise of America

Park's influence is clear in Wirth's focus in *The Ghetto* upon the shaping of personality by local culture. Furthermore, Park would evidently have approved of Wirth's closing words: 'is it not possible that in dealing with the ghetto as a natural phenomenon, without offering an apology and without presenting a program, we have made [the so-called "Jewish problem"] more intelligible?' (Wirth, 1928, p. 291). However, Wirth did not inherit Park's reluctance to immerse himself in social action directed at practical problems. Quite the reverse. According to the recollection of Reinhard Bendix, himself a German-Jewish refugee studying at Chicago in the late 1930s, Wirth 'would argue that, to be a better social scientist, the scholar must be a more active citizen. For Wirth this was a matter of professional competence, not of individual preference' (Bendix, 1954, p. 529).

As a young man during the First World War, Wirth had been active in anti-war groups on the campus and seized the opportunity offered in the later years of Small's regime to study theoretical approaches critical of capitalism, including Marxism. During Franklin D. Roosevelt's New Deal Administration, Wirth worked on testimony concerning urban affairs and unemployment for congressional committee hearings. He also served as a consultant to the National Resources Planning Board for eight years (1935–43), became Director of Planning for the Illinois Post-war Planning Commission in 1944 and, later, prepared background data which were used in the decision on school segregation taken by the Supreme Court in 1954. These activities fed back into his academic work for he wrote a number of papers on matters such as housing, race and the need for effective planning agencies operating at the levels of the metropolitan region and nation.

Wirth's other activities included advising the Federal Public Housing Authority and serving as president of the American Council on Race Relations. As Elizabeth Wirth Marvick notes, 'After 1945 he wrote scarcely any article that was not to be presented before a particular group on a specific occasion' (Marvick, 1964, p 340). Almost incidentally, Wirth was not only elected president of the American Sociological Association in 1946 but also became in 1950 the first president of the International Sociological Association.

Wirth preferred the international to the parochial. He certainly did not share Park's enthusiasm for the strategy of encouraging people to 'seek God in their own village'. As he wrote in *The Ghetto*, 'Not until the Jew gets out of the ghetto does he live a really full life'. Small enclaves of the kind typified by the ghetto were 'shallow in content and out of touch with the world'. The ghetto was 'the product of sectarianism and isolation, of prejudices and taboos . . . a closed community' (Wirth, 1928, pp. 225–6). Not that larger collectivities were free from disadvantages. As human societies became larger and more complex they increasingly suffered from the lack of a common universe of discourse. Special interest groups competed to get their own way. The secularisation of social life worked in the same direction. The scope for consensus and collective action was narrowed to the realm of means rather than ends as the 'public' replaced the 'crowd' and 'logic' superseded 'tradition' (ibid, p. 194).

However, Wirth had the vision of a consensual world society. Intellectuals could contribute towards realising this vision, as they already were doing (so he believed) in the realm of science. His adopted nation also had a special part to play: 'America for centuries has been the experimental proving ground for the principle that men irrespective of their race, creed, or origin can live and work together harmoniously for the common good' (ibid, p. 291). There was some way to go. As Wirth wrote in 1941, 'our society has not yet been fully knit together into a single, integrated national unit' (Wirth, 1964, p. 415). The article in which that comment appeared contained a passionate assertion of America's role: 'the United States is not merely a territory, a political unit, and a body of traditions, but a promise' (ibid, p. 433).

As an internationalist, an intellectual, and a recent immigrant, Wirth wanted to show that America's national culture – in spite of its tendency towards isolationism, anti-intellectualism, conservatism and parochial prejudice – could in fact contribute to the forging of an open and harmonious social order. The passage just quoted continued as follows:

> America is unfinished. Our principal source of national unity and strength, therefore, lies in the present and in the future. America belongs to the future, and it is in this sense that our minorities can share with the rest of the population a common set of objectives (ibid, p. 433).

This sense of America as 'unfinished' recalls Albion Small's comment in 1905 that the USA was still in a state of 'social childhood'.

Objectivity and the intellectual

Wirth's knowledge of life in Germany during and after his migration to the USA obviously helped him to arrive at the conclusion that, despite its imperfections, American democracy was the best hope for liberalism. However, democracy was insufficient unless it was founded upon consensus. Unfortunately, liberal assumptions could generate contradictory aspirations which required close examination: 'Are Christianity and capitalism mutually exclusive or compatible? Are socialism and equalitarianism mutually contradictory?' We find that 'The proponents of freedom and security . . . almost certainly are at war with each other. The same applies to . . . the advocates of progress and order' (Wirth, 1964, p. 52).

What were liberal academics to do in these circumstances? Knowledge by itself was of little practical use if you did not know how to put it into effect within a world dominated by powerful vested interests. As Wirth rather sardonically expressed it, there was 'no inherent reason why intellectuals should be totally unaware of the facts of life' (ibid, p. 155). In 'Ideas and Ideals as Sources of Power in the Modern World', published in 1947, Wirth showed that he was more troubled than was Park by capitalist control of the press. The market in ideas was 'highly monopolistic' (Wirth, 1964, p. 153) and subject to manipulation on behalf of half-truths. Lacking Park's faith in the robust good sense of the people, Wirth preferred Small's programme of giving a special role within society to advocates of the 'knowledge interest'.

Intellectuals, according to Wirth, had a special responsibility to uncover their own 'unstated assumptions'. In analysing social ideals, they should 'determine the degree to which they are congruent with the cultural configurations of the groups which are exposed to them' (ibid, p. 154), as well as examining their inconsistencies, interrelations and implications. Intellectuals should strive for greater understanding among themselves and learn to use the powerful means of world-wide communications at their disposal. Wirth himself was a frequent broadcaster. Between 1938 and 1952 he made several contributions to the University of Chicago Round Table, a radio series which included discussions of a range of topics such as 'How shall we solve the housing problem?', 'Should America feed Europe?' and 'Is the consumer getting his nickel's worth?'

Wirth's European background helps to account for a strain of caution and pessimism, especially in his earlier work. This tendency was evident in his introduction to the translation of Mannheim's *Ideology and Utopia* which appeared in 1936. He warned his readers that the conflicts which destroyed the liberal Weimar Republic had been felt throughout the world, not least in Western Europe and the United States. Furthermore, the troubles of a few German intellectuals had become 'the common plight of modern man' (Wirth, 1936, p. xiii).

In a rather Schumpeterian vein, Wirth observed with bemusement the distrustful critical spirit abroad in the contemporary world. Much that used to be taken for granted was now regarded as being in need of proof. Wirth's reaction to this was very mixed. On the one hand, the critical spirit was not all-pervasive since there still remained areas where enquiry was, in practice, forbidden: 'It is virtually impossible, for instance, even in England and America, to inquire into the actual facts regarding communism, no matter how disinterestedly, without running the risk of being labelled a communist'. Such investigations were condemned since they probed facts which touched the interests of powerful groups. On the other hand, the spirit of disbelief and disputatiousness had penetrated far enough to undermine the 'reign of the disinterested and objective search for truth'. The questioning spirit had, in effect, both gone too far and not gone far enough. It left untouched certain citadels of power while subjecting the very standards which guaranteed objectivity in the social sciences to destructive doubt. It seemed possible that under these conditions the era of scientific enlightenment in the West would turn out to have been 'a brief interlude between the eras of medieval, spiritualized darkness and the rise of modern, secular dictatorships' (ibid, pp. xiv–xvii).

How should social scientists react in this situation? In essence, Wirth wanted them to maintain a strong commitment to the values of disinterested and objective enquiry while at the same time subjecting the underlying social and psychic interests of themselves and others to the most searching scrutiny. However, there was more to it than that. Intellectuals should also, in Wirth's view, be actively helping to re-establish a social order characterised by 'a common purpose and common interests' (ibid, p. xxv). Enquiry and action motivated with reference to *this* purpose and *these* interests would necessarily be disinterested (that is, not serving a partial interest) and from this disinterestedness would flow objectivity. By critically scrutinising the vested interests bound up in their own and others' thinking, social scientists would be able to clarify the sources of the differences between competing views. Despite their disagreements, they would make efforts to achieve 'a working agreement' on the relevant facts and, develop 'universe of discourse' within which to 'communicate their results to one another with a minimum of ambiguity' (ibid, p. xxviii).

Wirth argued that there was a convergence in European and American thinking with regard to the problem of objectivity. He noted that Mannheim's conclusions on many issues were identical with those of the American pragmatists. Charles H. Cooley, R. M. MacIver, W. I. Thomas and Robert Park had all treated cognition and perception as aspects of action directed at fulfilling interests. Nevertheless, Mannheim's contribution marked 'a distinctive advance' (ibid, p. xxiii) over previous work in Europe and America. He had, argued Wirth, moved beyond Marx in drawing out specific connections between interest groups and modes of thought, distinguishing 'ideologies' which support the existing order from 'utopias' which predispose towards social change. It is ironic that Wirth should have been pointing out the convergence of a group of American thinkers upon an approach brought to fruition by a European scholar just a year before Talcott Parsons argued that a group of European thinkers had all made partial contributions to an intellectual system more fully clarified by himself.

Wirth's enthusiasm for Mannheim's work was couched within a broadly pessimistic view of tendencies at work in the modern world. He bemoaned 'our vanishing sense of a common reality' and the 'disintegration in culture and group solidarity'. In this anomic culture, 'much of life's activity loses its sense and meaning' (ibid, p. xxv). Wirth was appalled at the flimsiness of the defences that were being thrown up against the threats to rationality and objectivity in modern Europe and America. These conditions provided ample materials for a sociology of intellectual life but they were also depressing signs of 'the deepening twilight of modern culture. Such a catastrophe can be averted only by the most intelligent and resolute measures' (ibid, p. xxvii).

Among these measures there would have to be compromises. It was necessary to penetrate the barriers imposed by the citizenry's pervasive distrust and the tendency of people to retreat into a 'privatized . . . existence' (Wirth, 1964, p. 58). In doing so, intellectuals had to take up the weapons of their enemies: 'Propaganda has become the price we pay for our literacy and our suffrage'; it is 'the chief means for enlarging the scope of consensus' (ibid, p. 56). These words were originally published in 1940. They catch Wirth at a sort of moral turning-point which seems to have coincided with the war years.

From pessimism to optimism

In an earlier chapter we saw the urbane and optimistic Albion Small being gradually forced towards a pessimistic view of the chances for social improvement in America. Louis Wirth made the reverse journey, from pessimism to optimism. Before the war, Wirth's work (as has been noted) had a 'European' flavour with its sense of ambiguity, its consciousness of the overpowering onrush of events, and its residual emphasis upon the virtues of detachment as distinct from the obligation to act. After the war, Wirth threw himself wholeheartedly into the task of helping to build a better world, especially in the USA. His work from these years had a more full-blooded feeling of commitment to the American way. The differences can be seen by contrasting two pieces whose original dates of publication are a decade apart. The first is Wirth's most famous paper: 'Urbanism as a Way of Life' (Wirth, 1957) originally published in 1938. The second is his presidential address to the American Sociological Society: 'Consensus and Mass Communication' (Wirth, 1948).

Wirth defined the city as 'a relatively large, dense, and permanent settlement of socially heterogeneous individuals' (Wirth, 1957, p. 50). The 'central problem' for investigation was 'the forms of social action and organization that typically emerge' (ibid, p. 51) in such settlements. In 'Urbanism as a Way of Life' he treated the city as one pole of a continuum between 'urban–industrial' and 'rural–folk' society (ibid, p. 47). Although he claimed to be distinguishing between the effects of urbanism, industrialism and modern capitalism, in practice his remarks were confined to the modern capitalist industrial city in which (as Veblen might have put it) 'The operations of the pecuniary nexus lead to predatory relationships' (ibid, p. 54). Wirth did not in fact exclude from his analysis the workings of contemporary capitalist institutions such as the business corporation. Nor did he explain which aspects of their operations – for example, the 'premium put upon utility and efficiency' (ibid, p. 54) – derived from their capitalist as opposed to their urban nature. 'Urbanism' as used by Wirth in this paper is a term which, to exaggerate only slightly, means 'the way America seems to be going'.

Wirth mentioned in passing the part played by a 'technological structure' (ibid, p. 52) in bringing about the urban way of life. However, he was mainly concerned with effects rather than causes. He began by describing the ecological processes which were removing humankind from 'organic nature' (ibid, p. 46), concentrating people and functions within cities, and radiating the influence of these controlling centres over the rural hinterland. He was concerned to trace the consequence of these processes in the realm of culture and experience. By contrast, in 'Consensus and Mass Communications', Wirth treated the modern means of cultural transmission (radio, cinema, the press, education and so on) as an engine of great potential influence which could be used effectively to counteract the worst effects of 'urbanism' and strengthen democracy.

In 1938 and in 1948 the underlying model was the same: an ecological order comprising physical, demographic and technological aspects; a system of social organisation with characteristic institutions and patterns of social relationships; and an array of personality types, attitudes and ideas expressed in forms of collective behaviour. In both cases, similar characteristics of modern society were emphasised: large numbers, high density and extensive dispersion of collectivities, heterogeneity, anonymity, manipulability, and the coexistence of organised groups and detached individuals. However, the arguments were very different.

In 'Urbanism as a Way of Life' Wirth presented a broadly pessimistic picture of modern tendencies. The apparent blessings of urbanism were always accompanied by huge disadvantages. On the one hand, utility and efficiency were emphasised in social relationships. On the other hand, anomie was generated by the substitution of secondary for primary contacts, the weakening of kinship bonds, the decline of the family, the loss of the neighborhood, and the erosion of traditional bases of social solidarity.

On the one hand, urbanism was accompanied by the rapid spread of voluntary organisations pursuing 'as great a variety of objectives as there are human needs and interests' (ibid, p. 61). On the other hand, the crowding together of people who lacked emotional ties produced 'a spirit of competition, aggrandizement, and mutual exploitation' (ibid, p. 56).

On the one hand, urban life encouraged a wide range of types of personality and groups. Local areas became differentiated from each other in terms of race, ethnicity and status. The city was 'a mosaic of social worlds'. Inhabitants developed a relativistic outlook and 'a sense of toleration of differences' (ibid, p. 56). On the other hand, however, social contacts became increasingly 'impersonal, superficial, transitory and segmental' (ibid, p. 54). Men and women coping with the pace and congestion of the city became irritable, unstable and insecure. They were subject to a 'leveling' process as facilities were adapted to 'the needs of the average person' (ibid, p. 58). At worst, they were prey to 'Personal disorganization, mental breakdown, suicide, delinquency, crime, corruption, and disorder' (ibid, p. 61).

This is only a partial analysis of a complex paper but it indicates the sense of ambiguity, tension and bemusement conveyed by Wirth. The name and spirit of Georg Simmel run through the paper, although Wirth was less inclined than the former to applaud the opportunities for the intellectual to lead a sophisticated and cosmopolitan individual existence, more inclined to itemise the social and psychological costs which accompanied these gains. Ten years later, the mood had changed. 'Consensus and mass communication' was a rallying call, a demand that social scientists and other academics should actively work towards world consensus. It was no longer possible for 'the saints to sit in their ivory tower while burly sinners rule the world' (ibid, p. 15). In 1938, the emphasis was on achieving sociological understanding as a preparation for political action by others in the real world. In 1948, Wirth was calling for politically-relevant action by sociologists with a view to shaping the understandings of others in the real world.

Wirth was confident that in the post-war world the city had been mastered: 'we have . . . learned to live with people of diverse background and character to a degree sufficient at least to achieve the requirements of a fairly orderly, productive, and peaceful society' (Wirth, 1948, p. 13). The next task on the agenda was to create 'a social sensorium' which would serve as a 'mind' (ibid, p. 4) within society. To put it another way, means had to be found for shaping and interpreting a social consensus. Only on this basis could concerted action be effective within a democracy. Wirth quoted with approval Dewey's assertion that 'we need one world of intelligence and understanding, if we are to obtain one world in other forms of human activity' (ibid, p. 5).

Wirth had sufficient confidence in the spread of democracy to believe that the practice of achieving consent by the use of force was bound to decline. However, the break-up of traditional cultures had inaugurated an era of scepticism and ideological salesmanship. Subtle means of persuasion had been developed by modern propagandists. These were employed to sway public opinion within a political system which no longer permitted direct participation by all in discussion and decision-making. For good or ill, all modern societies had to come to terms with the fact that 'the engineering of public consent is one of the great arts to be cultivated' (ibid, p. 9).

What were the practical rules and guidelines for employing this art within a democracy? One essential was a willingness to compromise. Another was a spirit of tolerance. The limits of permitted disagreement had been 'worked out quite pragmatically in our democratic society' (ibid, p. 9). In a large and complex modern society it was also necessary to be aware of popular feelings on a variety of matters. These techniques were even being used by the Allies in the occupied countries after the Second World War: 'nowadays after enemies have surrendered, we send public opinion pollsters among them to learn how best to govern them' (ibid, p. 9). Consensus flourished where there was regular communication between individuals and groups, especially if this was buttressed by shared educational experiences. Where group identification and social participation were cultivated, then people would be more likely to accept group decisions 'unless the matter is fundamentally incompatible with our interests and dignity' (ibid, p. 10).

Communication among intellectuals such as scientists and artists was an important means of overcoming barriers to a democratic consensus. One very large barrier requiring special attention was the concentration of control over the mass media in a few hands. This fact had 'serious implications for mass democracy' since it tended to produce unbalanced presentation of minority views. Censorship and distortion of this land might 'threaten the free and universal access to the factual knowledge and balanced interpretation which underlie intelligent decision' (ibid, p. 11). Wirth made it quite clear that in modern society 'the control of these media of mass communication constitutes a central problem' (ibid, p. 12).

The issue which had been latent in Robert Park's work broke surface in Wirth's paper and became explicit. Public opinion was regarded by both Chicago sociologists as a mighty power which was a potential counterweight to capitalist influence. It was essential that the two juggernauts should not become tied too closely together. The mass media should not become the instrument of a few large business corporations. As Wirth expressed it:

In mass communications we have unlocked a new social force of as yet incalculable magnitude . . . It has the power to build loyalties, to undermine them, and thus by furthering or hindering consensus to affect all other sources of power. . . . It is of the first importance, therefore, that we understand its nature, its possibilities, its limits, and the means of harnessing it to human purposes (ibid, p. 12).

German history in the early twentieth century had provided ample evidence of the perils of both disorder and centralised repression. During the 1930s Wirth had helped many of his relatives to leave that country at a time of increasing danger. Subsequently, he developed a sociological approach which placed great emphasis upon achieving social harmony through voluntary consensus. The spirit of compromise was important. A middle way had also to be achieved in coping with the inescapable dilemmas of liberalism: between freedom and security, between efficiency and the toleration of dissent, and so on.

Wirth believed that sociologists could make a major contribution towards protecting and developing liberal ideals and practices. They could help to make democracy workable in modern urban industrial societies; for example, through the fashioning of effective planning techniques. He did pioneering work himself in this sphere, not least in the preparation of 'local fact books' on Chicago (for example, Wirth and Bernert, 1940). Sociologists could also, as has just been seen, point out some of the dangers to liberal democracy stemming from capitalism itself.

Note

1. On Wirth, see Wirth, 1964 (introduction by Albert J. Reiss Jr, and biographical note by Elizabeth L. Marwick); Smith, M. P. 1980a; Braude, 1970; Etzioni, 1959.

9
William Ogburn

More measurement

Louis Wirth, as has been seen, was deeply concerned with the issues posed by size and space as aspects of modern society. By contrast, William Ogburn was fascinated by speed and time. His best-known work is *Social Change* which originally appeared in 1922. At the time this book was published Ogburn was a sociology professor at Columbia University, the institution which he had earlier attended while carrying out doctoral research under the guidance of Franklin Giddings. Ogburn, whose fields of competence included not only sociology but also economics, history and statistics, joined the Chicago faculty in 1927. Born in 1886, he was over a decade older than Wirth. However, he entered the orbit of Chicago some years after Wirth and enjoyed a longer life, dying in 1959.[1]

Like Wirth, Ogburn gained a commanding position in the national profession. He was president of the American Sociological Society in 1929 and chairman of the Social Science Research Council from 1937 to 1939. He had considerable experience of working with government agencies. He was employed at Washington DC between 1918 and 1919, working on cost-of-living statistics for the National War Labor Board and the Bureau of Labor Statistics. In 1930 he became director of research of the President's Research Committee on Social Trends. He edited and contributed to *Recent Trends in the United States*, the Committee's report which appeared in 1933. Ogburn also served at various times as research consultant to the National Resources Committee, adviser to the Resettlement Administration, director of the Consumers' Advisory Board of the National Recovery

Administration and chairman of the United States Census Advisory Committee.

As a southerner from Georgia, Ogburn, like Wirth, was originally an outsider in Chicago. Wirth had warmly responded to the existing Chicago approach to sociology and, having incorporated it in his thinking, adapted it to the problems of social control in the era inaugurated by the New Deal. By contrast, in appointing Ogburn the Chicago department made a deliberate decision to adapt itself to the newcomer. As Ellsworth Faris put it in a letter to Ogburn in 1926, 'We are weak in statistical work and you would have full charge of as much of that as you cared to cultivate with courses of a general theoretical nature in so far as it would appeal to you' (quoted in Bulmer, 1984a, p. 170).

Although Chicago sociology was renowned for its richly descriptive ethnographic case-studies of aspects of urban life, statistical approaches were well established before Ogburn's arrival. Since before the First World War, sociology students had been directed to attend statistical courses run by the economics department. Furthermore, in 1924 Ernest Burgess had organised the Chicago Census Committee which included representatives from a wide variety of local interests. Its object, as set out in its rules was to organise 'the collection, correlation, tabulation, and publication of statistical data concerning Chicago in a manner that would insure their maximum usefulness to social, civic, and governmental bodies in Chicago' (quoted in Bulmer, 1984a, p. 158). Over the next few years Burgess directed a project whereby the city was divided for analytical purposes into seventy-five local community areas. In his local investigations Burgess drew upon and encouraged the use of both descriptive and statistical materials. In 1927, he argued that statistical and case-studies 'should be granted equal recognition and full opportunity for each to perfect its own technique' (Burgess, 1927, p. 120).

However, with the arrival of Ogburn that same year the balance of prestige and influence shifted perceptibly in the direction of quantitative methods. Ogburn set out his position in 'Folkways of a Scientific Sociology', his presidential address to the American Sociological Society. As far as Ogburn was concerned the science of sociology was 'not interested in making the world a better place in which to live, in encouraging beliefs, in spreading information, in dispensing news, in setting forth impressions of life, in leading the multitudes or in guiding the ship of state'. Having cast doubt on these broad ambitions, some of which had been very dear to the heart of (for example) Albion Small and W. I. Thomas, Ogburn set out his own formula: 'Science is interested in one thing only, to wit, discovering new knowledge' (Ogburn, 1930, p. 2). The same year as he made that address, the Social Science Research Building was erected. It bore the motto which Ogburn had decreed as chairman of the relevant subcommittee. The motto, taken from the works of Lord Kelvin, was: 'When you cannot measure your knowledge is meagre and unsatisfactory'.

Social trends and democracy

It is important not to exaggerate the differences between Ogburn's approach and that of his new colleagues. In the review of the findings of the President's Research Committee on Social Trends – a piece which bears the clear marks of Ogburn's style and for which he must have had overriding responsibility – it was made clear that the findings of social science were deeply relevant to the broad issues he had mentioned in the presidential address. The review mentioned such questions as:

Shall business men become actual rulers; or shall rulers become industrialists; or shall labor and science rule the old rulers? Practically, the line between so-called 'pure' economics and 'pure' politics has been blurred in recent years by the stress of the late war, and later by the stress of the economic depression.

The writer added that 'The American outcome, since all the possible molds of thought and invention have not yet been exhausted, may be a type *sui generis*, adapted to the special needs, opportunities, limitations and genius of the American people' (Ogburn, 1930, pp. lxii–lxiii).

Reviewing possible future adaptations of democracy in America, the writer concluded:

An interpretation which seems to have a margin of advantage is that of the prospect of a continuance of the democratic regime, with higher standards of achievement, with a more highly unified and stronger government, with sounder types of civic training, with a broader social program and a sharper edged purpose to diffuse more promptly and widely the gains of our civilization, with control over social and economic forces better adapted to the special social tensions of the time, with less lag between social change and governmental adaptation and with more pre-vision and contriving spirit (ibid, p. lxix).

Louis Wirth would have had little difficulty in subscribing to that description of a better America although in 1933 he would have had a more pessimistic view of the chances of its coming to pass. One difference between the two men is that while Wirth thought that it was a professional responsibility of the social scientist to strive for this better America, Ogburn wished to restrict the professional sociologist to the task of discovering the strength and direction of social trends already at work. Ogburn accepted that individual social scientists could do more than this but not in their professional capacity: 'I am not averse [he later wrote] to the sociologist writing essays or propaganda providing he does this merely as a human being and not as a scientist' (Odum, 1951, p. 151).

Knowledge and values

Wirth placed his faith in intellectuals, Ogburn in knowledge itself. Wirth was concerned that intellectuals should not give up their responsibility to promote the common good in the face of mighty social trends which seemed to be eroding the bases of stability and consensus. By contrast, Ogburn was determined that the ideological and utopian aspirations of intellectuals should not obstruct nor pervert scientific investigation into the nature of those trends which seemed to be in many respects, though not all, benevolent. Both men were fascinated by power. Wirth paid most attention to the influence of mass communications as a potential means of promoting adjustments between competing interests by increasing mutual understanding and emphasising shared values. Ogburn was more interested in the capacity of government and public agencies, armed with the knowledge discovered by social science, to ease the adjustments made necessary by social change between maladapted institutions, practices and beliefs.

Despite the tone of his presidential assertions in 1927, Ogburn was perfectly well aware that moral evaluations entered into the application of sociological terms such as 'adaptation' and 'maladaptation'. In *Social Change*, when discussing the process of adjustment between culture and human nature he almost casually made the comment: 'It should be observed that one's notion of adaptation in some cases depends somewhat on one's attitude towards life, one's idea of progress, or one's religious beliefs' (Ogburn, 1950, p. 50).

In fact, some of Ogburn's most engagingly humane and insightful writing dealt with the permeation of social life with distinctive values. In 1945 he wrote: 'Democracy has all the compelling force of the powerful mores. None dare speak against it. To criticize democracy is no more permitted than to praise fascism' (Ogburn, 1945, p. 338). Although the implicit reference of that remark was to the war against Germany, still in its final stages, it also revealed the special sensitivity of the American southerner who had come north to Chicago. It was a sensitivity he shared with, for example, Howard Odum, a fellow-Georgian and contemporary at Columbia, who served with him on the President's Research Committee on Social Trends.

Odum published his *Southern Regions in the United States* in 1936. The journal *Social Forces* had been founded by Odum in 1922 at the University of North Carolina at Chapel Hill. The comment by Ogburn which has just been quoted came from an article entitled 'Ideologies of the South in Transition' (Ogburn, 1945) which was published in *Social Forces*. In the article just mentioned, Ogburn pointed out that there was considerable confusion of attitudes in both North and South. For example, the South was becoming more liberal, the North more restrictive in regard to the treatment of blacks. His object, of which Wirth would surely have approved, was 'to try to bring some clarity and order in this confusion' (ibid, p. 335) with a view to overcoming a situation in which 'Neither region appreciates the social values of the others' (ibid, p. 341).

Ogburn compared the urban North with the Old South in a number of respects, constructing a 'somewhat idealized statement' of each. His intention was 'not to present them scientifically and objectively' but 'sympathetically' (ibid, p. 336). He discussed their different approaches to social class, democracy, the family, friendship and success. For example, class inequality was accepted without question in the Old South and family pride was a central concern of the Southern gentleman. The cultivation of friendship entailed standards of honour and discrimination which effectively debarred such a gentleman from the dishonourable and undiscriminating sphere of urban politics. Furthermore, such a Southerner would not sacrifice his values for the selfish personal satisfactions of material success.

By contrast, in the North there was a cult of success which encouraged ruthlessness: 'Accomplishment, speed, production, efficiency, streamlining, executive ability, aggressiveness, hustle are the particulars of these social values' (ibid, p. 340). The South found itself confronted by 'the new conquering mores' of the northern cities whose missionaries displayed 'narrowness of understanding and . . . intolerance'. Ogburn hoped that southerners would be able to overcome their own tendency towards narrowness: 'The ideologies of the South are in transition, the problem of the southerners is to preserve the best of the old values and to select from the virtues of the new'. He was cautious rather than optimistic since, as he put it, 'there is not complete freedom of will, for the socioeconomic systems are powerful forces in affecting ideologies' (ibid, p. 342).

Ogburn's response to Northern democracy was a mixed one. On the one hand, he believed that the findings of science were favourable to its basic assumptions: 'Democracy is supported by the sciences of sociology and biology which show no superiority of one race over another and which show the difference in ability of the classes to be much a matter of environment' (Ogburn, 1945, p. 338). On the other hand, he found the excesses of democracy distasteful. Ogburn sympathised with some aspects of the culture of the Old South where 'Among the self-sufficing landed gentry you like a friend for what he is, not for what you can get out of him. To "use" a friend for selfish purposes was much condemned in the Old South' (ibid, p. 339). This gentlemanly spirit in Ogburn found expression in a passage subheaded 'Selfishness' in *Social Change*:

> Perhaps the psychological factor underlying the largest number of social problems is selfishness. The fact that a great majority of individuals in most of the situations in life feel their interests more strongly than the interests of others and act accordingly is fundamental in nearly all social problems. A larger number of

modern social problems flow from the unequal distribution of property: one reason why wealth is so unequally accumulated is the pursuit of one's selfish interests with not enough considerations for the interests of others, and another reason is the scarcity of social limitations upon such selfish actions . . . A highly developed accumulation of material culture such as we have in modern society provides a wonderful opportunity for an apparently ruthless exploitation of selfish interests (Ogburn, 1950, pp. 334–5).

This is, among other things, a comment from a son of the Old South on the evils which accompanied the undoubted virtues of the urban North.

Freedom and organisation

In some respects, the Southern gentleman and the nineteenth-century European liberal-intellectual – two figures from 'the old world' – provided, for Ogburn and Wirth respectively, a point of comparison against which to assess contemporary developments in urban America as seen from Chicago. Both sociologists found repugnant the inequality and suffering built into the traditional social orders of Europe and the South. However, they responded positively to the values of humanity, stability and reason which were admired and sometimes put into practice within the upper reaches of those societies. They wanted to encourage the cultivation of those same virtues within modern America. If such virtues were successfully implanted within American institutions, the intrinsic dilemmas of liberalism – social justice *vs* individual freedom, individual happiness *vs* social efficiency, and so on – could be more easily handled in practice.

Ogburn confronted some of these issues in 'Thoughts on Freedom and Organization' which appeared in the journal, *Ethics*, in 1948. He was writing at the time when, on the one hand, big business was complaining loudly about the threat posed by government interference to the free enterprise system and, on the other hand, 'radicals are dismissed from their jobs, not because of anything they have done but because of what others say they think' (Ogburn, 1948, p. 260). Ogburn was very unsympathetic to the special pleading of big business and observed that the dismissal of radicals reduced 'our great tradition of liberty . . . to ritual' (ibid, p. 260). His main argument, however, concerned the potential threat to freedom posed by an increase in the size and scale of organisations.

Ogburn began by making two points. First, the spread of cities, the weakening of patriarchy within the family, the reduced power of organised religion and the growth of scientific education had all increased human freedom. Second, at the same time the influence and functions of big business and big government had expanded. In fact, business was currently complaining because the balance of power between the two had shifted in the direction of government. In these circumstances, it had to be realised that some aspects of increased organisation produced effects which gave us more freedom, for example through the application of more efficient technology. However, the costs imposed upon individual freedom by organisation could only be accepted if an organised society encompassed 'a substructure of justice and a superstructure of worthy purpose' (ibid, p. 261). On the assumption that this condition was met, Ogburn suggested a number of ideals 'to be added to our pantheon as suited to the concerted collective activities of twentieth-century society' (ibid, p. 259).

His formula was as follows:

> We should applaud good teamwork and admire the beauty of a smooth-running efficient organization. Loyalty should be rated high as a virtue, and we ought to be willing to sacrifice our narrow selfishness for the larger good. Effective organization rests upon respect for rules and leadership. Factionalism is disruptive of the unity necessary for a team to win. Unity becomes a major objective and cooperation a major method in attaining it. Behind all these attitudes there should be the driving power of an *esprit de corps*, evidenced sometimes in song and legend (ibid, pp. 259–60).

This ideology of team work was not supposed to displace the cause of liberty since 'a real emphasis upon freedom is good even though it may slow up development of an ideology of cooperation'. The two emphases – upon cooperation and upon freedom – were most easily reconciled when membership of an organisation was voluntary. We should participate enthusiastically in the programme adopted by the leader or by the majority. However, 'If one is a member other than by choice, as in a family or a state, it is best to act as if one had joined voluntarily' (ibid, p. 260). If this is a problem, 'the difficulty can be overcome sometimes by examining searchingly the sources of one's principles or the origins of one's prejudices' (ibid, p. 261).

Ogburn and Wirth approached the problem of freedom *vs* organisation from different angles. Wirth feared a widespread retreat of urban individuals and groups into privatised worlds between which communication occurred along increasingly narrow channels. Observing the same urban phenomena, Ogburn saw instead the overthrow of old means of repression such as superstition, religion and the traditional family. However, both men hoped to see the growth in modern America of a form of positive freedom embodied within encompassing organisations which would provide means of realising noble human purposes. These purposes would be such that free and rational human beings would, in any case, choose to adhere to them.

Science and social change

In 'Consensus and Mass Communication'. Louis Wirth evoked the process through which shared understanding would emerge in modern society. It would be 'always partial and developing and has constantly to be won. It results from the interpenetration of views based upon mutual consent and upon feeling as well as thinking together' (Wirth, 1964, p. 24). As has been seen, Wirth was very alive to the dangers posed by the special interests of big business; more so, perhaps, than Park. To oversimplify radically, Wirth's approach might be labelled as 'Dewey modified by Marx'. In the same spirit you could label Ogburn's approach as 'Veblen modified by Freud'. This comment requires further explanation.

In 1957, Ogburn denied that the concept of 'cultural lag' which he developed in *Social Change* was the same as Marx's materialistic version of history or a form of economic determinism. He also strongly resisted the idea that he had taken the idea of cultural lag from Veblen who had employed a similar concept in his book entitled *Imperial Germany and the Industrial Revolution* (Veblen, 1964b) in order to account for the persistence of a militaristic and autocratic government in industrialising Germany. Ogburn assured his readers that at the time *Social Change* was written 'I had never read him on this point' (Ogburn, 1964, p. 37). However, the case to be made here is not that Ogburn was reproducing Veblen's ideas but that on some key issues arising within American liberalism they adopted similar positions. Before developing this argument further it will be useful to recall Ogburn's approach to the analysis of social change.

Ogburn's early contacts with anthropologists such as Franz Boas and Alfred Kroeber persuaded him that the key to social change was to be found not in alterations of human biology or the human psyche but in cultural transformations. Having identified culture as the principal subject of investigation, he then distinguished between different aspects of culture. These included, on the one hand, 'the material culture' and, on the other hand, 'knowledge, belief, morals, law and custom' (Ogburn, 1950, p. 4). Different parts of the culture tended to change at different rates and 'since there is a correlation and interdependence of parts, a rapid change in one part of our culture requires readjustments through other changes in the various correlated parts of culture' (ibid, pp. 200–1).

A particularly important cause of maladjustment was the more rapid development of the material than the non-material culture. The cultural process in the material realm tended to be cumulative although the rate of accumulation depended upon the frequency of inventions. This in turn was to a considerable degree a reflection of the state of the culture at any particular time. The accumulation process in the material sphere was selective, reflecting in part the perceived utility of old and recent inventions. As the technology became more complex, diversification and specialisation occurred within the culture. To a considerable degree, though not entirely, the non-material culture could be understood as being 'adaptive' (ibid, p. 203), in other words, organised to manage, respond to, or complement the material culture. This applied to many aspects of the 'larger usages and adjustments, such as customs, beliefs, philosophies, laws, governments' (ibid, p. 202).

Cultural lags flowing from maladjustment might be the product of (for example) the vested interests of social classes, the power of tradition and habit or the tendency to nostalgia. The observation that material changes usually preceded changes in the adaptive culture was 'not in the form of universal dictum'. However, this was certainly the most common case and to avoid such lags would presume 'a very high degree of planning, prediction and control' (ibid, p. 211). Ogburn did not seriously discuss that possibility although he did comment that it was 'thinkable that the piling up of . . . cultural lags may reach such a point that they may be changed in a somewhat wholesale fashion. In such a case, the word revolution probably described what happens' (ibid, p. 280).

Ogburn did not credit either wholesale planning or revolution with as much significance in social development as the processes of discovery and technological innovation associated with the development of science. The main objects of social science were to discover social trends and seek their causes and consequences. In the course of doing this, investigators would learn, as he once wrote, that 'there is a sort of inevitability about social trends'. Since 'It is difficult to buck a social trend', planners 'should not start with a utopian urge and a clean slate and a belief in the unlimited potential of the human will' (Ogburn, 1964, p. 109).

Reviewing the 'dramatic events of the year 1933', for example, Ogburn pointed out that despite alterations in the sphere of social and economic welfare 'Births, deaths, marriages, divorces, crime, insanity and religion continue their respective courses' (Ogburn, 1934b, p. 729). From an examination of social trends he concluded that there was 'no crisis in the population problem . . . Neither is the crisis one of technology' (ibid, p. 735). However, there had been 'an unusual burst of energy' which was due to a particular relationship between cyclical forces, specifically 'the synchronizing of the business cycle and the political cycle' (Ogburn, 1934b, p. 842). Such a synchronisation had only occurred on one other occasion in recent American history, in late 1896. However, four years of depression in the early 1890s had culminated in the election, not of William Jennings Bryan, but of the presidential candidate representing 'the conservative sound money of the industrial East'. In 1932, by contrast, 'The protest party . . . got hold of the government machinery' (ibid, p. 843).

Ogburn argued that the political and economic pattern taken by the resultant burst of energy was 'determined by the secular trend', especially with regard to 'the framework of governmental and business relationships' (ibid, pp. 843–4). Measures relating to (for example) price-fixing, the regulation of credit, intervention in foreign trade and the establishment of federal relief agencies were the recent expressions of long-term trends. However, the heightened ideological atmosphere of the period, combined with the burst of energy, created a rare opportunity for action to change the social structure. Although 'fervor is by its nature not long sustained', ideals and social philosophies would for a while have importance 'in determining the direction we take towards economic fascism, communism, or a goal somewhere between' (ibid, p. 847).

In 1942, Ogburn reviewed changes over the previous decade, which had included the depression and the beginning of the Second World War. He found that the trends noticed in 1934, especially the rapid growth of government, were continuing but was cautious regarding the degree to which the expanded power of the executive would be maintained after the war was over. Ogburn's tone was optimistic. Democratic methods had undergone 'profound changes in their nature' but the effect had been very much 'in the service of the common man'. He argued that 'What has been done for labor unions, for Negroes, for farmers, for youth, for distressed businesses is unprecedented, a brilliant record unequaled in our history' (ibid, p. 807). There had indeed been some sacrifice of liberty and individualism but 'One can hardly live in comtemporary Chicago and have the kind of freedom that was Daniel Boone's as a scout in the wilds' (ibid, p. 809).

Ogburn noted that 'The war economy is clearly not the capitalist system of the eighteenth and nineteenth centuries which the classical economists described'. For example, 'The so-called captains of industry are not the money-makers but the men with managerial skill. The managers take over and operate for the government' (ibid, p. 814). This was a point which Thorstein Veblen would have relished and it leads directly into the question of this writer's relevance to an understanding of Ogburn.

The similarity between Ogburn and Veblen is threefold. First, and most obvious, both men paid particular attention to the strains introduced into a society when technological development generates actual or potential patterns of social action and perception which conflict with or are frustrated by established social rules and institutions. Second, as noted in the discussion of his paper 'Thoughts on Freedom and Organization', Ogburn hoped for (and, indeed, he perceived some evidence of) the strengthening of an ethos of team work and collective endeavour for the common good, an ethos which is reminiscent of what Veblen called 'the instinct of workmanship'. He shared Veblen's contempt for exploitative selfishness justified by ritualistic reference to ideological shibboleths. Third, Ogburn and Veblen were both reasonably confident that if it was left to do its work with as few restrictions or distortions as possible, science would, on balance, have a benevolent effect upon society. This last point can be developed further.

Ogburn defined sociology in the textbook he co-authored with M. F. Nimkoff as 'the scientific study of social life' (Ogburn and Nimkoff, 1959, p. 13). A discipline was scientific if it was capable of producing 'reliable knowledge' (ibid, p. 11), one test of reliability being the capacity to make accurate predictions. It was important to be cautious – not only about the potential for achieving statistical accuracy in social science but also about the contribution of science to human affairs. Ogburn stressed that the place of science was 'quite limited in scholarship, in intellectuality, in the control of human affairs, in leadership, in the determination of values, and in furnishing human happiness' (Ogburn, 1934c, p. 12). However, he was very interested in identifying the ways in which the potential contribution of science, including social science, could be maximised.

Ogburn set out his position clearly in his article entitled 'Three Obstacles to the Development of a Scientific Sociology' (Ogburn, 1930). The first obstacle was 'intellectualism', by which he meant the elaboration by scholars of ideas deriving from a *mélange* of experiences and emotions, freely and imaginatively interpreted. This approach, 'somewhere between day dreaming and scientific thinking' (ibid, p. 348), was enjoyable as well as being helpful in formulating initial hypotheses. However, it was a widespread error to confuse it with scientific research.

The second obstacle was 'the idea that the aim of science is mastery or control' with a view to 'making the world a better place to live in'. On the contrary, Ogburn insisted that for scientists 'The one objective is to learn and use the best procedures for the discovery of new enduring knowledge' (ibid, p. 348). This approach is strongly reminiscent of Veblen's distinction between the pragmatic attitude which is interested in 'knowledge of what had best be done' and the scientific attitude which is concerned with 'knowledge of what takes place' (Veblen, 1906, p. 599). This was related to the third obstacle to science which was 'the pressure for action and results' as a result of which 'Society won't let a scientist in the social field do good work even if he wants to' (Ogburn, 1930, p. 349). Just as Veblen mocked the eagerness of disciplines concerned with the application of pragmatic conventional wisdom to borrow the prestige of sciences based upon 'idle curiosity' (Veblen, 1906, p. 590), so Ogburn commented:

> The tendency of sociology is to deal more and more with practical social problems. As practical persons dealing with social problems, the force is to make us content with approximations to knowledge, with guesses, estimates, and provisional, contingent answers. Such approximations are not science – real knowledge – at all. We call them science, just as we call intellectuality and mastery science. The idea of science is becoming debased. Everybody wants to be scientific (Ogburn, 1930, p. 349).

A further problem for science was the distorting effect of psychological and social pressure, documented by Ogburn with regard to the prediction of football scores and students' grades (Ogburn, 1934d). He had examined the causes of bias in an early paper which included a critique of Dewey's account of 'reflective thinking' (Ogburn, 1964, p. 294; Dewey, 1975c). Although Dewey gave 'an excellent, clear-cut analysis of the logical processes of thought' he conveyed 'a totally inadequate idea of the great part emotion and desire play in thinking' (Ogburn, 1964, p. 297). Emotion was one of two 'fundamental conditions' (ibid, p. 291) of bias and prejudice, the other being ignorance. Both were present, argued Ogburn, in the realm of social science.

Happiness

In the analysis just discussed of 'Bias, psychoanalysis and the subjective in relation to the social sciences', Ogburn made use of Freudian ideas about 'association' and the 'mechanism of the night dream' (ibid, p. 292). Freudian theory was also evident in *Social Change*, as will be seen shortly. Ogburn drew upon Freud in two ways. First, he recommended to social scientists that 'The way of becoming less unscientific is to know the etiology of our own desires and the mechanisms of the behavior'. This could best be done by 'The study of abnormal psychology and of psychoanalysis' (ibid, p. 301). In a sense, by recommending careful *psychological* introspection, Ogburn was dealing with the same problem that Wirth coped with by recommending that intellectuals should be sensitive to the limitations upon perception and understanding imposed by their particular *social* situation. Second, Ogburn was impressed by Freudian analysis of the neurotic conditions supposedly caused by the repression of instinctual drives in modern society, although he was not convinced by the prominence given to sexuality by Freud:

> even if the non-hereditary influences that lay the foundation for neuroses are effective in childhood, nevertheless the precipitating factors in adult life commonly associated with emotional shock, strain, overwork, etc., may involve a repression of various other parts of man's psychological equipment (Ogburn, 1950, pp. 321–2).

Ogburn agreed with Wirth that modern urban society was ridden with psychological disorders, many of them the product of 'specialization, social pressure, morality, ambition, repression, necessary hours of labor, and the inherent inevitability of conflicting interests and motives' (ibid, p. 353). However, although his hopes were raised during the exceptional circumstances of the New Deal and the Second World War, Ogburn was generally rather pessimistic about the chances of overcoming 'the inherent inevitability' of social conflict, given the fact that humans were (*pace* Wirth) 'without any . . . deity-like power over culture as a whole' (ibid, p. 347). He was quite capable of offering a formula for a social order redolent with harmony and justice, as we have already seen, but he never came to share Wirth's conviction that it was the sociologist's professional mission to work for it.

Ogburn cautiously stalked a different animal: the happiness of individuals. In his view, happiness was strongly affected by the mode of adjustment between an individual and his or her particular cultural environment. Furthermore, 'Very probably the thing we call happiness is related to the state of the nerves more than to economic conditions or to material welfare' (ibid, p. 331). Given the difficulty of bucking social trends, a factor which apparently remained more daunting to him than it did to Wirth, Ogburn paid attention to two things. First, the possibility of alleviating human misery by promoting appropriate forms of individual adjustment to modern society. Second, the question of whether social trends were working in a way conducive, if not to justice in the public sphere, at least to happiness in the private sphere.

In *Social Change*, he considered a number of piecemeal solutions which might 'lessen the tension of life in modern civilization' by correcting 'the overuse of some instincts and the under-use of others' (ibid, p. 350). He paid most attention to the creative use of recreation as a way of expressing instincts such as 'fear, anxiety, anger, the desire for mastery, self-assertiveness, leadership [and] . . . sociability' (ibid, p. 353). In a later article, he went further and suggested that although in a changing society there was more disharmony within the social structure than in a stationary society, the relationship between culture and human nature actually became closer: 'it would seem that the influence of the factor of change alone is one to release the bonds holding back normal biological activity. Change thus helps to shape a culture more in conformity with biological nature' (Ogburn, 1964, p. 54).

A particular institution which exemplified this was the modern family. With his collaborator M. F. Nimkoff, Ogburn explored the causes and consequences of changes in the family such as: the decline in religious practices, family size and the influence of parental and patriarchical authority; and the increase in birth control, divorce, extra-marital sex, working wives and state benefits. They concluded that the family's 'productive and protective functions are gone . . . for the foreseeable future. But there remains the set of personality functions, immeasurably important though fewer in number'. The authors ended with the message: 'a major object of the exercise of the personality functions is to produce happy marriages and psychologically healthy children, and future scientific discoveries should make it easier to attain these objectives' (Ogburn and Nimkoff, 1955, p. 321).

A few years before *Technology and the Changing Family* (Ogburn and Nimkoff, 1955) appeared, Ogburn had raised the question 'Can Science Bring us Happiness?' (Ogburn, 1972) in the *New York Times Magazine*. He admitted that 'Social science does not yet have a great deal of achievement to point to in this field' but added 'Surely the promise is good'. He concluded: 'And there is reason to think that we may yet be a happier people' (Ogburn, 1972, pp. 38–9). As in the case of Veblen, a major object of Ogburn's sociological analyses was to show the social implications of advances in technology and the natural sciences.

Ogburn's confidence in the capacity of science and technology to produce benefits was fed by his work during the early 1950s. He presented statistical evidence that 'the standard of living of the people of the United States doubled in the first half of the twentieth century' (Ogburn, 1955a, p. 386). He argued that if the rise in living standards continued, as he predicted it would, its effect would be to 'reduce poverty, improve health, decrease the appeal of socialism, create a much bigger market for mass production [and] . . . lift the expenditure of the working class to those of the present middle classes' (Ogburn, 1955b, p. 541).

Furthermore, Ogburn carried out a statistical comparison of China, India, the UK, the USSR and the USA with the object of assessing the relative importance of population density, economic organisation and level of technological development in determining the standard of living. He demonstrated to his own satisfaction that technological development was much more important than population density and that 'communism or private ownership is not very significant in explaining . . . differences in standard of living, contrary to popular opinion' (Ogburn, 1951, p. 30).

Such a conclusion tended to confirm Ogburn's view that the cultivation of science and technology was likely to furnish the means of happiness. It also supplied ammunition for the position that it was not only very difficult but also probably a waste of time to tamper with the polity if your object was to advance the happiness of ordinary Americans.

Note

1. On Ogburn, see Ogburn, 1964 (Introduction by O. D. Duncan), Duncan, 1959; Huff, 1974, and see also Cash, 1973.

10
Morris Janowitz

The persuaders

All of the Chicago sociologists so far considered have been well aware both of the moral issues raised by American liberalism and of the practical constraints and opportunities flowing from American capitalism. Their responses to these pressures have inclined towards two broad approaches which may be labelled those of the 'activist' and the 'persuader'. None of the scholars discussed falls exclusively into one or the other of these rather arbitrary categories but most display a preference. Nearest to the activist pole is W. I. Thomas. William Ogburn and Louis Wirth each straddle the two categories. Closest to the persuader pole is Albion Small. Robert Park and Morris Janowitz both have strong leanings in that direction.

If you look at the occupational experience or training acquired by Small, Park and Janowitz immediately before they became full-time sociologists, a pattern emerges. They had all become professional persuaders. Small trained as a preacher; Park worked as (in effect) a public relations officer, and Janowitz served as a military expert in the techniques of propaganda. One of the first articles published by Janowitz, entitled 'German Reactions to Nazi Atrocities' (Janowitz, 1946), was based upon work he carried out in occupied Germany in his capacity as an intelligence officer for the Psychological Warfare Branch of the United States Army.

Morris Janowitz, the last of the major figures to be discussed in this book, made his own position clear in the last few pages of *The Last Half-Century* (Janowitz, 1978): 'I prefer to believe that the contribution of social scientists to societal changes must be indirect and must emphasize clarification more than direct political leadership and action' (ibid, p. 556). In fact, from the beginning of his career as a sociologist, Janowitz has focused upon subjects which are clearly relevant to policy. The first paragraph of the first chapter of his first major book, *Dynamics of Prejudice*, contained the assertion that:

'pure' science, without the practical applications implied in its findings, is a sterile abstraction. True [the passage continued], the development of social science depends upon objective study truly unbiased by any wish for immediate practical applications. But research into the significant problems confronting society today must, necessarily, arrive at findings which have important implications for social planning and action' (Bettelheim and Janowitz, 1975a, p. 105).

Morris Janowitz was the first of the Chicago sociologists studied here to have been born in the twentieth century. His birthplace (in 1919) was Paterson, New Jersey. Among his teachers at New York University was the philosopher Sidney Hook who combined a critical interest in Marxism with a subtle Deweyan perspective on the nature of ideas and action. Looking back to his undergraduate days at Washington Square College, Janowitz recalled that Hook's 'teaching of pragmatism saved me from the burdens of both materialism and idealism' (Janowitz, 1973, p. xii). Having completed his studies at New York, Janowitz carried out further training at Chicago University and was awarded his doctorate there in 1948. Although he taught at Chicago for a few years in the late 1940s and early 1950s, in 1951 he accepted an appointment at the University of Michigan. Janowitz returned to Chicago in 1961 and chaired the sociology department between 1967 and 1972. He subsequently remained at Chicago, playing a major part in the reinvigoration of sociology at that university in the wake of its period of relative decline during the 1950s.

Back to Germany

During the Second World War, Janowitz served as a propaganda analyst in the United States Department of Justice between 1941 and 1943. Later, as has been seen, he worked in a related capacity in the United States Army. It is deeply ironic that as a young man Janowitz should have taken part in the process of attempting to teach the defeated German people to hate Nazism and love democracy. Half a century previously, his predecessors at Chicago had derived a powerful inspiration from German academic debates, making frequent pilgrimages to Berlin, Leipzig and so on. They had revered German culture, even though, as has been seen, they tended to Americanise it when adapting it to their own domestic intellectual purposes.

By contrast, in his post-war work with Bruno Bettelheim which led to the publication of *The Dynamics of Prejudice* (Bettelheim and Janowitz, 1975a) Janowitz explored the forms taken in the USA by anti-semitism and other types of prejudice which had been virulent in Germany. In the course of half a century the question Americans were asking of Germany had changed from 'have the Germans got something grand and special in their culture which we might borrow and exploit?' to 'have the Germans got something mean and nasty in their make-up which might be infectious?'

As an analyst of contemporary Western societies, Morris Janowitz cut his teeth on the German case or in close contact with German scholars. As an example of this latter point, after the war he worked on American patterns of prejudice under the aegis of a research programme sponsored by the American Jewish Committee. The programme was directed by Max Horkheimer, a leading member of the Frankfurt School. Publications arising out of the programme included *The Authoritarian Personality* (1964) by Theodor Adorno and others. The authors of this particular study found evidence of a 'potentially fascist pattern' (ibid, p. 976) in the psyche of some Americans. A few years later Janowitz spent a period of time at the Institute of Social Research at Frankfurt University, a visit which enabled him to observe ways in which German society had altered in the period since the end of the war.

In fact, in his publications during the 1940s and 1950s, Janowitz identified what appeared to be a profound transformation of German society. When Janowitz conducted his research on reactions to Allied propaganda about Nazi atrocities in mid-1945 he encountered widespread 'ethical indifference' (Janowitz, 1946, p. 145). American public information campaigns were intent on overcoming this: 'The development of a sense of collective responsibility was considered a prerequisite to any long-term education of the German people' (ibid, p. 141). What was the character of the German consciousness? Janowitz conducted some research relevant to this issue during the 1940s in collaboration with Edward Shils. It concerned the relatively high level of stability and cohesion maintained by the Wehrmacht during the Second World War (Shils and Janowitz, 1975). Shils and Janowitz concluded that disintegration was inhibited by the fact that soldiers were closely bound into primary groups, their squads or sections, which fulfilled their main personality needs, including 'affection and esteem [and] . . . a sense of power' (ibid, p. 346).

The strong primary group was complemented by a strict military hierarchy:

> Domination by higher authority was eagerly accepted by most ordinary soldiers, who feared that if they were allowed to exercise their initiative their *innere Schweinhunde*, i.e. their own narcissistic and rebellious impulses, would come to the fore. On the one hand, rigorous suppression of these impulses constituted an appeasement of the superego which allowed the group machinery to function in an orderly manner' (ibid, p. 359).

Strong primary group cohesion and a rigid hierarchy were generally combined with relatively weak attachment to symbols of state authority.

Reviewing the situation once more in the mid-1950s, Janowitz found that where he had previously encountered a denial of collective responsibility there was now a strong social consensus. He also reported the existence not of a rigid and inegalitarian hierarchy but of a more egalitarian, open and fluid society:

> West Germany and the United States have been developing greater similarity in fundamental value systems. West Germany, like other highly industrialized Western societies, is increasingly a society in which social stratification is based on achievement rather than on ascription. In an achievement-oriented society more and more universalistic criteria for social differentiation are necessary; social consensus requires widespread acceptance of the belief that each individual should have an 'equal' opportunity for ascent. This is no utopian goal but rather a realistic and

pragmatic acceptance of the importance of skill as compared with social inheritance (Janowitz, 1958, p. 14).

During the late 1940s, Adorno and his colleagues had identified a potentially fascist substratum in America reminiscent of the seed-bed of Nazism. By contrast, in Germany during the 1950s Janowitz found a solid basis for democracy. Like the exiles from Frankfurt in the USA a few years previously, the visitor from America in Frankfurt found a mirror of the folks back home.

In the rest of this chapter, some major themes pursued by Janowitz in a very prolific academic career will be explored in the following sequence. First, his work on the military will be considered. Second, his research with Bruno Bettelheim on the psychology of prejudice will be examined. Third, attention will turn to the writings on various dimensions of the local community, especially the press and education. Fourth, his conception of the nature and purpose of sociology will be reviewed. Finally, an account will be given of his recent trilogy concerned with aspects of 'macrosociology and social control', contrasting some central points of the argument with the perspective adopted by Jürgen Habermas.

The modern military

His work on Germany apparently confirmed three aspects of Janowitz's approach to sociology. First, it was made dramatically clear by wartime and immediately post-war experience that the organisation and use of political power and military force had a very large part to play in the destruction and reconstruction of societies as well as in their regular management. Janowitz has paid far more attention than his predecessors at Chicago to political and military sociology. Second, it is evident that in this early work Janowitz was already focusing upon a general issue he would later approach from several different angles: the relationship between the individual and the collectivities to which he or she belongs. Third, in analysing the processes and relationships mentioned, Janowitz has drawn upon theoretical ideas strongly associated with (among others) Sigmund Freud and John Dewey. If Sidney Hook had demonstrated the potentiality of a Deweyan perspective, Harold Lasswell showed what could be done with Freud.

Janowitz's work contains frequent references to the writings of the political scientist Harold Lasswell, a student and subsequently a teacher at Chicago between the wars. Lasswell had been profoundly impressed by the work of Robert Park with whom he shared an interest in public opinion and propaganda techniques. However, Lasswell also incorporated a Freudian approach which he applied in various studies, including his research on the pathological motives expressed within political movements.

Lasswell was fascinated by the way values are shaped and shared within democratic societies. His attempts to specify relevant values such as income, safety and deference (Lasswell, 1936) or – more comprehensively – power, respect, rectitude, affection, well-being, wealth, skill, and enlightenment (Lasswell and Kaplan, 1950) recall the much earlier efforts of W. I. Thomas with his four wishes and Albion Small with his six higher interests. Janowitz has sympathised with the spirit of such enterprises but remains cautious: 'Each step in the elaboration of a categories system of value analysis makes the tasks of empirical research more complicated and the procedures of use more difficult and arbitrary'. However, he agrees with Lasswell that with regard to democratic societies 'the role of coercion and its reduction are still the central issue' (Janowitz, 1978, p. 52).

The 'central issue' of 'coercion and its reduction' has been on Janowitz's agenda for four decades. The military provided one convenient sociological laboratory for investigating, directly and indirectly, various dimensions of this issue. Like Ogburn, Janowitz acknowledged the importance of 'technological trends' (Janowitz, 1970c, p. 124). By the mid-twentieth century, expenditure upon an increasingly professional (rather than conscripted) military establishment had become a substantial and permanent item in the national account. Military skills had become so diverse and specialised that the 'organization line between the military and the non-military' (ibid, p. 125) had been weakened. Internal conflicts within the military had tended to increase.

How could modern societies avoid the undesirable options of aristocratic, totalitarian or garrison-state models of civil–military relationships, all of which would reduce the proper control of a democratic polity? A conceivable democratic model was one in which civilian political élites controlled a professional military establishment through formal rules defining the latter's functions. Some elements of this model had been achieved in a few societies with stable parliamentary institutions and widespread political consensus. However, the model did not take account of several important complexities. What realistic conclusions about ideals, practices and possibilities could be derived from sociological inquiry into contemporary military establishments, especially in the USA?

In *Sociology and the Military Establishment* (1974) and *The Professional Soldier* (1971) Janowitz concentrated upon patterns of morale, skills and authority within military bureaucracies with particular reference to the occupational culture of the military élite in the USA. His own research, based in part upon a historical sample of generals and admirals, a questionnaire survey of Pentagon staff officers and a number of intensive interviews, was most fully set out in *The Professional Soldier*.

Janowitz argued that during the half-century up to 1960, the basis of discipline and authority within the US military establishment had shifted. Authoritarian forms of domination had given way to an increased dependence upon manipulative techniques as a means of building a consensus within the group. The object was to inculcate not blind unthinking obedience but the intelligent and resourceful application of increasingly specialised skills within the organisation or team. In this respect, the military were undergoing changes similar to those occurring in civilian life. Success within the new forms of organisation which had developed within the military depended upon social and technical skills with direct equivalents in the civilian sphere.

Military commanders had to become more sensitive and political in managing both internal and external relations. Such individuals were being recruited from a broadening social base but the experience of inter-war Germany suggested that this fact, in itself, did not guarantee a more democratic outlook on the part of military élites. It might undermine traditional conceptions of honour related to family tradition which implied indifference to the opinion of society at large, replacing them with military leaders more dependent upon public acclaim and more likely to 'place a strain on traditional patterns of civilian–military relations' (Janowitz, 1971, p. 11). These tensions had to be handled in a situation where the military establishment had developed into 'a vast managerial enterprise with increased political responsibilities' (ibid, p. 12) encompassing not only legislative and administrative action on national security but also participation in an international arena. The old conservative 'military mind' was having to become more innovative.

The officer corps was moving towards new pragmatic self-conceptions which maintained 'a proper balance between military technologists, heroic leaders, and military managers' (ibid, p. 424). In doing this it was necessary, argued Janowitz, to ensure that officers obtained 'a full understanding of the realities of practical politics as it operates in domestic affairs'. Military education would have to move beyond 'moralistic exhortations regarding ideal goals' (ibid, p. 429). The modern military establishment also had to adapt to a 'constabulary concept' (ibid, p. 415). In other words, its duty was, to a great extent, the management of peace in the context of international tension rather than the practice of full-scale war. Janowitz warned that prolonged international tension might enable the military, in association with demagogic civilian politicians, to acquire inordinate power within a garrison state: However, by contrast

the constabulary force is designed to be compatible with the traditional goals of democratic political control. The constabulary officer performs his duties, which include fighting, because he is a professional with a sense of self-esteem and moral worth. Civilian society permits him to maintain his code of honor and encourages him to develop his professional skill. He is amenable to civilian political control because he recognizes that civilians appreciate and understand the tasks and responsibilities of the constabulary force. He is integrated into civilian society because he shares its common values. To deny or destroy the difference between the military and the civilian cannot produce genuine similarity, but runs the risk of creating new forms of tension and unanticipated militarism (ibid, p. 440).

Macrosociology

The question of 'the basic balance between the political party and the military' (Janowitz, 1970b, p. 18) is one amongst a number of issues within the sphere of what Janowitz refers to as 'macrosociology'. This is a form of sociological reasoning distinct from two other approaches: one concerned with processes of social stratification, the other concentrating upon formal and informal organisations such as political parties. Macrosociology, by contrast, is 'a form of sociological field theory, concerned with the whole in terms of the structure and interrelations of the parts' (ibid, p. 6).

This approach incorporates ecological considerations as well as analyses of class determinants and political élites. It also considers broader issues such as civil–military relations, 'the capacity of the economic and industrial sector to influence and control political decisions' (ibid, p. 17), and 'the articulation or disarticulation of local élite structure with the national socio-political balance' (ibid, p. 19). Its main concerns have been the impact of modern economic institutions on political representation and the cultural, ideological, and political conditions under which economic progress occurs.

Janowitz has found historical antecedents for his own macrosociological approach in the work of Alexis de Tocqueville, Thorstein Veblen and Max Weber (as well as Emile Durkheim and Joseph Schumpeter). He has written that a number of:

> social thinkers of the late nineteenth and early twentieth century . . . were responding to the transformation and disruption in social structure wrought by industrialism and rational ideologies. They were concerned with the reconciliation of individualism and the requirements of a social order. It was through the explicit effort of Talcott Parsons, in *The Structure of Social Action*, that the converging concerns of diverse sociological writers were made more explicit. Thereby the central focus of the sociological endeavour to explain and account for diverse patterns of social control emerged somewhat more clearly. The same line of reasoning developed in the Chicago school of sociology, which drew its intellectual sustenance from pragmatism and an emphasis on empiricism (ibid, pp. 20–1).

At the heart of Janowitz's approach to macrosociology has been the problem of achieving a satisfactory system of social control which will maximise the chances for social justice and individual happiness. Like his intellectual predecessors, he has paid a great deal of attention to the question of reconciling the demands of the individual and the social group. His analyses of the psyche in its social context have encompassed topics such as prejudice, race and violence. In his work upon the community he has researched the local press and urban education. In the latter part of his career, Janowitz has been drawing several threads together in a large-scale study of macrosociology and social control whose main results have been published in three books: *Social Control of the Welfare State* (1976), *The Last Half-Century* (1978) and *The Reconstruction of Patriotism* (1983). These complementary emphases and their intellectual fusion can now be discussed in more detail.

Prejudice and control

In *Dynamics of Prejudice* (1975a), Bruno Bettelheim and Morris Janowitz analysed the factors 'essentially associated with anti-Semitism and . . . anti-Negro attitudes' (p. 106). They drew upon psychoanalytic theory in spite of the fact that the application of this theory 'to the larger organization of society . . . was still relatively undeveloped' (ibid, p. 106). On the basis of intensive interviews with 150 veterans of the Second World War from Chicago, they explored a number of hypotheses. The first was that hostility towards 'outgroups' (ibid, p. 106) was a function of deprivations suffered in the past by the prejudiced individual. The second was that expectations of deprivation caused this individual to feel anxious when anticipating future tasks in which success was initially regarded as obligatory. Aggressive or amoral behaviour towards an outgroup was the result of an individual externalising the unacceptable personal characteristics held responsible for failure and projecting them onto the outgroup concerned. The third hypothesis was that such behaviour was 'the consequence of a lack of ego strength and of inadequate controls which favor irrational discharge and evasion rather than rational action' (ibid, p. 107).

The study's conclusions tended to confirm these hypotheses. The authors' findings were in apparent contradiction with those of Adorno *et al.*'s *The Authoritarian Personality* (1964) which appeared at about the same time. Theodor Adorno and his colleagues found prejudice among those who approved and conformed to existing social arrangements. By contrast, Bettelheim and Janowitz found that the prejudiced were those who resisted the values and established arrangements of society and had 'no feelings of consensus with social institutions' (Bettelheim and Janowitz,

1975b, p. 74). They agreed with Nathan Glazer (1950) that the difference of approach stemmed partly from the fact that their own study was of lower or lower-middle class Americans whereas *The Authoritarian Personality* dealt with people from the better-educated middle class. However, they point out that Adorno's team paid particular attention to patterns of childhood socialisation. By contrast, *Dynamics of Prejudice* took account of adult socialisation and the effects of 'controlling institutions' (Bettelheim and Janowitz, 1975a, p. 76) within the social structure.

How could prejudice be contained? Bettelheim and Janowitz offered proposals regarding 'the provision of more adequate outlets for the discharge of tension' as built up by, for example, factory routines involving the 'endless repetition of movements in a mechanical way' (ibid, pp. 286–7). Like Ogburn, who was concerned with a similar problem in *Social Change*, they were sceptical about the Freudian tendency to relate this problem exclusively to the question of sexuality. They stressed the importance of promoting education for ethnic tolerance and also developing 'gratifying interpersonal relationships within the family circle'. The human product of such a family would be confident, autonomous and independent, not especially vulnerable to feelings of dependence upon others outside the immediate family.

The authors speculated upon

> how such a personality structure would affect a democracy. Would it make for greater autonomy and independence of judgement [and therefore an active and responsible electorate] or would satisfaction with life in the private sphere foster indifference to public affairs [and therefore a citizenry easily manipulated for good or for ill]?

Having come face to face with a central dilemma of American liberalism – concerning the difficulty of combining individual happiness and social justice – the authors unfortunately backed speedily away, remarking that 'we have not yet known a society of wholly autonomous individuals, so that all speculation on this question remains hazardous' (ibid, p. 284).

Action at the social level should include, they believed, the introduction of more extensive social security and a wage system designed to fears of seasonal unemployment. Like Louis Wirth, they also placed great emphasis upon the task of mass communications to build up an appropriate social consensus. Such a system of shared values should not encourage 'unbridled aspirations' among ordinary people but, instead, teach 'greater acceptance of the facts of occupational status and opportunity as they now exist in the United States' (ibid, p. 279).

Running through this analysis is an acceptance of the need to find satisfaction and self-realisation in the very processes of negotiation, compromise and restraint, processes which should occur within a framework of realism and rationality. It is the same spirit that informs Janowitz's notion of the 'constabulary' function as applied to the military establishment. It reappears in his discussion of the social control of 'escalated riots' where he insists upon the need for 'domestic disarmament' in the wake of the urban riots of the 1960s (Janowitz, 1968, pp. 7–8).

In *Social Change and Prejudice* (1975b), which was originally published in 1964, Bettelheim and Janowitz returned to the issues broached in 1950. In the intervening years, there had been a decline in the 'over-all level of anti-Jewish and anti-Negro attitudes' (ibid, p. 5). However, to a considerable extent this was restricted to the elimination of social barriers (as in school desegregation) rather than the promotion of positive integration. The latter entailed not merely the modification of social controls embedded in institutional arrangements but also changes with respect to personal controls and attitudes. In their opinion, there was an urgent need for a body of theory concerning psychological change which 'practice-oriented professionals, such as the educator, social worker, and the like' could use 'in handling interracial tension at the interpersonal level'. Such 'doctrine' was 'essential' 'if a democratic society is to mobilize its full resources for change' (ibid, p. 92). As we have seen, a similar approach was to be found in *The Polish Peasant*.

Turning from personal controls to social control, Bettelheim and Janowitz emphasised the role of 'urban renewal'. This included not only individual housing projects but also 'comprehensive interracial community planning' as in the Hyde Park–Kenwood scheme sponsored by (and adjacent to) the University of Chicago. The object of such a scheme was the development of 'a stable interracial community' through institution-building in the spheres of education, housing, religion and so on. Although the relative success of this particular scheme was partly due to 'self-selection' of residents, some general conclusions were suggested by the experience. Among these was the need for a major academic or medical organisation to supply local middle-class professional leadership, and for residents to participate in community organisations deliberately designed to achieve 'managed integration' (ibid, p. 89). Local structures should include mechanisms allowing organised bargaining among interests and their leaders within a decentralised community political system.

Janowitz has always displayed sensitivity to the interplay between morale and organisation. This was evident in his analysis of the relative failure of the inchoate American fascist movements of the 1930s (Janowitz, 1970d) and also in his discussion of the anatomy of racial violence during the twentieth century, developing as it did through 'communal' and 'commodity' riots to planned and deliberate attempts by black street-leaders to export violence to white neighbourhoods (Janowitz, 1970e). When Bettelheim and Janowitz wrote a prologue to the 1974 edition of *Social Change and Prejudice* they were able to report that in the aftermath of the urban riots of the 1960s there had been important shifts in respect of attitudes and social organisation. The changes were not in all respects benevolent. The principles of racial and social equality were more firmly entrenched within the institutional order but George Wallace had demonstrated the continued force of racial hostility among certain white groups.

Although tolerance had tended to increase overall, partly because of increased interracial contact at work, it was largely a consequence not of positive strengthening of democratic values but rather of indifference. American society faced the challenge of incorporating new groups within its mass while retaining widespread democratic participation. In these circumstances, it was necessary to overcome the dangers of privatisation which confined individuals to 'particular, parochial groupings'. Positive social learning through the medium of active voluntary associations was preferable to an 'often unstable and self-centred' search for particularistic attachments 'at the expense of the larger collectivity' (ibid, p. xxx). Like Thomas and Znaniecki, Bettelheim and Janowitz pointed out the importance, in times of rapid social and cultural transformation, of 'the person with strong inner controls . . . [and] strong personal convictions . . . [who] is not swayed by the pressure of social change' (ibid, p. xxxii). Along with trained professionals active in the local community, such men and women could take the lead in overcoming the temptations of prejudice, demonstrating self-control, self-confidence and self-respect.

Life at the local level

In a stream of research and writing complementary to the work just examined, which begins with and repeatedly returns to the psychology of prejudice, Janowitz has investigated the social mechanisms through which 'community' is constituted or undermined: especially, the press and education. Two years after the appearance of *Dynamics of Prejudice* Janowitz published *The Community Press in an Urban Setting* (1952). This book bore the imprint of Louis Wirth's concern with the relationship between social consensus and mass communications. However, Janowitz developed his own distinctive approach, suggesting that the perception of urban inhabitants as 'rootless' was not unrelated to the fact that intellectuals and critics were themselves 'marginal' and 'stood in a highly impersonal relation to society' (ibid, pp. 18–19).

In some respects, Janowitz was closer to Park than to Wirth in his perception that 'the modern metropolis is a collection of little worlds and local communities'. The local community areas of Chicago, for example, were 'not mere statistical devices' as was shown by the persistence of a thriving community press. This press, which cultivated 'local consensus' by its 'emphasis on common values', was 'one of the social mechanisms through which the individual is integrated into the urban social structure'. The consciousness of these functions by all concerned was, perhaps, a reason why the content of the community press 'appeared less commercialized than that of the daily newspapers' (ibid, pp. 20–3). Again, this is nearer to Park than to Wirth.

Janowitz argued that the community press was a powerful medium for expressing strong local attachments. This was an important function since 'individuals who display strong local community identifications are people who display a higher sense of political competence required for democratic consensus than those who have low or no local community identifications' (ibid, p. 26). The local press helped such people to fight 'the individuating tendencies and impersonality of urban existence' (ibid, p. 72). By reflecting and moulding group pressures it also helped to manage 'the clash between individual motives and effective social organization' which was an aspect of 'Social control at all levels' (ibid, p. 216).

However, on the other side, the community press also helped to mobilise local resistance to federal public housing projects and the entry of black residents to local districts. Janowitz met this issue head on:

> Although the elimination of segregation is a basic and fundamental democratic value its achievement through the destruction of local autonomy would be undesirable. The destruction of all local community autonomy and all sense of local identification would seem to lead the individual . . . to a sense of personal incompetence which can only result in an even greater anti-democratic potential than is present today' (ibid, pp. 221–2).

Like Park, Janowitz acknowledges the difficulty of combining a high degree of group solidarity with a low degree of inter-group prejudice.

Although Janowitz shares with Park a strong sense of the contribution made to social control by local attachments, he acknowledges that in a modern city these attachments are attenuated. Janowitz has introduced the concept of the 'community of "limited liability"' (ibid, p. 223) from which the individual demands a clear return upon his or her (always provisional) investment. However, although the commitment of the individual to the community through such attachments is limited, the 'impact of industrialism and large-scale organization on the local community' (ibid, p. 225) is, nevertheless, softened by them. The test of local institutions such as the community press was, in any case, the pragmatic one of whether they helped to make democracy 'work':

> Social cohesion grounded in local community integration supplies an important ingredient for mobilizing our human resources. Social cohesion, whether it be in an army or in a local community, means, in effect, the existence of a communications

system by means of which individuals are oriented towards group action (ibid, p. 232).

Two decades later, in association with John D. Kasarda, Janowitz once again explored the character 'of community attachment in mass society' (Kasarda and Janowitz, 1974), this time using data collected in London. He concluded that Louis Wirth was wrong to stress the size and density of the urban population when evaluating its tendency to generate strong local attachments. A more important factor was length of residence which was also strongly associated with the strength of bonds of kinship and friendship.

Janowitz has been concerned not only to reveal the residual strength (as he sees it) of inherited social arrangements, understood as resources for democracy, but also to suggest ways in which these arrangements could be improved. A major example of this latter enterprise was his *Institution Building in Urban Education* (1969). This work drew upon his own involvement in education and other aspects of urban renewal in the Near South Side of Chicago as well as upon Gayle Janowitz's investigations of the part played by volunteers in urban education (Janowitz, G., 1965). Morris Janowitz conducted a critical analysis of existing educational strategies for coping with the problems of slum schools and the (mainly) black neighbourhoods with which they were associated. For example, he saw serious limitations to a 'specialization model' of promoting educational change which maintained and even strengthened the boundaries between educational professionals and the communities from which their pupils came. He recommended instead an 'aggregation model' (Janowitz, 1969, pp. 44–5) which linked academic goals to broader socialisation, stressed labour-intensive approaches and saw 'the school as a coordinating unit of community development' (ibid, pp. 58–9).

As in his analysis of the community press, Janowitz avoided extremes. He opposed both the wholesale 'breaking up' (ibid, p. 79) of the slum school by bussing and physical relocation and, equally, the idea that the schools should try to manage 'the total life space' of its pupils. Instead, he proposed that the school should become 'the stimulus for insuring relevant policy and practices' (ibid, p. 57) by agencies such as local medical practitioners, the police and social workers. When Janowitz referred to 'school–community relations' (ibid, p. 101) he meant the distinctively local contacts between the school and local families and organised groups. The promotion of such links was not the task for a specialist trouble-shooter but 'a natural extension of the teacher–manager's responsibility for his pupils' (ibid, p. 106). The pupils, too, should have ample opportunity to experience and strengthen the links between school and the rest of the community through various types of paid work, for example on community improvement programmes.

Janowitz was seeking to give educational professionals a model for social intervention which was not vulnerable to the charge of 'welfare colonialism' (ibid, p. 113) and which recognised the limitations of self-help deprived of technical support from outside the local community. He sketched various approaches within the general aggregation model, including the encouragement of housing patterns involving 'mutual or collective support', a kind of 'modified and urbanized version of the Israeli kibbutz' (ibid, p. 115). Another approach was the development of a community centre as a 'single stop "supermarket"' without the confusion and rigidity of a referral system'. It would be 'operated like a hospital on a continuous-day basis'. He continued:

> A model for one community on the South Side of Chicago, for example, projects a medical facility as the central unit, but in this building would be found the welfare agency, family service and legal assistance, and an employment unit. This consolidated agency would serve the area of a school district. The artificial barriers between agencies would be weakened and deemphasized . . . This approach requires the construction of a central building facility to this specific purpose. In essence, the purpose is to create a focal point where residents can obtain information and assistance without regard to the existing organization of agencies, but in response to persistent problems that require resources from outside the community (ibid, pp. 113–14).

Contrast the following:

> I think that time has . . . justified our early contention that the mere foothold of a house, easily accessible, ample in space, hospitable and tolerant in spirit, situated in the midst of the large foreign colonies which so easily isolate themselves in American

cities, would be in itself a serviceable thing for Chicago (Addams, 1960, originally 1910, p. 76).

The spirit of Hull House was evidently still powerful, though modernised, in the late 1960s.

Enlightenment and social control

Attention has mainly been focused so far upon Janowitz's work, in early and mid-career, on German society, prejudice, the military, education and the press. Since the early 1970s, Janowitz has been drawing these and related themes together and developing them further in a series of books and subsidiary papers exploring aspects of macrosociology and social control. Before examining them, it will be useful to review Janowitz's views on the nature and purposes of sociology and related disciplines.

Janowitz has been open to the possibilities offered by interchanges between sociology and related disciplines such as psychology, economics and anthropology. This receptively has been within the framework of an intellectual strategy concerned with 'closing the gap between general theoretical formulations and empirical research procedures' (Janowitz, 1963, p. 154). He has also been preoccupied with the question of the relationship between social scientists and policy-makers outside the academic world. He noted in the mid-1950s that psychologists had become very self-conscious about their 'social resonsibility' (Janowitz, 1970g, originally 1954, p. 261). This was part of a more widespread concern already expressed, for example, in works by Robert Lynd (1939) and Harold Lasswell (1936).

In presenting his own approach, Janowitz has made a distinction between an 'engineering model' and an 'enlightenment model' (Janowitz, 1970f, p. 247). The engineering model makes a strict division between basic research and applied research. The basic researcher's task is 'to develop and test a logico-deductive system of hypotheses' (ibid, p. 247) which will lead to general, systematised knowledge of a highly abstract or statistical kind. By contrast, applied researchers are commissioned to solve specific problems for those who make policy and engage in professional practice by collecting relevant empirical data. The two kinds of researcher have diverging career patterns and different institutional affiliations.

In the enlightenment model, to which Janowitz adheres, the pure/applied distinction is not stressed. Instead, the search for generalisations encompasses both the elaboration of formal propositions and the gathering of relevant hard data. The link between sociology and social policy is a complex and subtle one. First, sociologists collect data and present evidence about social trends which is highly relevant to policy-makers. Second, sociologists also test specific hypotheses about particular institutions or problems and in doing so may develop useful generalisations or sensitising concepts. Third, in the course of the activities just mentioned, sociologists are evaluating actual or potential strategies for handling conflict and change in terms of causes and consequences.

Fourth, the sociologist may develop models of complex social systems or carry out empirical research on such systems. Their findings 'may help society to clarify or even alter its social and political goals and objectives' (ibid, p. 251). This fourth sphere is where Janowitz has sought to pitch his most ambitious efforts in the realm of macrosociology. More generally, the enlightenment model is concerned not just with specific answers to particular practical problems but also with 'creating the intellectual conditions for problem-solving. Its goal is a contribution to institution-building' (ibid, p. 252).

The professionalisation of sociology and its 'natural history' as an 'applied' discipline (Janowitz, 1972b, p. 106) may be interpreted with reference to these models which in many respects encapsulated the respective ideologies of Columbia sociology and Chicago sociology as seen through the eyes of the latter. Janowitz has pointed out that efforts to create an applied sociology have been relatively unsuccessful. These efforts he has argued, are, largely a consequence of the tradition of 'a liberal and "left of center" personal ideology' among sociologists. Their failure is a result not of ideology but of the fact that, unlike engineering or the clinical psychology, sociology is by its nature a 'staff-type profession' based on 'The teacher–researcher format' (ibid, p. 106). This format, which is more congruent with an enlightenment than an engineering model, has prevailed in spite of the determined efforts of (for example) Ernest Burgess, Louis Wirth, Paul Lazarsfeld and

William Ogburn to engage in 'the search for an applied sociology' (ibid, p. 116).

Despite the failure to develop a strong applied sociology implementing practical reforms within society, Janowitz has no sympathy with the suggestion that sociologists have instead contributed to a flight from reason. His own view has been that sociologists have indeed 'neglected to place sufficient emphasis on key topics such as the social and psychological preconditions for a democratic society' (ibid, p. 133). However, there are no grounds for accepting the argument that by the 1970s there was a full-blown 'crisis in sociology' (Janowitz, 1975b, p. 100) as suggested by Alvin Gouldner (Gouldner, 1970).

Writing in the early 1970s, Janowitz commented that if there was a 'crisis', it was a personal crisis experienced by some sociologists who were frustrated by their failure to influence social change and disenchanted with their lives in academe. Janowitz distanced himself from the approach of Gouldner and those who despaired of the capacity of human reason to cope with contemporary society: 'We are not dealing with a Hegelian dialectic in which rational inquiry produces its own seeds of self-destruction but a pragmatic thrust in which human motives and voluntaristic commitments fashion and are fashioned by rational pursuits' (Janowitz, 1972b, p. 133).

Having 'cleared the decks' so to speak, in 1975 Janowitz set out his own version of the problemmatic which should be at the centre of American sociology. In doing so, he located himself four-square in the Chicago tradition. The perspective of 'social control' delineated by Janowitz was a response to the inadequacy of individualistic models of economic self-interest as a means of explaining collective social behaviour and social order. The echoes of Talcott Parsons are not accidental, as has already been seen. The social-control perspective assumed a commitment to reducing coercion, eliminating human misery and enhancing rationality in social life.

Janowitz resisted the accusation that social control necessarily implied 'stability or repression' (Janowitz, 1975b, p. 85). On the contrary, it was most effective when it motivated social groups 'to realize their collective goals' (ibid, p. 88). Analysis of social control should not be restricted to a 'normative conception of elements of social organization and society' but 'incorporate the ecological, technological, economic and institutional dimensions' (ibid, p. 8). Within this context, 'voluntaristic action' involving 'articulated human purpose and actions' (ibid, p. 88) was stressed.

Despite the acknowledged influence of Auguste Comte, Karl Marx, Emile Durkheim, Max Weber, Georg Simmel and Karl Mannheim, all of whom are invoked, Janowitz is clear in his claim that writing on social control is 'mainly an American stream' (ibid, p. 87). Charles Cooley, W. I. Thomas, Robert Park, Thorstein Veblen, Edward Shils and Barrington Moore are all mentioned in this context. Karl Mannheim, whose writings on planning presented 'freedom [as] . . . a particular type and quality of social control', had 'followed the American literature closely and served as a focal point of interpretation' (ibid, p. 95).

By contrast, the emergence by 1940 of a 'constricted and narrow' understanding of the term social control as 'a process of socialization leading to conformity' could partly be blamed on an inappropriate American appropriation of certain European ideas:

> the power analysis and modified version of economic determinism derived from the writings of Karl Marx had the unanticipated consequence of weakening a concern with the voluntaristic and purposeful process of modifying the social order. This occurred during the Great Depression and the New Deal, which created ideological and political currents that impinged on sociology in a fashion comparable with the events of the 1960s and made the idea of social control or any equivalent unpopular (ibid, pp. 95–6).

Beyond selfishness

Having established his commitment to macrosociology, the enlightenment model and an exploration of the issue of social control, what specific conclusions has Janowitz arrived at as a consequence of his work since the early 1970s? Before answering that question, Janowitz's enterprise must be seen in its proper context. The scale of ambition it represents has been immense. His self-assigned tasks have been to analyse the development of the USA as an advanced industrial society since the First World War, identify its fundamental weaknesses and strengths from the point of view of personal and social control, and indicate the strategies which could (and should) be adopted in order to remedy the weaknesses and capitalise upon the strengths. These tasks are carried out in *Social Control of the Welfare State* (1976), *The Last Half-Century* (1978), and *The Reconstruction of Patriotism* (1983).

This trilogy, in the author's words, 'reflects a fusion of my continuing exposure to the various strands of the Chicago school of sociology, with its multiple research traditions, and my interest in political sociology' (Janowitz, 1978, p. xii). In fact, Janowitz incorporates Ogburn's deep interest in social trends with Wirth's concern with the consequences of the mass media for social control. Like his predecessors in Chicago (especially, Small, Park and Ogburn), Janowitz is sensitive to the interplay between normative/ moral/political processes on the one hand and ecological/ technological/economic processes on the other. He shares with all the Chicago sociologists already discussed a bemused determination to cope with the problems of size and complexity in modern urban society, not least by seeking ways to alleviate the more blatant forms of unhappiness and injustice. Finally, although Janowitz has paid far more attention than his predecessors to military matters, some of these predecessors, especially Park and Ogburn, displayed considerable awareness in their writings of the impact of warfare upon American society.

Although Janowitz stresses the need for 'conservation of the effective heritage of sociology' (Janowitz, 1978, p. xi), he is not merely derivative. Apart from the original research contributions mentioned earlier in this chapter, he has undertaken a task of theoretical and empirical integration which – to recall *The Professional Soldier* – must have drawn upon resources both 'heroic and managerial' (Janowitz, 1971, p. 19). Janowitz elaborates what might be called 'a Chicago stance' on the limitations and opportunities confronting America in the late twentieth century. He also looks beyond the Chicago tradition, indicating bonds of intellectual sympathy with (for example) Talcott Parsons, Barrington Moore and Clifford Geertz.

In *Social Control of the Welfare State*, Janowitz argued that the apparently chronic features of the contemporary welfare state, such as federal budget deficits, limited economic growth and stagflation were due in part to 'Institutional barriers inherent in the organization of industry and labor force' (Janowitz, 1976, p. 58).

However, these barriers were just one aspect of a more fundamental problem: 'we are dealing with a pattern of "ordered segmentation", and the central problem is the extent and nature of the articulation and disarticulation of these social elements' (ibid, p. 73). An intricate system of social stratification had developed structured around occupation, membership of voluntary associations, race and ethnicity and, not least, the institutional orders associated with the welfare state.

The imperatives of capitalist industrial development combined with the impact of military mobilisation during the Second World War had generated an overwhelming demand for the expansion of citizenship rights in the sphere of education, health, social security, housing and so on. The welfare state which took shape generated a complex set of equity claims. As home-ownership became more widespread, the categories of wage-earner and property-owner overlapped to an increasing extent. More people came to depend upon a mixture of wage payments, government income-maintenance programmes and a range of benefits such as public education. In such circumstances, 'The task of assessing one's self-interest becomes continuous and more complex, and pursuing one's personal or group goals almost defies programmatic articulation' (ibid, p. 83).

In these circumstances, fundamental liberal goals were being frustrated. Janowitz noted that happiness had become an explicit topic of empirical research during the 1960s. Trend data did not justify the assumption that higher living standards increased measurable happiness: 'If anything, the contrary appears to be the case' (ibid, p. 108). This was probably due in large measure to the absence of clear normative standards. This hiatus was also evident in the treatment of specific social groups by social welfare agencies. The system required transformation to ensure that in its operation 'the moral criteria are those of distributive justice' (ibid, p. 112).

The Last Half Century took up arguments developed in *Social Control of the Welfare State* and carried them further. Both works shared the assumption that modern America faces a deep crisis of political legitimacy. However, Janowitz's 'crisis' is different from the 'legitimation crisis' identified by Habermas (1976). The German writer was, like Janowitz, concerned with the implications of an unmanageable expansion in the state's involvement in economic and social life. However, Habermas assumed that the subsequent rationality crisis would exacerbate attempts to disguise the contradiction entailed in the state's attempt simultaneously to satisfy the demands of capital for special treatment and the people for fair play. The state would undergo a weakening of its authority. The people would become unwilling to satisfy its demands upon them.

By contrast, Janowitz described a crisis which is constituted not by the people's refusal to cooperate with demands made upon them through superordinate political structures but by the unwillingness of citizens to provide the trust and support which will enable the political system to engage in coherent policies on their behalf. The outcomes that each writer would ideally like to see were very similar to each other, as has been noticed. However, their shared vision of health was contrasted with two very different diagnoses of national disorder. Habermas envisaged that rational collective self-mastery would be a defence against authoritarian rule. Janowitz hoped that it could be conjured out of the scattered building blocks of 'a highly "fragmented" electorate with a considerable solidarity within its component social fragments' (Janowitz, 1978, p. 10). I will return to this comparison shortly.

The Last Half-Century (subtitled 'Societal Change and Politics in America') is a large *opus* in which theoretical argument and empirical evidence are densely interwoven. It is a kind of Michelin guide to the development of American institutions and practices with regard to social and personal control from the 1920s to the 1970s. It has a distilled quality about it. It is necessary when discussing it to make a radical choice between confronting in detail the specific debates to which it contributes on practically every page and/or concentrating upon the central argument which serves as backbone to this intellectual structure. The latter is attempted here.

Janowitz wants US democracy to work. In *The Last Half-Century* he accepted that the principal mechanism by which American society regulates itself was, indeed, the electoral process – especially so when the market was trammelled with legislative regulations as in advanced industrial societies. However, there had been downward trends in the levels of voting participation and expressed confidence in the political system. Americans gave their vote less consistently than they used to, shifting allegiance and splitting tickets more frequently. At the same time, the growth of the welfare state had helped to shape a system of social stratification which was highly differentiated.

The resulting pattern of segmentation combined with changing electoral practices made it difficult for political leaders to produce stable coalitions upon which to base their electoral appeal and their legislative programmes. Unstable administrations were the result. Further cleavages had been generated by the decline of the mass armed force and its replacement by an all-volunteer force. Janowitz argued that the growth of the modern military establishment, accompanied as it was by shifts in recruitment practices and the recent trauma of Vietnam, provided 'a direct analogy with the growth of the welfare state' – although the strains imposed by the former appeared to be 'more intractable' (Janowitz, 1978, p. 217).

Institutional disarticulation had effects in several spheres. Discontent and resistance abounded in industrial and service bureaucracies, despite the decline in violence and the shift from overt domination to manipulative techniques by management. Residential communities were divided from each other by economic, ethnic and racial segregation. Work and home were geographically separate. The suburbs and the city centre were worlds apart.

How could these cleavages be overcome? In the medium term, Janowitz placed great emphasis upon the possibility of cultivating an increased sense of shared responsibility among Americans by giving practical shape to the obligations – as opposed to the rights – of citizenship. This theme was explored in *The Reconstruction of Patriotism*. Returning to roots with a vengeance, Janowitz argued that 'Military experience during the American Revolution operated as a form of civic education in support of the democratic polity' (Janowitz, 1983, p. 17). Indeed, military service continued, until the Second World War, to educate the citizen–soldier in attitudes favourable to the maintenance of American democracy.

Janowitz also paid attention to mass education and its contribution to 'the search for national citizenship' (ibid, p. 73). He noted a decline in the effectiveness of public education in this regard after 1890 and a further decline after 1940. The Depression of the 1930s contributed to this process because the prevailing social climate facilitated a shift of approach away 'from traditional patriotism to various forms of political dissent' (ibid, p. 98). These years also witnessed the emergence of a radical student movement.

This very incomplete summary of the early chapters is mainly intended to establish their main point which is that the bases of civic consciousness within the USA had, in Janowitz's view, been very seriously eroded. Many of the more recent immigrant groups posed particular difficulties with respect to acculturation or assimilation. In his fascinating discussion of Mexican-Americans, relevant in this respect, Janowitz noted their reluctance to be deeply affected by American civic education. His bemusement was mixed with admiration at the resilience of their culture. The discussion is reminiscent, in some respects, of Park's much earlier analysis of the peculiar situation of the Japanese on the West coast.

However, Janowitz's principal point – one which he had been advocating for over thirty-five years – was that national service of some kind or another would be a valuable means 'to improve and clarify one's sense of civic obligation' (ibid, p. 195). Through this means, however it was organised, it would be possible to overcome the pervasive 'lack of group identity and group spirit' (ibid, p. 168). National service was an ambition for the future. At this point, the analysis returns to the past and present.

In *The Past Half-Century*, Janowitz noted that the mass media had, historically, played a large part in developing controls at the personal and societal level. However, they had also encouraged violence and material gratification at the expense of control. Meanwhile, the legitimacy of the legal system had been eroded as a consequence of decisions which were perceived by the people as being too lenient with regard to the poor and the weak, too generous with regard to social groups subject to popular discrimination. Finally, Janowitz turned to more informal attempts to manage interpersonal relations. The tide of hedonism, he found, was being partially countered by professional and lay movements with therapeutic intentions. Such movements helped to strengthen normative support for efforts to increase personal controls.

Community participation was also being restructured in a helpful direction by the emergence of at least three levels of organisation: the very localised 'social bloc', the more formalised 'organizational community' and the 'aggregated metropolitan community' (Janowitz, 1978, p. 487). This movement Janowitz found particularly encouraging given his view that such local organisations 'supply a matrix by which the weakness of party organization is contained, if not corrected' (ibid, p. 543). However, he resisted the conclusion that institution-building to repair American democracy must only work from the bottom upwards. Elite leaders had to acquire 'strong, clear conceptions of the special role of the political tasks of societal coordination' (ibid, p. 544).

Unfortunately, academics who made it their business to support promising candidates rather than concentrate on developing objective understanding of relevant social processes were not helping since they tended to reflect 'the model of immediate self-interest as the basis of political effectiveness' (ibid, p. 545). By contrast, Janowitz made an appeal to his fellow-social-scientists, to industrialists, to union bosses and to political leaders: 'The essential strategy [writes Janowitz] is for each group of organized adversaries to confront and deal with broader sets of issues than normally encountered in routine practice in order to enhance its collective responsibilities' (ibid, p. 553).

This is the classic Chicago stance: a determination to use the intellectual resources of sociology to wrest a fuller realisation of liberal values from a society whose predominating groups were unwilling or unable to reach beyond the selfish interests of their occupational group or ecological niche. Within the limits imposed by the sacred symbols of the capitalist market and the democratic election, Janowitz and his predecessors have looked for ways of turning competition into cooperation rather than conflict. By and large, also, they have placed faith in the fruitfulness of science and technology rather than capitalist enterprise as such. More has been expected of the professional (often a public servant) than the business person. In combating the vested interests of the latter they have encouraged the former to strengthen his or her links with the agencies which shape public opinion. The scholars studied here have not in every case and in all respects trusted the people to know their own best interests but they have, in general, thought it prudent to educate this mighty force.

11

Is Our Republic to Fail?

A static agenda

Between the 1890s and the 1980s three major changes have occurred. First, social science has become institutionalised within American educational, governmental and business organisations. Second, these organisations have grown enormously in size. Third, the USA has achieved, maintained and is only just beginning to relinquish a position of global domination. It is fascinating to note that Chicago sociology began to lose its own hegemony within the profession at about the time that American society at large was on the brink of asserting its pre-eminent world position during the Second World War. Now, at a time when this world position is being gradually yielded, the Chicago sociology department is well on the way to re-establishing its claim to pre-eminence among its peers. The enormously difficult moral and political task of adjustment to international decline deserves a special place upon its intellectual agenda.

This last point is pertinent in view of the fact that, in spite of the considerable social and political changes that have occurred since the 1890s, the actual intellectual agenda of Chicago sociology, as far as it is represented by the six scholars discussed in this book, has remained remarkably stable. It is an agenda set by American liberalism at whose centre is a series of dilemmas focusing upon the difficulties of achieving justice and happiness in a vast modern society undergoing rapid change. Each scholar was most sensitive to particular aspects of this problematic. Small believed that it was the sociologist's duty to discover and communicate knowledge of how to manage a just and harmonious society in the general interest.

Thomas stressed the need to improve the means available to 'social technicians' whose task was to help individuals develop the personal controls which could alleviate individual misery.

Park attempted to weigh in the balance the losses and gains produced by civilisation from the point of view of social order and the realisation of human nature. Wirth attempted to advance social consensus not by simply making available the appropriate knowledge (Small's strategy) but by accepting a professional responsibility to shape popular opinion. Ogburn emphasised the sociologist's vocation to discover knowledge but (unlike Small and Wirth) concentrated mainly upon the implications for individual freedom and satisfaction rather than collective harmony. Janowitz has displayed affinities with all these predecessors in his efforts to identify effective means of personal and social control.

In the first part of this book, a comparison was made of certain ideas of Dewey and Veblen in order to illustrate contrasting tendencies within American liberalism. Veblen was located, along with C. W. Mills and Alvin Gouldner, in a radical tradition whose adherents considered that at some point in its development (exactly *when* being in dispute) the Chicago school of sociology became an acquiescent servant of the establishment within American corporate capitalism. In fact, all six of the Chicago schoolmen discussed have strongly criticised social tendencies within contemporary America from within the liberal tradition, two of them (Small and Ogburn) in terms sometimes reminiscent of Veblen. The other four, more clearly 'Deweyan', have all been interested in the creation of forms of democratic consciousness appropriate for modern America. As has been seen, it probably cost at least one of them his career. Thomas and Wirth were very active in working for practical reforms pitched at the levels of, respectively, the individual and the whole society. Park and Janowitz have incorporated investigation at both levels in analyses which also focused upon the local community. Both have investigated the possibilities for and limits upon human intervention to bring about reform. Janowitz, in particular, has produced a number of schemes for institution-building.

Unfinished business

'Is our republic to fail?' remains the haunting question. How to make America work is still the problem. In the 1940s and 1950s Wirth and Ogburn were relatively optimistic. Even more recently, a spirit of dogged confidence has persistently broken through the rather sardonic tone of Janowitz. However, during the 1970s and 1980s the willingness of the American electorate to fund and implement extensive programmes of social amelioration has greatly diminished. It seems that the era of the New Deal is finally over. Meanwhile, the rise in influence of other political and moral orders in societies throughout the world, not least in Western Europe, offers challenging alternatives to the 'American way'. The USA is now neither completely dominant over its global neighbours nor relatively isolated from their influence. However, there is a 'cultural lag' (to coin a phrase) between this harsh politico-economic fact and its permeation within American national consciousness.

Complex and highly-charged debates are under way concerning the fate of the public philosophy of the New Deal (for example, Storing, 1981; Schambra, 1982). They are complemented by a vigorous academic controversy about the historical character and intellectual consequences of American political ideology (for example, Diggins, 1984; Diggins 1985; Shalhope, 1972; Appleby, 1984). It is important that equivalent attention be paid to the task of easing America's cultural adaptation to the process of relative decline. In fact, American sociology could contribute to all these tasks by engaging in sympathetic exchanges with other intellectual traditions, not least across the Atlantic. The comparisons between Simmel and Veblen in the early part of this book illustrate the contrasting meanings that may be derived from processes which at first sight appear very similar. Such meanings could usefully be explored on progressively equal terms as the balance of political and economic advantage becomes (as it has gradually been doing for some time now) less heavily weighted in America's favour.

To take just one example, not necessarily the most significant: might not the respective traditions of Chicago and Frankfurt, including their more recent manifestations, have something to offer each other? Their strengths (which in excess become weaknesses) complement each other: on the one side, a sturdy tradition of empirical analysis and a commitment to core values of American liberalism; on the other side, a close adherence to a dialectical philosopher approach and a continuing debate with the Enlightenment; on both sides, an interest in Freudian approaches, the nature of mass communication and the interplay between capitalism and democracy. Members of these schools, and their successors, bear different scars: those of the Frankfurt school are the product of cultural loss and political exclusion; the Chicago school, by contrast, has had to wrestle with the temptations and frustrations of incorporation within a society whose ideology cannot be too harshly attacked since it contains the outlines of the desired 'utopia' (to recall Mannheim).

It must be admitted that Chicago sociology has not recently taken a lead in this respect. For example, Janowitz dismisses approaches which assume a 'crisis in sociology' (Gouldner, 1970) or the 'eclipse of reason' (Horkheimer, 1974). Having worked quite closely with scholars of the Frankfurt school in the early part of his career, he has, it seems, concluded that its perspective is quite incompatible with his own pragmatist philosophy. His own approach recognises 'the extensive distortions and exaggerations of purpose and achievement resulting from mechanical scientism in the social sciences'. However, Janowitz rejects 'the argument that organized social investigation of the real world undermines reason, and thereby necessarily and automatically contributes to the attenuation of the social order and to the weakening of social control' (Janowitz, 1978, p. 401).

Janowitz and Habermas

In the light of Janowitz's views it is intriguing to notice that in 1976, the same year that *Social Control of the Welfare State* was published, there appeared the English translation of Jürgen Habermas's *Legitimation Crisis*. Both works were concerned with the origins, nature and implications of crises in advanced capitalist industrial societies, paying particular attention to a crisis of legitimation in the political sphere. Neither author makes reference to the work of the other and, in his subsequent writings, Janowitz does not pay attention to the publications of Habermas, a distinguished latter-day contributor to the critical tradition exemplified by the Frankfurt school. This silence is interesting and should be placed in context.

In the course of the eight or nine decades that have passed since the establishment of the Chicago sociology department the relationship between German and American intellectual culture has undergone a sea-change. Albion Small, founder of the department, deliberately soaked himself in German academic culture. He visited Germany as a pilgrim. By contrast, Morris Janowitz, along with thousands of his fellow-Americans in uniform, entered Germany as a conqueror. His native tradition acquired prestige and influence from its association with global economic and military power. Why look abroad for ideas?

In fact, the initiative with respect to the exploration of possibilities for transatlantic intellectual interchange has shifted to the European side since the Second World War. Habermas has contributed to this process. He has 'brought Kant, Fichte, and Hegel into contact with Wittgenstein, Popper and Peirce . . . [and] fashioned a language in which Marx, Dilthey, and Freud as well as Dewey, Mead and Parsons can all have their say' (McCarthy, 1976, p. vii). It will be useful to compare the argument set out by Janowitz in his trilogy with the formulations presented by Habermas, for example in *Legitimation Crisis*. Only the broadest comparisons can be made, indicating some major similarities and differences.

Habermas shares with the American pragmatists an interest in the interplay between human interests, knowledge and action. Science, in his view, is the product of efforts to overcome obstacles or disturbances which arise in the course of human interaction with nature. He is sympathetic to Charles Peirce's approach in this regard and also, with reservations, to the spirit of John Dewey's treatment of the relationship between technocratic administrators and the public within modern society:

the successful transposition of technical and strategic recommendations into practice is, according to the pragmatist model, increasingly dependent on mediation by the public as a political institution . . . For Dewey it seemed self-evident that the relation of reciprocal guidance and enlightenment between the production of techniques and strategies on the one hand and the value-orientations of interested groups on the other could be realized within the unquestionable horizon of common sense and an uncomplicated public realm. But the *structural change in the bourgeois public realm* would have demonstrated the naiveté of this view even if it were not invalidated by the internal development of the sciences. For the latter have made a basically unsolved problem out of the appropriate translation of technical information even between individual disciplines, let alone between the sciences and the public at large (Habermas, 1971, pp. 68–9; italics in original).

The rational pursuit of the collective interest is complicated by the distorting effect of capitalist power structures and ensuing difficulties of communication. In analysing these issues, Habermas makes a much clearer distinction than does Dewey between three kinds of human interest, organisational form and science. He distinguishes between: technical interests which are pursued through instrumental action and the empirical–analytic sciences; practical interests which are expressed through the medium of language and the historical–hermeneutic sciences; and emancipatory interests, relating to the distorting impact of constraint and dependency, which find expression through critical theory. Critical theory is necessary in order to unmask the ideology embedded in the modern fusion of industry, technology and science, an ideology which disguises the practical interests of particular classes as technical problems relating to means. The distorted perceptions imposed by 'the system' had to be overcome so that people would know what their real interests were and would be able to reassert mastery over their own lives.

As part of its emancipatory project, critical theory has a responsibility to analyse tendencies and contradictions within the structures of modern societies. Habermas argues that the bourgeois liberal ideal of rational discussion and decision-making by citizens within the public sphere has been radically undermined by the development of capitalism. For example, the mass media have become commercialised. Big business and government have made compacts for their mutual convenience which diminish the democratic participation of others. Government, science, technology and industry have drawn more closely together. At the same time, however, new citizenship rights and new claims upon the state have been created through the expansion of social welfare. State intervention in the economy has increased in order to reduce disruptive tendencies within the market. Several spheres previously subject to the (supposedly neutral) rule of *laissez-faire* have become, potentially, arenas of political dispute. They can be depoliticised only if the people can be persuaded that the relevant issues are, in Habermas's terms, technical rather than practical.

Advanced capitalist societies are structured through steering systems which regulate their complex internal workings and external environments. Their members participate in symbolically structured life-worlds expressed in their speech, action and sense of identity. The steering system of an advanced capitalist society may undergo crisis in its economic or political sectors. Crises in the life-world of the society may manifest themselves in either the political sphere or the socio-cultural subsystem, according to Habermas. These themes are developed in *Legitimation Crisis*.

Crises in the economic sphere within advanced capitalist societies may be displaced to the political sphere, for example through increased government spending and the expansion of public bureaucracies. However, while attempting in this way to safeguard accumulation processes, the government is likely to be faced with the selfish demands of particular economic interests which may be so pressing as to undermine any strategic logic directed at general interests. The result may be a rationality crisis in the political sphere. At the same time as maintaining the interests of the economically powerful, the state has also to convince the people at large that the liberal principles of justice and freedom are being upheld. In the nature of things within a capitalist society, this entails attempting to disguise a fundamental contradiction. By expanding its sphere of intervention, the state opens up to question the moral appropriateness of its actions over a wider range of actions and becomes susceptible to a withdrawal of public confidence in the form of a legitimation crisis.

Meanwhile, in the socio-cultural sphere the capacity of privatism to motivate the population is liable to erosion. As social life becomes increasingly rationalised, moral tenets are subject to criticism from a relativistic and subjectivist perspective and so lose their absolute force. In such circumstances, faith in the market is undermined. The expansion of the state weakens possessive individualism. People become less used to the rigours of the wage relationship and adapt to the habits and expectations induced by social welfare. Universalism and the habit of critique grow predominant within the cultural sphere and some groups (feminists, students) begin to question the rationality underlying the social order. Thus, the legitimation crisis may be complicated by a motivation crisis. In these circumstances, capitalism may develop oppressive forms of domination to overcome mounting opposition. Or, it may be transformed by the emergence of a participatory democracy within which 'reciprocal behavioral expectations raised to normative status afford validity to a *common* interest ascertained *without deception*' (Habermas, 1976, p. 108; italics in original).

The rather dense sentence just quoted actually states an ideal shared by all the Chicagoans discussed in this present book. Like Habermas, they hoped for a social order in which the people would mutually determine their common interest through open communication and rational discussion, freely accepting the obligation to behave in ways which would serve it. If the European version of this ideal drew upon memories of the eighteenth-century *salon*, the American version recalled the early New England town meeting or the rough democracy of the idealised frontier settlement in the old north-west. It is an ideal lying behind Janowitz's view that although 'every statement of fact threatens the interest of some social group', sociologists could 'overcome distortions'. This was because 'Social research is a collective and professional enterprise, and it can and does make progress by means of its own norms of consensual validity. It remains a system of control by colleagues because sociologists have a significant degree of group autonomy' (Janowitz, 1976, p. xv).

Habermas and Janowitz both sympathise with the aspirations embedded in the writings of Freud and Dewey. Janowitz has noted that 'Both psychoanalysis and pragmatism . . . emphasize the importance of individual and collective problem solving and of strengthening patterns of personal and social control as opposed to the prospects of conformity and coercion' (ibid, p. 28). This was thoroughly compatible with Janowitz's view of the welfare state as 'a strategy for making use of collective symbols and practices to achieve goals that are cast in an individualistic mould. Thus, [he continued] the welfare state is an extension of the main lines of liberal democracy that are embodied in the political aspirations of the Western nation-state' (ibid, p. 106).

Habermas and Janowitz have worried about different things. Habermas most fears a steady drift towards a form of bureaucratic repression which extinguishes human freedom. By contrast, Janowitz is much more concerned that a lack of coordination and control in several aspects of personal and collective life is preventing liberal democracy from fulfilling its potential. This difference in emphasis is understandable given the intellectual roots of each. Habermas, born in 1929, was brought up in Nazi Germany. He later became the assistant of Theodor Adorno, who had been forced to go into exile during the period of Hitler's rule. Members of the Frankfurt school had witnessed the crushing of a weakened liberal culture by a deeply unsympathetic regime. By contrast, the repeated experience of members of the Chicago school, as we have seen, was that the values to which they were committed were officially revered but often ignored or very imperfectly realised. Furthermore, because of the sacred status of core institutions such as the market and the ballot they had to be very careful when criticising them even when they had damaging effects in human terms.

In fact, the seeds of a potentially fruitful interchange have already been planted. As has already been seen, Habermas has drawn freely upon the American pragmatists. In a discussion of Park's work on the mass media Alvin Gouldner argued that 'The analysis of the public as a sphere of rational discourse – of reflective and critical discourse – that had been stimulated by the Chicago School well before World War II languished without significant development until 1962' when Habermas took up these themes (Habermas, 1976, p. 138). Hans Joas, in a recent critical study of G. H. Mead, makes the case that the American advanced beyond the point reached by Habermas. Mead, he argues, 'roots perception and meaning in a common praxis of subjects, not . . . as Habermas . . . in a communication that is severed from active engagement with nature' (Joas, 1985, p. 166). As was noted much earlier, Jim Thomas has argued that the critical theory of the Frankfurt school could usefully be related to the emancipatory impulse of the early Chicago tradition.

The comments just made are not intended to plead the cause of a 'Chicago–Frankfurt' hybrid. It is enough to notice that a debate is getting under way. Other debates are equally possible and valuable. For example, Peter Jackson and Susan J. Smith have argued strongly for an approach drawing upon the interactionism of the early Chicago tradition, a Simmelian perspective on conflict and

Anthony Giddens's concept of structuration (Jackson and Smith, 1984). However things develop, it is to be hoped that the intellectual products of such debates contribute to the strategy, well expressed by Morris Janowitz, of 'closing the gap between general theoretical formulations and empirical research procedures' (Janowitz, 1963, p. 154). It will also be an achievement if they are as readable as *The Polish Peasant* or *The Ghetto*.

Bibliography

Adams, H. (1961) *The Education of Henry Adams: An Autobiography* with an introduction by D. W. Brogan; Boston, Houghton Mifflin, originally published in 1918.

Addams, J. (1960) *Twenty Years at Hull House*, New York, Signet, originally published in 1910.

Adorno, T. W. *et al.* (1964) *The Authoritarian Personality*, New York, John Wiley, originally published in 1950.

Adorno, T. W. (1967a) 'Veblen's Attack on Culture' in Adorno, 1967b, pp. 73–94.

Adorno, T. W. (1967b) *Prisms*, translated by Samuel and Shierry Weber, London, Neville Spearman.

Alihan, M. A. (1938) *Social Ecology*, New York, Columbia University Press.

Anderson, E. (1976) *A Place on the Corner*, Chicago, Chicago University Press.

Anderson, N. (1923) *The Hobo: The Sociology of the Homeless Man*, Chicago, University of Chicago Press.

Angell, J. R. (1909) 'The Influence of Darwin on Psychology' *Psychology Review*, 16(3) pp. 152–69.

Appleby, J. (1984) *Capitalism and the New Social Order: The Republican Vision of the 1790s*, New York, New York University Press.

Arnold, M. (1888) 'Civilisation in the United States', *Nineteenth Century*, 134, pp. 481–96).

Axelrod, C. (1977) 'Towards an Appreciation of Simmel's Fragmentary Style', *Sociological Quarterly*, 18, 185–96.

Baker, P. J. (1974) 'The Life Histories of W. I. Thomas and Robert E. Park', *American Journal of Sociology*, 79(2) 243–60.

Ballis Lal, B. (1986) 'The "Chicago School" of American Sociology, Symbolic Interactionism, and Race Relations Theory', in Rex and Mason, 1986, pp. 281–98.

Barnes, H. E. (1926) 'The Place of Albion Woodbury Small in Modern Sociology', *American Journal of Sociology*, 32(1) pp. 15–48.

Baylen, J. O. (1964) 'A Victorian's "Crusade" in Chicago 1893–94', *Journal of American History*, 60(3), pp. 418–34.

Becker, E. (1971) *The Lost Science of Man*, New York, Braziller.

Becker, H. and Boskoff, A. (eds) (1957) *Modern Sociological Theory in Continuity and Change*, New York, The Dryden Press.

Beetham, D. (1985) *Max Weber and the Theory of Modern Politics*, Cambridge, Polity.

Ben-David, J. and Clark, T. N. (1977) *Culture and Its Creators: Essays in honor of Edward Shils*, Chicago, University of Chicago Press.

221

Bender, T. (1982) *Towards an Urban Vision: Ideas and Institutions in Nineteenth-Century America*, Baltimore, Johns Hopkins Press.

Bendix, R. (1954) 'Social Theory and Social Action in the Sociology of Louis Wirth', *American Journal of Sociology*, 59(6) pp. 523–9.

Benjamin, W. (1979a) 'A Berlin Chronicle', in Benjamin (1979b), pp. 293–346.

Benjamin, W. (1979b) *One-way Street and Other Writings*, translated by Edmund Jephcott and Kingsley Shorter with an introduction by Susan Sontag, London, New Left Books.

Bettelheim, B. and Janowitz, M. (1975a) '*Dynamics of Prejudice*' in Bettelheim and Janowitz, 1975b, pp. 99–337, originally published 1950.

Bettelheim, B. and Janowitz, M. (1975b) *Social Change and Prejudice*, New York, Free Press, originally published in 1964.

Blackbourn, D. and Eley, G. (1984) *The Peculiarities of German History: Bourgeois Society and Politics in Nineteenth-century Germany*, Oxford, Oxford University Press.

Blackwell, J. E. and Janowitz, M. (1974) *Black Sociologists: Historical and Contemporary Perspectives*, Chicago, University of Chicago Press.

Blumer, H. (1979) *Critiques of Research in the Social Sciences: An Appraisal of Thomas and Znaniecki's The Polish Peasant in Europe and America*, New Brunswick, New Jersey, Transaction Books, originally published in 1939.

Bottomore, T. (1984) *The Frankfurt School*, London, Tavistock.

Bowles, S. and Gintis, H. (1976) *Schooling in Capitalist America: Educational Reform and the Contraditions of Economic Life*, London, Routledge & Kegan Paul.

Boyer, P. (1978) *Urban Masses and Moral Order in America 1820–1920*, Cambridge, Harvard University Press.

Bradbury, M. and McFarlane, J. (eds) (1976) *Modernism 1890–1930*, Harmondsworth, Penguin.

Bramson, L. (1961) *The Political Context of Sociology*, Princeton, New Jersey, Princeton University Press.

Braude, L. (1970) 'Louis Wirth and the Locus of Sociological Control', *American Sociologist*, 5(?) pp. 233–9.

Brill, A. A. (1939) 'The Introduction and Development of Freud's Work in the United States', *American Journal of Sociology*, 45(3) pp. 318–25.

Brookings Institution (1931) *Essays on Research in the Social Sciences*, Washington, The Brookings Institution.

Bullen, R. J. *et al.* (eds) (1984) *Ideas into Politics: Aspects of European History 1880–1950*, London, Croom Helm.

Bulmer, M. (1984a) *The Chicago School of Sociology: Institutionalization, Diversity, and the Rise of Sociological Research*, Chicago, University of Chicago Press.

Bulmer, M. (1984b) 'Philanthropic Foundations and the Development of the Social Sciences in the Early Twentieth Century: A Reply to Donald Fisher', *Sociology*, 18(4) pp. 7552–79.

Burgess, E. W. (1927) 'Statistics and Case Studies as Methods of Sociological Research', *Sociology and Social Research*, vol. 12, pp. 103–20.

Burgess, E. W. (1939) 'The Influence of Sigmund Freud upon Sociology in the United States', *American Journal of Sociology*, 45(3) pp. 356–74.

Burgess, E. W. (1967) 'The Growth of the City: An Introduction to a Research Project' in Park and Burgess, 1967, pp. 47–62, originally published in 1925.

Burns, L. R. (1980) 'The Chicago School and the Study of Organization–Environment Relations', *Journal of the History of the Behavioral Sciences*, 16(4) pp. 342–58.

Buxton, W. (1985) *Talcott Parsons and the Capitalist Nation-State: Political Sociology as a Strategic Vocation*, Toronto, University of Toronto Press.

Carey, J. T. (1975) *Sociology and Public Affairs: The Chicago School*, Beverly Hills, Sage.

Carnegie, A. (1886) *Triumphant Democracy or Fifty Years March of the Republic*, London.

Cash, W. J. (1973) *The Mind of the South*, Harmondsworth, Penguin, originally published in 1941.

Castells, M. (1976) 'Theory and Ideology in Urban Sociology' in Pickvance, 1976, pp. 60–84, originally published in 1969.

Castells, M. (1983) *The City and the Grassroots: A Cross-cultural Theory of Urban Social Movements*, Berkeley, University of California Press.

Chapin, F. S. (1934) 'The Present State of the Profession', *American Journal of Sociology*, 39(4) pp. 506–19.

Commager, H. S. (1950) *The American Mind: An Interpretation of American thought and character since the 1880s*, New Haven, Yale University Press.

Coughlan, N. (1975) *Young John Dewey: An Essay in American Intellectual History*, Chicago, University of Chicago Press.

Cressey, P. G. (1932) *The Taxi-Dance Hall: A Sociological Study in Commercialized Recreation and City Life*, Chicago, University of Chicago Press.

Croly, H. (1964) *The Promise of American Life*, New York, Capricorn, originally published in 1909.

Dedmon, E. (1953) *Fabulous Chicago*, New York, Random House.

Deegan, M. J. and Burger, J. S. (1981) 'W. I. Thomas and Social Reform: His Work and Writings', *Journal of the History of the Behavioral Sciences*, 17(1) pp. 114–25.

Denzin, N. K. (1984) 'On Interpreting an Interpretation' (review of Lewis and Smith, 1980) *American Journal of Sociology*, 89(6) pp. 1426–33.

Dewey, J. (1902a) 'Interpretation of the Savage Mind', *The Psychological Review*, 9(3) pp. 217–30.

Dewey, J. (1902b) 'Academic Freedom', *Educational Review*, 23 pp. 1–14.

Dewey, J. (1930) *Individualism, Old and New*, New York, Minton, Batch & Co.

Dewey, J. (1975a) 'Moral Theory and Practice' in Dewey, 1975, pp. 93–109 (originally published in 1891).

Dewey, J. (1975b) 'Outline of a Critical Theory of Ethics, in Dewey, 1975, vol. 3, pp. 239–388 (originally published in 1891).

Dewey, J. (1975c) 'The Reflex Arc Concept in Psychology', in Dewey, 1975, vol. 5, pp. 96–109, originally published in 1896.

Dewey, J. (1975) *The Early Works, 1882–1898*. 5 vols, edited by J. A. Boydston, Carbondale and Edwardsville, Southern Illinois University Press.

Dibble, V. (1975) *The Legacy of Albion Small*, Chicago, Chicago University Press.

Diggins, J. P. (1978) *The Bard of Savagery: Thorstein Veblen and Modern Social Theory*, Brighton, Harvester Press.

Diggins, J. P. 'The Socialization of Authority and the Dilemmas of American Liberalism', *Social Research*, 46(3) pp. 454–86.

Diggins, J. P. (1984) *The Lost Soul of American Politics: Virtue, Self-interest, and the Foundations of Liberalism*, New York, Basic Books.

Diggins, J. P. (1985) 'Comrades and Citizens: New Mythologies in American Historiography', *American Historical Review*, 90(3) pp. 614–38.

Diner, S. J. (1975) 'Department and Discipline: the Department of Sociology at the University of Chicago, 1892–1920', *Minerva*, 13(4) pp. 514–53.

Diner, S. J. (1980) *A City and its Universities: Public Policy in Chicago, 1892–1919*, Chapel Hill, University of North Carolina Press.

Dorfman, J. (1935) *Thorstein Veblen and his America*, London, Gollancz.
Dreiser, T. (1981) *Sister Carrie*, edited by Neda M. Westlake *et al.*, Philadelphia, University of Pennsylvania Press, originally published in 1900.
Duffey, B. (1954) *The Chicago Renaissance in American Letters*, Michigan, Michigan State College Press.
Duncan, H. D. (1965) *Culture and Democracy; The Struggle for Form in Society and Architecture in Chicago and the Middle West during the Life and Times of Louis H. Sullivan*, Totowa, New Jersey, Bedminster Press.
Duncan, O. D. (1959) 'An Appreciation of William Fielding Ogburn', *Technology and Culture*, 1(i) pp. 94–9.
Eksteins, M. (1984) 'When Death was Young . . .: Germany, Modernism and the Great War', in Bullen *et al.*, 1984, pp. 25–35.
Eldridge, J. (1983) *C. Wright Mills*, London, Tavistock.
Ellwood, C. A. (1909) 'The Influence of Darwin on Sociology', *Psychology Review*, 16(3) pp. 188–94.
Encyclopedia of the Social Sciences (1930–5) New York, Macmillan.
Etzioni, A. (1959) The Ghetto – A Reevaluation', *Social Forces*, 37(3) pp. 255–621.
Eubank, E. E. (1936) 'European and American Sociology: Some Comparisons', *Social Forces*, 15(2) pp. 147–84.
Faris, E. (1934) 'Too many Ph.D.'s?' *American Journal of Sociology*, 39(4) pp. 509–12.
Faris, R. E. L. (1967) *Chicago Sociology 1920–1932*, Chicago, University of Chicago Press.
Farrell, J. T. (1979) *Studs Lonigan*, London, Granada, originally published 1932–5.
Featherstone, J. M. (1974) 'Human Ecology and Sociology: The Development of Human Ecology in the Department of Sociology at the University of Chicago 1914–1939', MA thesis, Durham University.
Firey, W. (1947) *Land Use in Central Boston*, Cambridge, Massachusetts, Harvard University Press.
Fischer, C. (1972), '"Urbanism as a Way of Life": A Review and an Agenda', *Sociological Methods and Research*, 1(2) pp. 187–242.
Fischer, C. (1981) 'The Public and Private Worlds of the City', *American Sociological Review*, 46(2) pp. 306–16.
Fisher, D. (1983) 'The Role of Philanthropic Foundations in the Reproduction and Production of Hegemony: Rockefeller Foundation and the Social Sciences', *Sociology*, 17(2) pp. 206–33.
Fisher, D. (1984) 'Philanthropic Foundations and the Social Sciences: A Response to Martin Bulmer', *Sociology*, 18(4) pp. 580–7.
Fleming, D. and Bailyn, B. (eds) (1969) *The Intellectual Migration: Europe and America 1930–1960*, Cambridge, Massachusetts, Belknoff Press of Harvard University Press.
Frazier, P. J. and Gaziano, C. (1979) 'Robert Ezra Park's Theory of News, Public Opinion and Social Control', *Journalism Monographs*, 64, Minneapolis, Association for Education in Journalism.
Fries, M. S. (1978) 'The City as Metaphor for the Human Condition: Alfred Doblin's *Berlin Alexanderplatz*', *Modern Fiction Studies*, 24(1) pp. 41–64.
Frisby, D. (1978) 'Introduction to the Translation' in Simmel, 1978.
Frisby, D. (1981) *Sociological Impressionism: A Reassessment of Georg Simmel's Social Theory*, London, Heinemann.
Frisby, D. (1984) *Georg Simmel*, London, Tavistock.
Frisch, M. H. (1982) 'Urban Theorists, Urban Reform, and American Political Culture in the Progressive Period', *Political Science Quarterly*, 97(2) pp. 295–315.

Furner, M. O. (1975) *Advocacy and Objectivity: A Crisis in the Professionalization of American Social Science 1865–1905*, Lexington, University Press of Kentucky.

Garson, R. and Maidment, R. (1981) 'Social Darwinism and the Liberal Tradition: The Case of William Graham Sumner', *South Atlantic Quarterly*, 80(1) pp. 61–76.

Gay, P. (1967a) *The Enlightenment: An Interpretation. Volume One: The Rise of Modern Paganism*, New York, Alfred A. Knopf.

Gay, P. (1967) *The Enlightenment: An Interpretation. Volume Two: The Science of Freedom*, New York, Alfred A. Knopf.

Glazer, N. (1950) 'The Authoritarian Personality in Profile: Report on a Major Study of Race Hatred', *Commentary*, 4, pp. 573–83.

Goebel, J. (1914) *Der Kampf im deutsche Kietur in Amerika*, Leipzig, Düss.

Goffman, E. (1963) *Behavior in Public Places*, New York, Free Press.

Goffman, E. (1971) *Relations in Public: Microstudies of the Public Order*, Harmondsworth, Penguin.

Gouldner, A. W. (1970) *The Coming Crisis of Western Sociology*, London, Heinemann.

Gouldner, A. W. (1976) *The Dialectic of Ideology and Technology: The Origins, Grammar and Future of Ideology*, London, Macmillan.

Guest, A. M. (1984) 'Robert Park and the Natural Area: A Sentimental Review', *Sociology and Social Research*, 69(1) pp. 2–11.

Gurfein, M. I. and Janowitz, M. (1946) 'Trends in Wehrmacht Morale', *Public Opinion Quarterly*, 10(1).

Habermas, J. (1971) *Towards a Rational Society: Student Protest, Science, and Politics*, London, Heinemann.

Habermas, J. (1976) *Legitimation Crisis*, London, Heinemann.

Hamilton, P. (1983) *Talcott Parsons*, London, Tavistock.

Hannerz, U. (1980) *Exploring the City*, New York, Columbia University Press.

Hartz, L. (1955) *The Liberal Tradition in America*, New York, Harcourt Brace Jovanovich.

Haskell, T. L. (1977) *The Emergence of Professional Social Science: The American Social Science Association and the Nineteenth-Century Crisis of Authority*, Urbana, University of Illinois Press.

Hatt, P. K. and Reiss, A. J. (1957) *Cities and Society. The Revised Reader in Urban Sociology*, Glencoe, Illinois, Free Press.

Hawley, A. (1950) *Human Ecology: A Theory of Community Structure*, New York, Ronald Press.

Hawley, E. W. (1978) 'The Discovery and Study of a "Corporate Liberalism"', *Business History Review*, 52(3) pp. 309–20.

Hawthorn, G. (1976) *Enlightenment and Despair: A History of Sociology*, Cambridge, Cambridge University Press.

Hayes, E. C. (1926) 'Masters of Social Science: Albion Small', *Social Forces*, 4(4) pp. 669–77.

Held, D. (1980) *Introduction to Critical Theory: Horkheimer to Habermas*, London, Hutchinson.

Henderson, C. R. (1896) 'Business Men and Social Theorists', *American Journal of Sociology*, 1(4) pp. 385–97.

Herbst, J. (1965) *The German Historical School in American Scholarship*, Ithaca, New York, Cornell University Press.

Hinkle, G. J. 'Sociology and Psychoanalysis' in Becker and Boskoff, 1957, pp. 574–603.

Horkheimer, M. (1974) *The Eclipse of Reason*, New York, Seabury.

Howe, F. C. (1905) *The City: The Hope of Democracy*, New York, C. Scribner.

Huff, T. E. (1974) 'Theoretical Innovation in Science: The Case of William F. Ogburn', *American Journal of Sociology* 79(2) pp. 261–77.

Hughes, E. C. (1928) 'A Study of a Secular Institution: The Chicago Real Estate Board', unpublished Ph.D. dissertation, University of Chicago.

Hughes, *et al.* (1950–5) *The Collected Papers of Robert Ezra Park*, 3 vols, Glencoe, Illinois, Free Press.

Hughes, E. C. (1971) *The Sociological Eye*, Chicago, Aldine–Atherton.

Hughes, E. C. (1971a) 'The Cultural Aspects of Urban Research', in Hughes, 1971, pp. 106–17.

Hunter, A. (1974) *Symbolic Communities: The Persistence and Change of Chicago Local Communities*, Chicago, Chicago University Press.

Hunter, A. (1980) 'Why Chicago? The Rise of the Chicago School of Urban Social Science', *American Behavioral Scientist*, 24, pp. 215–27.

Hunter, A. (1983) 'The Gold Coast and the Slum Revisited: Paradoxes in Replication Research and the Study of Social Change', *Urban Life* 11(4) pp. 461–76.

Hunter, R. (1901) *Tenement Conditions of Chicago: Report by the investigating Committee of the City Homes Association*, Chicago, City Home Association.

Jackson, P. (1983) 'Social Disorganization and Moral Order in the City', *Transactions of Institute of British Geographers*, 9, pp. 168–80.

Jackson, P. and Smith, S. J. (1984) *Exploring Human Geography*, London, Allen & Unwin.

Jacobs, J. (1963) *The Life and Death of Great American Cities*, New York, Vintage Books.

James, E. J. (1900) 'The City Council of Berlin', *American Journal of Sociology*, 6(3) pp. 407–15.

James, W. (1904) 'The Chicago School', *The Psychological Bulletin*, 1(1) pp. 1–5.

James, W. (1917a) 'On a Certain Blindness in Human Beings' in James, 1917b, pp. 1–21.

James, W. (1917b) *Selected Papers on Philosophy*, with introduction by C. M. Bakewell, London, Dent.

Janowitz, M. (1946) 'German Reactions to Nazi Atrocities', *American Journal of Sociology*, 52(2) pp. 141–6.

Janowitz, M. (1952) *The Community Press in an Urban Setting*, Glencoe, Illinois, Free Press.

Janowitz, M. (1958) 'Social Stratification and Mobility in West Germany', *American Journal of Sociology*, 64(1) pp. 6–24.

Janowitz, M. (1963) 'Anthropology and the Social Sciences', *Current Anthropology*, 4(2) pp. 139–54.

Janowitz, M. (1964a) 'Organizing Multiple Goals: War-making and Arms Control', in Janowitz, 1964b, pp. 11–31.

Janowitz, M. (ed.) (1964b) *The New Military: Changing Patterns of Organization*, New York, Russell Sage Foundation.

Janowitz, M. (1965) *Helping Hands: Volunteer Work in Education*, Chicago, Chicago University Press.

Janowitz, M. (1968) 'Social Control of Escalated Riots', Chicago, University of Chicago Center for Policy Study (pamphlet).

Janowitz, M. (1969) *Institution Building in Urban Education*, New York, Russell Sage Foundation.

Janowitz, M. (1970a) *Political Conflict: Essays in Political Sociology*, Chicago, Quadrangle Books.

Janowitz, M. (1970b) 'The Logic of Political Sociology' in Janowitz, 1970a, pp. 5–35.

Janowitz, M. (1970c) 'Military Elites and the Study of War', in Janowitz, 1970a, pp. 119–34.

Janowitz, M. (1970d) 'Native Fascism in the 1930s' in Janowitz, 1970a, pp. 149–70.

Janowitz, M. (1970e) 'Patterns of Collective Racial Violence' in Janowitz, 1970a, pp. 243–59.

Janowitz, M. (1970f) 'Sociological Models and Social Policy' in Janowitz, 1970a, pp. 243–59.

Janowitz, M. (1970g) 'The Ideology of Professional Psychologists' in Janowitz, 1970a, pp. 260–8.

Janowitz, M. (1971) *The Professional Soldier: A Social and Political Portrait*, New York, Free Press.

Janowitz, M. (1972a) 'Volunteer Armed Forces and Military Purpose', *Foreign Affairs*, 80(3) pp. 427–43.

Janowitz, M. (1972b) 'Professionalization of Sociology', *American Journal of Sociology*, 78(1) pp. 105–35.

Janowitz, M. (1973) 'The US Forces and the Zero Draft', *Adelphi Papers*, 94, London, International Institute for Strategic Studies.

Janowitz, M. (1974a) 'Introduction' in Blackwell and Janowitz, 1974, pp. xi–xxi.

Janowitz, M. (1974b) 'Towards a Redefinition of Military Strategy in International Relations', *World Politics* 26(4) pp. 473–508.

Janowitz, M. (1975a) 'The All-volunteer Military as a "Sociopolitical" Problem', *Social Problems*, 22, pp. 432–49.

Janowitz, M. (1975b) 'Sociological Theory and Social Control', *American Journal of Sociology*, 80(1) pp. 82–108.

Janowitz, M. (1976) *Social Control of the Welfare State*, New York, Elsevier.

Janowitz, M. (1977) 'The Journalistic Profession and the Mass Media' in Ben-David and Clark, 1977, pp. 72–96.

Janowitz, M. (1978) *The Last Half-Century: Societal Change and Politics in America*, Chicago, Chicago University Press.

Janowitz, M. (1983) *The Reconstruction of Patriotism: Education for Civic Consciousness*, Chicago, Chicago University Press.

Janowitz, M. (in collaboration with Little, R. W.) (1974) *Sociology and the Military Establishment*, Beverly Hills, Sage.

Janowitz, M. and Suttles, G. D. (1978) 'The Social Ecology of Citizenship' in Sarri and Hasenfeld, 1978, pp. 80–104.

Jarausch, K. H. (1985) 'The Crisis of German Professions 1918–33', *Journal of Contemporary History*, 20(3) pp. 379–98.

Jay, M. (1973) *The Dialectical Imagination: A History of the Frankfurt School and the Institute of Social Research, 1923–1950*, Boston, Little, Brown & Co.

Joas, H. (1985) *G. H. Mead: A Contemporary Re-examination of His Thought*, Cambridge, Polity Press.

Judson, H. P. (1895) 'Is our Republic a Failure?', *American Journal of Sociology*, 1(1) pp. 28–40.

Kammen, M. (1980) *People of Paradox: An Inquiry Concerning the Origins of American Civilization*, New York, Oxford University Press.

Karier, C. (1977) 'Making the World Safe for Democracy: An Historical Critique of John Dewey's Pragmatic Liberal Philosophy of the Welfare State', *Educational Theory*, 27(1) pp. 12–47.

Karl, B. E. (1976) 'Philanthropy, Policy Planning and the Bureaucratization of the Democratic Ideal', *Daedalus*, 105(4) pp. 129–49.

Karl, K. D. and Katz, S. N. (1981) 'The American Private Philanthropic Foundations and the Public Sphere 1890–1930', *Minerva*, 19(2) pp. 236–70.

Kasarda, J. D. and Janowitz, M. (1974) 'Community Attachment in Mass Society', *American Sociological Review*, 39(3) pp. 328–39.

Kettler, D. *et al*. (1984) *Karl Mannheim*, London, Tavistock.

Kocka, J. (1980) *White Collar Workers in America 1890–1940: A Socio-political History in International Perspective*, translated by Maura Kealey, London, Sage.

Kohler, R. E. (1978) 'A Policy for the Advancement of Science: The Rockefeller Foundation 1924–29', *Minerva*, 16(4) pp. 480–515.

Kornblum, W. (1974) *Blue-Collar Community*, Chicago, Chicago University Press.

Kracauer, S. (1963a) 'Georg Simmel' in Kracauer, 1963b, pp. 238–9, originally published in 1920.

Kracauer, S. (1963b) *Das Ornament der Masse*, Frankfurt, Suhrkamp.

Kuklick, H. (1973) 'A "Scientific Revolution": Sociological Theory in the United States, 1930–1945', *Sociological Inquiry*, 43(1) pp. 3–22.

Kuklick, H. (1980a) 'Restructuring the Past: Towards an Appreciation of the Social Context of Social Science', *The Sociological Quarterly*, 21, pp. 5–21.

Kuklick, H. (1980b) 'Boundary Maintenance in American Sociology: Limitations to Academic "Professionalization"', *Journal of the History of the Behavioral Sciences*, 16(3) pp. 201–19.

Kuklick, H. (1980c) 'Chicago Sociology and Urban Planning Policy: Sociological Theory as Occupational Ideology', *Theory and Society*, 9(6) pp. 821–45.

Kuklick, H. (1984) 'The Ecology of Sociology' (review of Lewis and Smith, 1980) *American Journal of Sociology*, 89(6) pp. 1433–40.

Kurtz, L. R. (1984) *Evaluating Chicago Sociology: A Guide to the Literature, With an Associated Bibliography*, Chicago, Chicago University Press.

Landesco, J. (1968) *Organized Crime in Chicago*, Chicago, University of Chicago Press, originally published in 1927.

Landmann, M. (1957) 'Einleitung' to G. Simmel, *Brucke and Tur*, Stuttgart, K. F. Koehler, p. v.

Lantz, H. R. (1984) 'Continuities and Discontinuities in American Sociology', *The Sociological Quarterly*, 25(4) pp. 581–96.

Lasch, C. (1965) *The New Radicalism in America (1889–1963): The Intellectual as a Social Type*, New York, Random House.

Lasswell, H. (1936) *Politics: Who Gets What, When and How*, New York, McGraw-Hill.

Lasswell, H. and Kaplan, A. (1950) *Power and Society*, New Haven, Yale University Press.

Lengermann, P. M. (1979) 'The Founding of the *American Sociological Review*: The Anatomy of a Rebellion', *American Sociological Review*, 44 pp. 185–98.

Lerner, M. (1958) *America as a Civilization: Life and Thought in the United States Today*, London, Jonathan Cape.

Levine, D. *et al*. (1976) 'Simmel's Influence on American Sociology', *American Journal of Sociology*, 81(4–5) pp. 813–45, 1112–32.

Lewis, D. J. and Smith, R. L. (1980) *American Sociology and Pragmatism: Mead Chicago Sociology and Symbolic Interactionism*, Chicago, University of Chicago Press.

Lofland, L. (1983) 'Understanding Urban Life: The Chicago Legacy', *Urban Life*, 11(4) pp. 491–511.

Lustig, R. J. (1982) *Corporate Liberalism: The Origins of Modern American Political Theory*, Berkeley, University of California Press.

Lynd, R. (1939) *Knowledge for What: The Place of Social Science in American Culture*, Princeton, Princeton University Press.

McCarthy, T. (1976) 'Translator's Introduction' in Habermas, 1976, pp. vii–xxiv.

McCaul, R. L. (1959) 'Dewey's Chicago', *School Review*, 67, pp. 255–30.

McFarlane, J. (1976) 'Berlin and the Rise of Modernism' in Bradbury and McFarlane, 1976, pp. 105–19.

McQuaid, K. (1978) 'Corporate Liberalism in the American Business Community, 1920–1940', *Business History Review*, 52(3) pp. 342–68.

Madge, J. (1962) *The Origins of Scientific Sociology*, New York, Free Press.

Mannheim, K. (1936) *Ideology and Utopia*, translated with an introduction by Louis Wirth, London, Routledge & Kegan Paul.

Marvick, E. W. (1964) 'Louis Wirth: A Biographical Memorandum' in Wirth, 1964, pp. 333–40.

Masur, G. (1971) *Imperial Germany*, London, Routledge & Kegan Paul.

Matthews, F. H. (1977) *Quest for an American Sociology: Robert Park and the Chicago School*, London, McGill–Queen's University Press.

Matza, D. (1969) *Becoming Deviant*, Englewood Cliffs, New Jersey, Prentice-Hall.

Mayer, H. M. and Wade, R. C. (1969) *Growth of a Metropolis*, Chicago, University of Chicago Press.

Mead, G. H. (1934) *Mind, Self and Society: From the Standpoint of a Social Behaviorist*, edited with an introduction by Charles W. Morris, Chicago, Chicago University Press.

Mellor, J. R. (1977) *Urban Sociology in an Urbanized Society*, London, Routledge & Kegan Paul.

Mills, C. W. 'The Professional Ideology of Social Pathologists', *American Journal of Sociology*, 49(2) pp. 165–80.

Mills, C. W. (1966) *Sociology and Pragmatism: The Higher Learning in America*, edited with an introduction by I. I. Horowitz, New York, Oxford University Press.

Molotch, H. (1972) *Managed Integration: Dilemmas of Doing Good in the City*, Berkeley, University of California Press.

Molotch, H. (1984) 'Romantic Marxism: Love is [Still] Not Enough' (review of Castells, 1983) *Contemporary Sociology*, 13(2) pp. 141–3.

Moore, B. (1967) *Social Origins of Dictatorship and Democracy: Lord and Peasant in the Making of the Modern World*, Harmondsworth, Penguin.

Moore, W. E. (ed.) (1972) *Technology and Social Change*, Chicago, Quadrangle.

Moreno, J. D. and Frey, R. S. (1985) 'Dewey's Critique of Marxism', *Sociological Quarterly*, 26(1) pp. 21–34.

Nicolson, M. (1917) *The Valley of Democracy*, London, Andrew Melrose.

Odum, H. W. (1951) *American Sociology: The Story of Sociology in the United States through 1950*, New York, Longmans, Green.

Ogburn, W. F. (1926) 'The Great Man versus Social Forces' *Social Forces*, 5(2) pp. 225–31.

Ogburn, W. F. (1930) 'Three Obstacles to the Development of a Scientific Sociology', *Social Forces*, 8(3) pp. 347–50.

Ogburn, W. F. (1931) 'Considerations in Choosing Problems of Research' in Brookings Institution, 1931, pp. 161–71.

Ogburn, W. F. (1934a) 'Limitations of Statistics', *American Journal of Sociology*, 40(1) pp. 12–20.

Ogburn, W. F. (1934b) 'The Background of the New Deal', *American Journal of Sociology*, 39(6) pp. 729–37.

Ogburn, W. F. (1934c) 'The Future of the New Deal', *American Journal of Sociology*, 39(6) pp. 342–3.

Ogburn, W. F. (1934d) 'Studies in Prediction and the Distortion of Reality', *Social Forces*, 13(2) pp. 224–9.

Ogburn, W. F. (1936a) 'Regions', *Social Forces*, 15(1) pp. 6–11.

Ogburn, W. F. (1936b) 'Stationary and Changing Societies', *American Journal of Sociology*, 42(1) pp. 16–31.
Ogburn, W. F. (1940) 'On Economic Interpretation of the Social Characteristics of Cities', *American Journal of Sociology*, 46(3) pp. 305–15.
Ogburn, W. F. (1942) 'Our Times', *American Journal of Sociology*, 47(6) pp. 803–15.
Ogburn, W. F. (1945) 'Ideologies of the South in Transition', *Social Forces*, 23(3) pp. 334–44.
Ogburn, W. F. (1948) 'Thoughts on Freedom and Organization', *Ethics*, 58(3) pp. 256–61.
Ogburn, W. F. (1950) *Social Change with Respect to Culture and Original Nature*, New York, The Viking Press, originally published in 1922.
Ogburn, W. F. (1951) 'Population, Private Ownership, Technology, and the Standard of Living', *American Journal of Sociology*, 56(4) pp. 314–19.
Ogburn, W. F. (1955a) 'Implications of the Rising Standard of Living in the United States', *American Journal of Sociology*, 60(6) pp. 541–6.
Ogburn, W. F. (1955b) 'Technology and the Standard of Living in the United States', *American Journal of Sociology*, 60(4) pp. 380–6.
Ogburn, W. F. (1964) *W. F. Ogburn on Culture and Social Change*, edited with an introduction by O. D. Duncan, Chicago, University of Chicago Press.
Ogburn, W. F. (1972) 'Can Science Bring us Happiness?' in Moore, 1972, pp. 31–9, originally published in 1949.
Ogburn, W. F. (ed.) (1974) *Social Changes During Depression and Recovery (Social Changes in 1934)*, New York, Da Capo Press, originally published in 1935.
Ogburn, W. F. and Nimkoff, M. F. (1955) *Technology and the Changing Family*, Boston, Massachusetts, Houghton Mifflin.
Ogburn, W. F. and Nimkoff, M. F. (1959) *A Handbook of Sociology*, London, Routledge & Kegan Paul.
Park, R. E. (1922) *The Immigrant Press and Its Control*, New York, Harper.
Park, R. E. (1950) *Race and Culture: The City and Human Ecology* (vol. 1 of Hughes *et al.* 1950–5).
Park, R. E. (1952) *Human Communities* (vol. 2 of Hughes *et al.* 1950–5).
Park, R. E. (1955) *Society: Collective Behavior, News and Opinion, Sociology and Modern Society* (vol. 3 of Hughes *et al.* 1950–5).
Park, R. E. (1967) *Robert E. Park on Social Control and Collective Behavior*, edited with an introduction by Ralph H. Turner, Chicago, University of Chicago Press.
Park, R. E. and Burgess, E. W. (1921) *Introduction to the Science of Sociology*, Chicago, University of Chicago.
Park, R. E. and Burgess, E. W. (1967) *The City*, with an introduction by Morris Janowitz, Chicago, University of Chicago Press, originally published in 1925.
Park, R. E. and Burgess, E. W. (1970) *Introduction to the Science of Sociology: Student Edition*, abridged, with a preface by Morris Janowitz, Chicago, Chicago University Press.
Parsons, T. (1930–5) 'Service' in *Encyclopaedia of Social Sciences*, p. 673.
Parsons, T. (1937) *The Structure of Social Action*, New York, McGraw-Hill.
Parsons, T. (1951) *The Social System*, New York, Free Press.
Parsons, T. (1964) *Essays in Sociological Theory*, Cleeve, Ill., Free Press.
Parsons, T. (1966) *Societies: Evolutionary and Comparative Perspectives*, Englewood Cliffs, New Jersey, Prentice-Hall.
Parsons, T. (1970) 'On Building a Social System Theory: A Personal History', *Daedalus*, 99, pp. 826–81.
Parsons, T., Bales, R. F. and Shils, E. (1953) *Working Papers in the Theory of Action*, New York, Free Press.

Philpott, T. L. (1978) *The Slum and the Ghetto: Neighbourhood Deterioration and Middle-class Reform in Chicago 1880–1930*, New York, Oxford University Press.

Pickvance, C. G. (1975) *Urban Sociology: Critical Essays*, London, Tavistock.

Plato (1955) *The Republic*, Harmondsworth, Penguin.

President's Research Committee on Social Trends (1933) *Recent Social Trends in the United States*, 2 volumes, New York, McGraw-Hill.

Rex, J. and Mason D. (eds) (1986) *Theories of Race and Ethnic Relations*, Cambridge, Cambridge University Press.

Riesman, D. (1950) *The Lonely Crowd: A Study of the Changing American Character*, Princeton, New Jersey, Yale University Press.

Ringer, F. K. (1979) *Education and Society in Modern Europe*, Bloomington, Indiana University Press.

Rocher, P. (1974) *Talcott Parsons and American Sociology*, translated by Barbara and Stephen Mennell with an introduction by Stephen Mennell, London, Nelson.

Rock, P. (1979) *The Making of Symbolic Interactionism*, Totowa, New Jersey, Rowman & Littlefield.

Rodgers, D. T. (1982) 'In Search of Progressivism' *Reviews in American History*, 10(4) pp. 113–32.

Rytina, J. H. and Loomis, C. P. (1970) 'Marxist Dialectic and Pragmatism: Power as Knowledge', *American Sociological Review*, 35(2) pp. 308–18.

Sarri, R. C. and Hasenfeld, Y. (eds) (1978) *The Management of Human Services*, New York, Columbia University Press.

Schambra, W. A. (1982) 'The Roots of American Public Philosophy', *Public Interest*, 67, pp. 36–48.

Schwendinger, H. and Schwendinger, J. R. (1974) *The Sociologists of the Chair: A Radical Analysis of the Formative Years of North American Sociology (1883–1922)*, New York, Basic Books.

Seidman, S. (1983) *Liberalism and the Origins of European Social Theory*, Berkeley, University of California Press.

Sennett, R. and Cobb, R. (1972) *The Hidden Injuries of Class*, Cambridge, Cambridge University Press.

Sennett, R. (1977) *The Fall of Public Man*, New York, Knopf.

Shalhope, R. (1972) 'Towards a Republican Synthesis: The Emergence of an Understanding of Republicanism in American Historiography', *William and Mary Quarterly*, 29, pp. 49–80.

Shaw, C. R. (1966) *The Jack-Roller: A Delinquent Boy's Own Story*, Chicago, Chicago University Press (with an introduction by Howard Becker, originally published in 1930).

Sheehan, J. J. (1971) 'Liberalism and the City in Nineteenth-century Germany', *Past and Present*, 51, 116–37.

Shideler, E. H. (1927) 'The Chain Store: A Study of the Ecological Organization of a Modern City', unpublished Ph.D. dissertation, University of Chicago.

Shils, E. (1970) 'Tradition, Ecology, and Institution in the History of Sociology', *Daedalus*, 99, pp. 760–825.

Shils, E. (1975) *Center and Periphery: Essays in Macrosociology*, Chicago, University of Chicago Press.

Shils, E. (1980a) 'The Contemplation of Society in America' in Shils, 1980b, pp. 95–133.

Shils, E. (1980b) *The Calling of Sociology and Other Essays on the Pursuit of Learning*, Chicago, University of Chicago Press.

Shils, E. (1981) 'Some Academics, Mainly in Chicago', *American Scholar*, 50(2) pp. 179–96.

Shils, E. (1982) 'The University – A Backward Glance', *American Scholar*, 51(2) pp. 163–79.

Shils, E. and Janowitz, M. (1975) 'Cohesion and Disintegration in the Wehrmacht in World War II' in Shils, 1975, pp. 345–83, originally published in 1948.

Short, J. F. (ed.) (1971) *The Social Fabric of the Metropolis, Contributions of the Chicago School of Urban Sociology*, Chicago, University of Chicago Press.

Short, M. (1984) *Crime Inc: The Story of Organized Crime*, London, Thames Methuen.

Sills, D. L. (ed.) (1968) *International Encyclopaedia of the Social Sciences*, London, Collier-Macmillan.

Simmel, G. (1896) 'Berliner Gewerbe-Ausstelling', *Die Zeit*, 8, 25 July.

Simmel, G. (1950a) 'The Stranger' in Wolff, 1950, pp. 402–3, originally published in 1908.

Simmel, G. (1950b) 'The Metropolis and Mental Life' in Wolff, 1950, pp. 409–24, originally published in 1903.

Simmel, G. (1959) 'The Adventure' in Wolff, 1959, pp. 243–58, originally published in 1911.

Simmel, G. (1968) 'The Concept and Tragedy of Culture' in Simmel 1968a, pp. 27–46.

Simmel, G. (1968a) *The Concept of Culture and Other Essays*, translated and edited with an introduction by K. P. Etzkorn, New York, Teachers College Press.

Simmel, G. (1978) *The Philosophy of Money*, translated by T. Bottomore and D. Frisby with an introduction by D. Frisby, London, Routledge & Kegan Paul.

Simmel, G. (1980) *Essays on Interpretation in Social Science*, translated and edited with an introduction by G. Oakes, Manchester, Manchester University Press.

Simich, J. L. and Tilman, R. (1980) 'Critical Theory and Institutional Economics: Frankfurt's Encounter with Veblen', *Journal of Economic Issues*, 14(3) pp. 631–48.

Sinclair, U. (1985) *The Jungle*, Harmondsworth, Penguin, originally published in 1906.

Small, A. W. (1895a) 'The Civic Federation of Chicago: A Study in Social Dynamics', 1(1) pp. 79–103.

Small, A. W. (1895b) 'Free Investigation' *American Journal of Sociology*, 1(2) pp. 210–14.

Small, A. W. (1895c) 'Scholarship and Social Agitation', *American Journal of Sociology*, 1(1) pp. 564–82.

Small, A. W. (1905) *General Sociology: An Exposition of the Main Development in Sociological Theory from Spencer to Ratzenhofer*, Chicago, University of Chicago Press.

Small, A. W. (1909) *The Cameralists, The Pioneers of German Social Polity*, Chicago, Chicago University Press.

Small, A. W. (1913) *Between Eras from Capitalism to Democracy*, Chicago, T. W. Bruder.

Small, A. W. (1914) 'The Social Graduations of Capital' *American Journal of Sociology*, 19(6) pp. 721–52.

Small, A. W. (1919–20) 'Some Structural Material for the Idea "Democracy"' *American Journal of Sociology* 25(3) pp. 257–97; 405–44.

Small, A. W. (1920) 'Christianity and Industry', *American Journal of Sociology*, 25(6) pp. 673–91.

Small, A. W. (1925) 'The Sociology of Profits', *American Journal of Sociology*, 30(4) pp. 439–61.

Small, A. W. and Vincent, G. E. (1894) *An Introduction to the Study of Society*, New York, American Book Company.

Smith, C. R. (1984) *Chicago and the American Literary Imagination 1880–1920*, Chicago, University of Chicago Press.

Smith, D. (1983) *Barrington Moore: Violence, Morality and Political Change*, London, Macmillan (published in USA by M. E. Sharpe as *Barrington Moore Jr: A Critical Appraisal*).

Smith, M. P. (1980a) *The City and Social Theory*, Oxford, Basil Blackwell.

Smith, M. P. (1980b) 'Critical Theory and Urban Political Theory' *Comparative Urban Research*, 7(1) pp. 5–23.

Smith, T. V. (1928) 'Philosophical Ethics and the Social Sciences', *Social Forces*, 7(1) pp. 17–24.

Smith, T. V. and White, L. D. (1968) *Chicago: An Experiment in Social Science Research*, New York, Greenwood Press, originally published in 1929.

Snodgrass, J. (1983) 'The Jack-Roller: A Fifty-year Follow-up', *Urban Life*, 11(4) pp. 440–59.

Sombart, W. (1913) *The Jews and Modern Capitalism*, translated and edited by M. Epstein, London, T. Fisher Unwin.

Sombart, W. (1915) *The Quintessence of Capitalism: A Study of the History and Psychology of the Modern Business Man*, translated and edited by M. Epstein, London, T. Fisher Unwin.

Sontag, S. (1979) 'Introduction' in Benjamin, 1979b, pp. 7–28.

Spencer, M. E. (1977) 'History and Sociology: An Analysis of Weber's *The City*', *Sociology* 11(3) pp. 507–25.

Spengler, O. (1923) *The Decline of the West*, London, originally published in 1918.

Stead, W. T. (1894) *If Christ Came to Chicago!: A Plea for the Union of All Who Love in the Service of All Who Suffer*, London, Review of Reviews.

Stern, B. J. (1933) 'The Letters of Albion W. Small to Lester P. Ward' *Social Forces*, 12(2) pp. 163–73; 13(3) pp. 323–40; 15(2) pp. 174–87; 15(3) pp. 805–27.

Stone, N. (1983) *Europe Transformed 1878–1919*, London, Fontana.

Storing, H. J. (1981) *What the Anti-federalists Were For*, Chicago, University of Chicago Press.

Strout, C. (1964) 'A note on Degler, Riesman and Tocqueville', *American Quarterly*, 16, pp. 100–02.

Sullivan, L. H. (1956) *The Autobiography of an Idea*, New York, Dover, originally published in 1924.

Sumner, W. G. (1940) *Folkways*, with an introduction by William Lyon Phelps, New York, Mentor, originally published in 1906.

Sutherland, E. H. (1983) *White Collar Crime: The Uncut Version*, with an introduction by Gilbert Geiss and Colin Goff, New Haven, Yale University Press.

Suttles, G. (1968) *The Social Order of the Slum*, Chicago, University of Chicago Press.

Suttles, G. (1972) *The Social Construction of Communities*, Chicago, University of Chicago Press.

Thomas, E. A. (1978) 'Herbert Blumer's Critique of *The Polish Peasant*; a *post mortem* on the Life History Approach in Sociology', *Journal of the History of the Behavioral Sciences*, 14(1) pp. 124–31.

Thomas J. (1983a) 'Chicago Sociology: An Introduction', *Urban Life* 11(4) pp. 387–95.

Thomas, J. (1983b) 'Towards a Critical Ethography: A Reexamination of the Chicago Legacy', *Urban Life*, 11(4) pp. 477–90.

Thomas, W. I. (1895) 'The Scope and Method of Folk-psychology', *American Journal of Sociology* 1(3) pp. 434–45.

Thomas, W. I. (1897) 'On a Difference in the Metabolism of the Sexes' *American Journal of Sociology*, 3(1) pp. 31–63.

Thomas, W. I. (1898) 'The Relation of Sex to Primitive Social Control', *American Journal of Sociology*, 3(6) pp. 754–76.

Thomas, W. I. (1899a) 'Sex in Primitive Industry', *American Journal of Sociology*, 4(4) pp. 474–88.

Thomas, W. I. (1899b) 'Sex in Primitive Morality', *American Journal of Sociology*, 4(6) pp. 774–87.

Thomas, W. I. (1905) 'The Province of Social Psychology', *American Journal of Sociology*, 10(4) pp. 445–55.

Thomas, W. I. (1907) *Sex and Society: Studies in the Social Psychology of Sex*, Chicago, University of Chicago Press.

Thomas, W. I. (1908) 'The Significance of the Orient for the Occident', *American Journal of Sociology*, 13(6) pp. 739–55.

Thomas, W. I. (1909a) *Source Book for Social Origins: Ethnographical Materials, Psychological Standpoint, Classified and Annotated Bibliographies for the Interpretation of Savage Society*, Chicago, University of Chicago Press.

Thomas, W. I. (1909b) 'Standpoint for the Interpretation of Savage Society', *American Journal of Sociology*, 15(2) pp. 145–63.

Thomas W. I. (1914) 'The Prussian–Polish Situation: An Experiment in Assimilation', *American Journal of Sociology*, 19(5) pp. 624–39.

Thomas, W. I. (1966) *W. I. Thomas on Social Organisation and Personality*, selected papers edited with an introduction by Morris Janowitz, Chicago, University of Chicago Press.

Thomas, W. I. Park, R. E. and Miller, H. A. (1969) *Old World Traits Transformed*, New York, Arno Press, originally published in 1921.

Thomas, W. I. and Znaniecki, F. (1927) *The Polish Peasant in Europe and America*, 2 vols, New York, Knopf, originally published in 1918–19.

Thrasher, F. M. (1963) *The Gang: A Study of 1313 Gangs in Chicago*, Chicago, University of Chicago Press, originally published in 1927.

Thurnwald, R. (1932) 'Sociology: Its Content and Application. I. Sociology in America: Impressions of a Visitor', *Social Forces*, 11(2) pp. 161–75.

Tocqueville, A. de (1968) *Democracy in America*, 2 vols, edited by J. P. Mayer and Max Lerner, translated by George Lawrence, New York, Fontana, originally published 1835–40.

Tufts, J. H. (1909) 'Darwin and Evolutionary Ethics', *Psychology Review*, 16(3) pp. 195–206.

Veblen, T. (1898a) 'Why is Economics Not an Evolutionary Science?' *Quarterly Journal of Economics*, 12, pp. 56–81.

Veblen, T. (1898b) 'The Beginnings of Ownership', *American Journal of Sociology*, 4(3) pp. 352–65.

Veblen, T. (1898c) 'The Instinct of Workmanship and the Irksomeness of Labor', *American Journal of Sociology*, 4(2) pp. 187–201.

Veblen, T. (1899) 'The Barbarian Status of Women', *American Journal of Sociology*, 4(4) pp. 503–14.

Veblen, T. (1899–1900) 'The Preconceptions of Economic Science', *Quarterly Journal of Economics*, pp. 13–14, 121–50, 240–69, 396–426.

Veblen, T. (1906) 'The Place of Science in Modern Civilisation', *American Journal of Sociology*, 11(5) pp. 535–609.

Veblen, T. (1910) 'Christian Morals and the Competitive System', *International Journal of Ethics*, 20(2) pp. 168–84.

Veblen, T. (1919) 'The Intellectual Preeminence of Jews in Modern Europe', *Political Science Quarterly*, 34.

Veblen, T. (1964a) *The Instinct of Workmanship*, New York, Norton, originally published in 1914.

Veblen, T. (1964b) *Imperial Germany and the Industrial Revolution*, New York, Augustus M. Kelley, originally published in 1915.

Veblen, T. (1965a) *The Higher Learning in America: A Memorandum on the Conduct of Universities by Businessmen*, New York, Augustus M. Kelley, originally published 1918.

Veblen, T. (1965b) *The Theory of Business Enterprise*, New York, Augustus M. Kelley, originally published in 1904.

Veblen, T. (1967) *Absentee Ownership*, Boston, Beacon, originally published in 1923.

Veblen, T. (1970) *The Theory of the Leisure Class*, London, Allen & Unwin, originally published in 1899.

Vizetelly, H. (1879) *Berlin Under the New Empire: Its Institutions, Inhabitants, Industry, Monuments, Museums, Social Life, Manners, and Amusements*, 2 vols, London, Tisley Bros.

Wallas, G. (1914) *The Great Society: A Psychological Analysis*, London, Macmillan.

Ward, D. (1983) 'The Progressives and the Urban Question: British and American Responses to the Inner City Slums 1880–1920', *Transactions of Institute of British Geographers*, 9, pp. 299–314.

Ward, L. (1883) *Dynamic Sociology*, New York, A. D. Appleton & Co.

Ward, L. (1900) Review of *The Theory of the Leisure Class*, *American Journal of Sociology*, 5(6) pp. 329–37.

Weber, M. (1975) *Max Weber: A Biography*, translated by Harry Zohn, New York, Wiley.

Weber, M. (1976) *The Protestant Ethic and the Spirit of Capitalism*, translated by Talcott Parsons and with an introduction by Anthony Giddens, originally published in 1930.

Weber, M. (1978a) 'Economic Policy and the National Interest in Imperial Germany', in Weber, 1978b, pp. 263–8, originally published in 1895.

Weber, M. (1978b) *Max Weber: Selections in Translation*, edited by W. G. Runciman and translated by E. Matthews, Cambridge, Cambridge University Press.

White, M. and White, L. (1962) *The Intellectual versus the City: From Thomas Jefferson to Frank Lloyd Wright*, New York, Mentor.

Wiebe, R. H. (1967) *The Search for Order 1877–1920*, New York, Hill & Wang.

Wiley, N. (1985) 'The Current Interregnum in American Sociology', *Social Research*, 52(1) pp. 179–207.

Williams, R. (1973) *Drama from Ibsen to Brecht*, Harmondsworth, Penguin.

Wirth, L. (1928) *The Ghetto*, Chicago, University of Chicago Press.

Wirth, L. (1936) 'Preface' in Mannheim, 1936, pp. xiii–xxxi.

Wirth, L. (1939) 'Review of Parsons 1937', *American Sociological Review*, 4(3) pp. 399–404.

Wirth, L. (ed.) (1940) *Eleven Twenty-Six: A Decade of Social Science Research*, Chicago, University of Chicago Press.

Wirth, L. (1941) 'Morale and Minority Groups', *American Journal of Sociology*, 47(3) pp. 415–33.

Wirth, L. (1957) 'Urbanism as a Way of Life', in Hatt and Reiss (1957), pp. 46–63 (originally published in 1938).

Wirth, L. (1948) 'Consensus and Mass Communication; *American Sociological Review*, 13(1) February, pp. 1–15.

Wirth, L. (1964) *On Cities and Social Life: Selected Papers*, edited with an introduction by Albert J. Reiss, Jr. Chicago, University of Chicago Press.

Wirth, L. and Bernert, E. W. (eds) (1940) *Local Community Fact Book of Chicago*, Chicago, University of Chicago Press.

Wolff, K. H. (1950) *The Sociology of Georg Simmel*, New York, The Free Press.

Wolff, K. H. (ed) (1959) *Georg Simmel, 1858–1918*, Columbus, Ohio State University Press.

Young, K. (1962–3) 'The Contribution of William Isaac Thomas to Sociology', *Sociology and Social Research*, 47(1–4) 3–24, 123–37, 251–72, 381–97.

Znaniecki, F (? 'A European') (1920) 'Intellectual America', *Atlantic Monthly*, vol. 125, pp. 188–99.

Znaniecki, F. (1969) *Florian Znaniecki on Humanistic Sociology*, edited with an introduction by Robert Bierstedt, Chicago, University of Chicago Press.

Zorbaugh, H. (1929), *The Gold Coast and the Slum*, Chicago, University of Chicago Press.

Zueblin, C. (1902) *American Municipal Progress*, New York, Macmillan.

Index